You won't find a more amazing account of how God's grace can change lives than what you have here in the life of my brother, Dimas Salaberrios.

TIMOTHY KELLER
Senior pastor, Redeemer Presbyterian Church

A complex and thrilling narrative. I dare anyone to read *Street God* and come away unchanged. This is *The Cross and the Switchblade* for a new generation.

JOSH McDOWELL
Author and speaker

This is a powerful story of the relentless love of God. There is no pit so deep that his grace and mercy can't find you.

SHEILA WALSH
Author of *Five Minutes with Jesus*

A powerful story of emerging leadership founded in personal transformation.

DR. A. R. BERNARD
Pastor of Christian Cultural Center, Brooklyn, NY

STREET GOD

Street God

The explosive true story
of a former drug boss on
the run from the hood—
and the courageous mission
that drove him back

DIMAS SALABERRIOS

with Dr. Angela Hunt

TYNDALE
MOMENTUM™

The nonfiction imprint of
Tyndale House Publishers, Inc.

Visit Tyndale online at www.tyndale.com.

Visit Tyndale Momentum online at www.tyndalemomentum.com.

TYNDALE, *Tyndale Momentum*, and Tyndale's quill logo are registered trademarks of Tyndale House Publishers, Inc. The Tyndale Momentum logo is a trademark of Tyndale House Publishers, Inc. Tyndale Momentum is the nonfiction imprint of Tyndale House Publishers, Inc., Carol Stream, Illinois.

Street God: The Explosive True Story of a Former Drug Boss on the Run from the Hood—and the Courageous Mission That Drove Him Back

Designed by Mark Anthony Lane II

Published in association with the literary agency of The Fedd Agency, Inc., P.O. Box 341973, Austin, TX 78734.

For information about special discounts for bulk purchases, please contact Tyndale House Publishers at csresponse@tyndale.com or call 800-323-9400.

Library of Congress Cataloging-in-Publication Data

Salaberrios, Dimas.
    Street god : the explosive true story of a former drug boss on the run from the hood—and the courageous mission that drove him back / Dimas Salaberrios, with Angela Hunt.
        pages cm
    Includes bibliographical references.
    ISBN 978-1-4964-0278-3 (sc : alk. paper)
    1. Salaberrios, Dimas. 2. Evangelists—New York (State)—New York—Biography. 3. Church work with youth with social disabilities—New York (State)—New York. 4. Evangelistic work. 5. Christian converts—New York (State)—New York—Biography. I. Title.
    BV3785.S1655A3 2015
    277.3'083092—dc23
    [B]   2015019554

Printed in the United States of America

23 22 21 20 19 18 17
11 10 9   8   7   6

To my lovely, amazing wife, Tiffany,
and my three girls: Shirley Ann, Dallas, and Skylar.
They so generously share their husband and dad
with the world for the cause of Jesus Christ.

Author's Note

THE FOLLOWING IS my story to the best of my memory . . . with some names changed and identifying details blurred, particularly for the sake of my family, the people I grew up with, and the dear people whom God has now called and equipped me to serve.

CHAPTER ONE

POP! POP-POP!

As several shots rang out, I crouched behind a dumpster. Then I glanced behind me and caught Black Sean's eye. What were we doing in the middle of a shoot-out? This was serious stuff, not exactly what I'd expected when Black Sean had approached me earlier in school.

"Hey," Black Sean had said, grinning. My eyes focused on the serious gold jewelry around his neck. "Wanna go get some money?"

He didn't have to ask twice. I followed him without a backward glance. We caught a city bus at the corner and got off at a stop in South Jamaica, Queens, where we spotted Jamal, a kid I knew to be a drug hustler.

"Hey, come on," Jamal called, moving down the sidewalk in a hurry. "We gotta go."

Black Sean and I didn't know what was happening, but the

excitement in Jamal's voice sent a surge of adrenaline through my bloodstream. A couple of other guys joined us for whatever was going down. Then Jamal crouched behind a dumpster in an alley and peered around the corner. What was he doing? Were we in the middle of some kind of drug deal, or what?

Before I even realized Jamal was carrying, he pulled out a gun, held it in both hands, and started shooting at a guy across the street. What?

Instinct had told me to duck, so I crouched behind Jamal. My heart pounded. I barely had time to think before he yelled, "Let's go," so off we went.

I glanced over my shoulder, looking for a body in the street, but I didn't see one. Good. I wanted no part of killing.

Next thing I knew I was standing with Jamal, Black Sean, and some other guys. A dealer named Abdul stood with us, and he grinned at Jamal. "Way to go," he said. Then he looked at Black Sean and gestured in my direction. "Who's this guy?"

Black Sean looked at me. "Slim."

"You wanna deal, Slim?" Abdul asked me.

Of course I did. Dealing meant money, and money meant everything on the street. Abdul must have figured that if I had the courage to run with Jamal, I had what it took to be a dealer.

I nodded, and Abdul grinned.

"Give 'im a package," he said to one of the other guys. Then he narrowed his eyes at me. "This is how it works—you don't sell to nobody you don't know. You keep the stuff hidden, you take the money, and then you go get a capsule and hand it over. If you follow my rules, you'll be okay." His smile broadened. "Be smart, dude, and you'll be cool."

He walked away, and another kid handed me a bag of crack cocaine. Then I grinned at Black Sean.

I felt the weight of the drug bag in my hand.

It was a lot lighter than my schoolbooks.

Ever since I'd been old enough to recognize the signs of success, I'd wanted to be a dealer. And there I stood among dudes with guns, attitude, and a supplier. I was on my way . . . and I was only fourteen years old.

*   *   *

A couple of months later I found myself lying on the sidewalk with blood gushing from my head. I felt the roughness of concrete beneath my hands and heard a throbbing in my ears. What had happened this time?

I pushed myself up to a sitting position. A group of my friends stood around me, but most of them were silent and still.

Jamal came over and glared at me. "Yo, you stupid, son. Why would you mess around with Abdul's money, trying to flip it? You dumb stupid, you ought to be happy you ain't gettin' capped."

I pressed my hand to my head and felt a swelling lump over my temple. "How'd my head get like this?"

Jamal's mouth twisted in a smirk. "Abdul smashed his phone into your skull till it exploded and then stomped his boots on your head."

I ran my hand over my jaw, which felt swollen, and tasted the metallic tang of blood mixed with dirt—*dirt?* Oh yeah, Abdul had tried to kick out my teeth once I was down. As my boss, he'd felt it his duty to administer a little discipline to a wayward worker.

Somehow I managed to stumble into a Korean grocery store, where someone finally looked at me with compassion. The owner hooked me up with some rubbing alcohol and a pack of Band-Aids so I could clean my wounds. As I braced myself for the alcohol burn, I realized I might have to patch the Band-Aids together to stop the bleeding.

I finished with the bandages and, without skipping a beat, went right back to hustling. I walked out of the store and yelled at anyone who looked like a potential customer. "I've got the good stuff here. Don't go to Jamal—his crack is whack. I've got the good stuff right here."

People stopped—they always did. After looking at the crazy patchwork on my head and face, a couple of my faithful customers summoned up the courage to ask what had happened.

I said what everyone in my condition said: "Don't sweat it. Man, this is just part of the business."

And it was . . . yet it wasn't. Everyone in the life I'd chosen got beat up; beatings were part of the game. But unlike the vast majority of other kids my age who were hustling, I wasn't content to be *just* a drug dealer. I wanted to be a kingpin, a boss, a street *god*, so I was constantly looking for ways to broaden my scope and increase my profit. By doing that, I was asking for more trouble. This time I had taken Abdul's money, purchased additional drugs, and made a sweet personal profit for myself even though I knew that "flipping" was an offense that drug bosses dealt with quickly and furiously, lest others wise up to the same idea.

Drug bosses were abusive by nature. If they wanted to survive for any length of time, they had to develop reputations for toughness or they'd face challenges from other bosses who wanted to take their turf. Most of us realized that the infighting among a guy's crew wasn't personal; it was simply part of the business. It wasn't unusual to take a beating and later on smoke a blunt with the guy who had just opened up a can of whiptail on you.

I knew I made a lot of money for Abdul, so I expected him to chill out for a while and then come back to reassure me that I was a valuable worker. He needed to lock in my loyalty in case I was ever busted. A drug boss needed to be able to count on his workers and know they wouldn't rat out the operation if arrested.

Only a few minutes after I'd gone back to the block, I watched Black Sean come limping around the corner with his expensive

Adidas shirt ripped in two. In his wake trailed an unmarked police car with two detectives, who made sure we saw them pointing us out.

My heart nearly leaped out of my chest. Black Sean yelled and cussed at the cops as blood poured out of his mouth—at fourteen, he was already a loose cannon. Once the police car moved on down the street, he turned to fill us in. He said the cops had jacked him up. They'd rolled up on him and asked how he could afford a hundred-dollar Adidas shirt. Then they had cuffed him, made him get in the back of their car, and beaten him up, ripping his shirt in the process.

"Be cool," I told him. "This is all part of the life."

We hustlers got it from all sides. Cops routinely picked us up and beat us, and sometimes they even stripped us down in the street. They hated our operation because it was almost impenetrable. We were disciplined enough not to sell to anyone we didn't know, a strategy that made it difficult for cops to catch us on a simple buy-and-bust. The drugs stayed in our possession only for a minute—just long enough for us to retrieve a packet from a hiding place and hand it to our customer.

We'd all become experts at swallowing small plastic capsules of crack whenever a cop pulled up in the middle of a sale. And our bosses—the guys who gave us the drugs and told us where to sell—rarely handled drugs on the street. Decked out with the flyest gold chains and gear, they'd roll onto the scene and flash their fancy cars and hot girlfriends. Their job was to intimidate and discipline, not to sell.

I expected Abdul to come find me after my beating, and about an hour after Black Sean's run-in with the cops, Abdul pulled up in his car and opened the door. "Slim, get in."

Being invited into Abdul's black Suzuki Samurai was a bigger perk than I had expected. The car had been pimped out to win admiration from and strike fear into the man's employees. Those big fat tires reminded us that he could roll over us if he wanted to, and the bright chrome trim reminded us that he would always draw more respect than we underlings. And the sound system—we could feel the *boom boom* of the bass while the car was a block away, and our bodies vibrated with every beat. That car had been designed to intimidate, and it fulfilled its purpose very well.

Yet I was grateful for the invitation to climb into the vehicle with Abdul. To everyone watching, that invitation meant not only that he wanted to keep me on his team but also that he thought I was cool enough to hang out with for a while. Riding in a drug dealer's car earned me major props, or proper respect.

"You know," Abdul said, handling the car as if it needed to be taught a lesson, "I can't have you playing with my money and flippin' it."

I nodded and kept my eyes on the road ahead.

"But hey—you do good and one day you can be a boss like me. And when that happens, you gonna have to keep your hustlers in line. You gonna have to bust some heads. It's business, man."

Abdul was full of it, deceiving me with every word. He was trying to gas me up enough to believe I could be the next boss on his team, but he wasn't fooling me. Though he was the boss of my crew, he worked for the Supreme Team, a vicious operation. Abdul was simply a franchisee of Fat Cat, Supreme, and James Corley, a notorious trifecta that ran operations in half of South Jamaica, Queens, at the height of the crack business. And me? I wasn't even close to being a lieutenant on his team.

I sat and listened, pretending to heed his advice, but that beating must have knocked some sense into my head. After getting out of the car, I realized I was finished working for that abusive psycho—I'd had enough. The only way an ambitious guy like me could reach the top of that particular organization would be through murdering people, and murder wasn't my style. My chosen street name was Daylight, not Nightmare.

Black Sean lived and breathed South Jamaica, but I'd come from a different background. My mother was a sophisticated, intelligent woman who worked as an elementary school principal, and my father was a former Air Force man who served as a captain of corrections on Rikers Island. Though we weren't wealthy, my roots were middle class, so my worldview was vastly different from most of the hustlers on the street.

I counted myself fortunate to have grown up in Cambria Heights, a community of homeowners, manicured lawns, and few, if any, welfare recipients. But even though my neighborhood was composed of upper-middle-class families, it wasn't immune from the allure of mind-altering drugs. As in all "good" communities, people used drugs.

By the time I was eleven, I was peddling mescaline tablets in middle school. Like anyone intent on being successful, I wanted to diversify my inventory and be a well-rounded player in the game. By fourteen, I had an advanced knowledge of the drug trade and knew what it would take to rise to the top. I also had drive and ambition. Even at that age, I wanted to be a boss, the most powerful player in the game—a street god.

*   *   *

Neither my father nor my mother wanted to raise a drug dealer. Though they never married (they spoke of themselves as "separated"), they both played an active role in my life. Dad, a strong and handsome Puerto Rican, worked at Rikers Island until he retired. He had a strong work ethic and tried to pass it on to me, even buying me a hot dog stand when I turned twelve.

Like many fathers, Dad would pick me up every Saturday and take me to places he thought I ought to visit. He was a visionary. He wanted me to be smart, so he enrolled me in memorization classes. He wanted me to be confident, so he enrolled me in karate class. He wanted me to be skilled, so he signed me up for wood shop. He wanted me to be multicultural, so he paid for tennis lessons and placed me in situations where I mixed with white, Asian, and Hispanic kids. My father lived in a diverse world, and he wanted me to share it.

We never finished those classes or perfected those skills, but by the time I'd lost interest in one activity, he'd come up with some other program he wanted me to try. He also taught me by example—how to greet people, how to repeat their names after meeting them so I'd remember them. I didn't realize it at the time, but I was picking up skills that would serve me well over the years.

My mother's world, on the other hand, was almost completely African American. I lived with her in a middle-class house on a nice street in Cambria Heights, home to lawyers and city leaders and officials. My mother was married when she had her first three children—my siblings Dawn, Emerald, and Chad—all by her husband. They divorced, and many years later, she met my father and I was born. On our street, all the families but mine and one other had mothers *and* fathers. I felt the difference keenly.

Cambria Heights was definitely not the ghetto; but every area has an underbelly, and Queens had a flourishing drug culture, especially in the eighties. Most of the drug action was in upper Manhattan, particularly Harlem and Washington Heights. Dealers there bought large quantities of cocaine and distributed it in the Bronx, Brooklyn, and later Queens. By the time they reached my neighborhood, the drug dealers and crime syndicates had become highly organized—they'd made all their mistakes in Brooklyn and the Bronx. Wealthy drug dealers bought nice homes in Queens and set up shops to take advantage of all that middle-class money.

Along with the Supreme Team, Lorenzo Nichols (aka "Fat Cat") controlled South Jamaica, a working-class neighborhood only four miles from my home. Most of the residents lived in either older two-family homes or the projects. Jamaica Avenue, part of the neighborhood's northern border, was filled with people every night, crowds who strolled the cracked sidewalks past razor wire on fenced parking lots, past hand-lettered signs in storefronts, and past homes with bars over the windows.

Drugs drew people to South Jamaica, and the dealers controlled the street. I'd heard that one corner drug spot made $150,000 a day. These guys robbed, murdered, and dealt drugs, but they caught the nation's attention in February 1988 when Howard "Pappy" Mason, a drug dealer associated with Fat Cat, ordered his men to kill a cop. Twenty-two-year-old police officer Eddie Byrne was shot to death in his patrol car, provoking national outrage and an intense police crackdown on drug dealing in Queens. George H. W. Bush carried Eddie Byrne's police badge with him on the presidential campaign trail, even as Nancy Reagan continued to tell kids to "just say no."

You might think all that crime and murder would frighten a kid so much that he'd want to avoid the drug dealer's lifestyle. Unfortunately, I'd been attracted to it long before crime in Queens hit the national radar. I'd been hooked as a youngster, baited by flashy toys and expensive rides.

When mopeds first came out, one kid had a blue-and-white moped everyone talked about. Rumor had it that it had cost thousands of dollars and that he got it because his family was connected to the mob (a rumor that seemed to be confirmed later when I was told his uncle had been discovered chopped up in the trunk of a car). That kid was the only sixteen-year-old in Queens with a moped, and everyone knew he could afford it because his family ran drug spots.

Despite the serious pockets of poverty in the area, a seventeen-year-old from the neighborhood bought a Cadillac Seville. One afternoon when I was nine or ten, a friend and I walked the block and a half to McDonald's. We were sitting outside when we saw the kid with the Cadillac approaching the drive-through line, but an ambulance pulled in first. My friend and I were wondering if someone was sick when we heard, "Freeze! Don't move, don't move!"

Fifteen armed undercover cops leapt out of the ambulance and surrounded the guy in the Cadillac. Then they pulled him out, laid him on the ground, and cuffed him.

"Drug dealer," my friend said.

My young brain connected the dots. *Oh! So that's how he got the Cadillac.*

My parents were always telling me, "If you work hard, you can do things and buy things when you get older." But I saw kids not much older than I buying nice things whenever they wanted them. To have that kind of power . . . the idea boggled my young brain. To be able to go where I wanted, buy what I wanted, walk down the street and hear others whispering about how cool and powerful I was . . . that was the life of a street god.

Also, unlike my older siblings, I had difficulty escaping the influence of drugs because they seemed to be everywhere. I remember going into a new little store one afternoon and buying a bottle of Nestlé Quik chocolate milk. When I carried my drink outside, I took a sip and gagged. I tipped the bottle and watched the contents spill onto the sidewalk like oatmeal, all clumped together. When I went home and told my mother, anger flared in her eyes. "That's not a store," she said, giving me a hard look. "You don't go in there again. Never buy anything from that place."

I don't know why I went in the first time—the Jamaican woman who ran it used to yell at all the kids who went inside. But we noticed that all the tough guys hung out there, and later we heard that someone had killed the store's owner and the owner's brother. The killer was connected to a man called Mr. McNally.

That's when I realized that the drug trade had a hierarchy. I'd hear people say, "Oh, you gotta see Mr. McNally" or "You need to meet Mr. McNally."

By the time I entered middle school, I understood that the drug world was complicated and ruthless. Yet I no longer wanted to be just a cool dealer—I wanted to be the man at the top of the ladder.

I got my start in drug dealing shortly after I met Blaze, a kid from Harlem, in middle school. He pulled me aside one afternoon and gestured toward his pocket. "Yo, I have these mess-tabs," he said, lowering his voice. "They're little pills. You take one, man, you'll be on a joyride."

I gaped at him. "Really?"

He grinned. "I'll give you one, and then I'd love for you to help me sell 'em. They sell for three dollars each, and you can keep a dollar for each one you sell."

I liked the idea of making money, and I liked the idea of the pills. So I swallowed one and went back to class. The teacher stood up in front of us and said we were about to have a special assembly led by a group that had come in to talk to us about drugs.

Meanwhile, nothing seemed to be happening to me. I couldn't believe it. Here I'd just taken my first pill, but I couldn't feel anything. I didn't think the pill was going to do anything.

I sat near Tamera, a girl I liked, and somehow I found the nerve to tell her so.

She looked at me like I'd grown an extra head. "You like me? Are you serious?"

When she said that, I don't know why, but I started to laugh and cry literal tears. The bell rang and we stood and went out to go hear about drug abuse, and for some reason I couldn't stop giggling. I managed to control it at first, but the more the drug counselor talked, the harder it was for me to control myself. I finally burst out laughing, and the counselor shot me a look that said, *I think you're high right now, but how could you be? You're only a kid.*

In that second, I realized I was high. That drug had messed with my mind and lowered my self-control. I didn't like being out of control.

Later I told Blaze I didn't want to use the drugs, but I'd help him sell them. I started to walk around with the other drug dealers, and they'd buy mescaline tablets from me. But Blaze ran out and was never able to get any more, so for a while my drug dealing ended. Then a girl gave Blaze and me a half pound of weed, which we sold on weekends at my hot dog stand. Eventually that supply ran out too.

Yet I'd had a taste of money and success, and I wanted more. I knew it was only a matter of time before I would pick up selling again.

*   *   *

When I was five, my older sister Dawn went away to Sarah Lawrence College—big news for our family, since the school was one of the top one hundred colleges in the country.

I was glad to see her when she came home for Christmas break, but I wasn't sure what she meant when she told us she'd been saved. "I have Jesus," she told me, her eyes glowing. "I'm different now."

"That's great," I told her, but I still wasn't sure what she meant. She didn't look different, but she sure acted different. For one thing, she began to play Andraé Crouch music, and I just couldn't get into it.

So I walked into her room with my hands over my ears. "Why are you playing that lame music?"

She smiled at me. "I'm worshiping Jesus."

"What? Man, put on some Earth, Wind & Fire. Put on anything else."

Dawn didn't change her music; she just kept playing Andraé Crouch, who kept singing "To God Be the Glory."

Then Dawn really went off the deep end. She began playing tapes—not of people singing, but of people *talking*. They were men, mostly, and they talked and talked, their voices coming through the walls and driving me crazy. I asked her who was doing all that talking on tape, and she said Oral Roberts.

"Who's he?"

"He's a preacher."

"Man." I shook my head. You had to be some kind of crazy if having Jesus meant that you sat around listening to people talk all the time. I thought Dawn had fallen off the planet. She wouldn't hang out with us as she used to but instead sat in her room, worshiping and listening to those talking tapes.

One day some of our younger cousins came over. One of them, Terry, went up to hug Dawn. "Hey, Dawn! I hear you're saved!"

"Yes!" she said, her eyes shining again.

"That's so cool! I am too!"

They were practically jumping for joy, but all I could think was, *More people got Jesus? What's happening around here?*

My family weren't what you'd call regular churchgoers. We went to church once in a blue moon—on Easter and Christmas, mostly, when we knew we had to get dressed up, go to church, and tolerate a man who yelled at us for an hour or so. It wasn't fun.

But Dawn and Terry were doing something different. They were playing tapes and singing, and in every conversation they seemed to sneak in a reference to what God had to say about every subject under the sun.

I just couldn't connect the two experiences. My church experience was nothing at all like what Terry and Dawn were doing and saying.

After Terry and the other cousins left, Dawn called me into her room and gave me a little box. "Open it," she said. "It's for you."

I opened it and found an illustrated Bible.

"It's about God," she said, watching me flip through the pages to see the pictures.

I shook my head and repeated what I'd heard my father say at least a dozen times. "I don't believe in God."

Dawn sighed heavily, and I could tell she was frustrated. "You know what, Dimas?" She tilted her head to meet my eye. "If you want to see God, you go into the other room and you ask him to show himself to you. He will, if you ask him."

"All right."

With the simple determination of a child, I went into my mother's bedroom and got on my knees. I squeezed my eyes shut and said, "God, if you're real like my sister says, show me. I want to know you're real."

When I opened my eyes, I was somewhere else, as if I were in a vision. I saw a grassy field, where two men stood measuring something with a long ruler. They stopped what they were doing long enough to look over at me, and I could tell they were smiling. They had beards, but I was so struck by those peaceful smiles that I couldn't tell if the men were black or white.

I freaked out and closed my eyes, desperate to block out the sight.

When I opened my eyes again, I was back in my mother's room. I got up and ran, terrified, back to Dawn. "I believe!" I yelled, my feet pounding the floor. "I really believe! I saw these men measuring grass and fields, and everything was bright and shiny, and I got scared and ran. And now I'm back here."

Dawn smiled. "Good. Now we've got to start reading the Bible together."

After that, I would sit with her every day, and she would read Bible stories to me. I was too young to read the big words on the page, but I could always tell where she was reading. Sometimes she'd get interrupted and look away. When she was ready to read again, she'd say, "Now, where was I?" and I could always tell her exactly where she'd stopped.

Dawn had to go back to school after that holiday break, and after that nobody read the Bible to me. My interest in spiritual things faded, but my sister had planted seeds. Oh yes, she had.

CHAPTER TWO

AFTER SUFFERING the beating from Abdul, I realized that I had to change teams. I needed more experience before I could run an operation on my own, so I thought about switching my allegiance to either the Top Guns or the Ice Boys.

Though the Supreme Team controlled South Jamaica, Mr. McNally ran the drug trade in Cambria Heights. His family had been indicted for several homicides, and his influence had spawned a brutal group called the Top Guns. I didn't want anything to do with killing, but if I only sold drugs, maybe I wouldn't have to resort to violence.

A mile away from Mr. McNally's empire, another family operated a lucrative crack industry under the name of the Ice Boys. Rocco, the head of the group, was a smart boss who kept his distance from the drugs. As a former addict, he'd learned the business from the inside out. His clients were wealthy addicts from affluent Long Island communities who traveled down to Jamaica Avenue for their drug supply.

Rocco's organized crew was fronted by his twin younger brothers, ruthless enforcers named Mick and Nick. Tough as nails, they'd beat up any dealer who came up short with the money. Tommy, the Ice Boys' lieutenant, bought and cooked up the cocaine. Once he'd transformed it into crack, other guys would distribute the product to team members who passed the drugs on to hustlers, who either worked noon to midnight or slugged it out on the midnight-to-noon shift, Sunday through Saturday. For just three hundred dollars a week, those hustlers risked arrest and sometimes their lives.

Convinced that I wanted to change my allegiance, I approached a member of the Top Guns and offered to hustle on Springfield Boulevard, part of Mr. McNally's territory. As soon as I'd made my offer, the guy backed away and narrowed his eyes, looking at me with suspicion. He walked over to another dude, a guy called Homicide, and I heard him mutter, "Yo, man, he could be a cop or something."

I've always been tall for my age, but I didn't see how anyone could mistake me for a cop. Still, Homicide sauntered over and said one of his sons could get me started if I was interested in dealing for them.

By that time I'd had serious second thoughts. Those guys had to be crazy—what kind of dude took the street name *Homicide*? I couldn't shake the feeling that if I went with the Top Guns, I'd probably end up in a body bag.

Since the Top Guns seemed to be more about violence than money, I moved on. Too many kids in my neighborhood got killed, and chalk outlines were a daily reality because the cops had to get bodies off the streets in a hurry. Even young kids knew about murder, and they knew drug dealers held the reins of power.

One of my childhood heroes, a personable seventeen-year-old named Jerry, had been killed in a crack house on Springfield. He was a brave and popular guy who brawled with the best of them, and the community was saddened when someone murdered him. Over a thousand stunned teens tried to get into his funeral, most of them in complete shock that he'd been killed over some drug foolishness.

I hadn't known Jerry well, but like lots of other young guys, I'd looked up to him and wanted to be like him. But I didn't want to be murdered over a drug deal. The cold-blooded look in the eye of the Top Guns hustler made me think of Jerry's murder, so I left their territory and vowed never to return.

My other option was to join the Ice Boys. They were known for being smart, raking in money, and sporting fly cars; plus, their organization had a family vibe around it. They even owned a rap group that had enjoyed a decent career. Everyone in Hollis, another neighborhood in Queens, loved Jamaica Park, and the Ice Boys controlled the park.

Different drug enterprises held down different blocks along the Avenue. The dangers of selling on Jamaica were high, but the huge profits from a wealthy clientele outweighed the risks. My friend Blaze introduced me to the Ice Boys, and their operation picked me up right away.

Meanwhile, the police had focused a spotlight on drug operations along Jamaica Avenue. Ninety percent of the clients going to Jamaica were white business professionals from well-to-do communities: Wall Street brokers, Broadway dancers, artists, and designers. In a mostly black community, these people were as out of place as a mouse in a meat loaf, so they drew narcotics squads to Jamaica Avenue like high-powered magnets. Cops began to stake out the park and made dozens of arrests.

When I joined up with the Ice Boys, they were hemorrhaging from drug busts. I quickly realized that the dealers from Cambria Heights didn't have the business acumen of the Supreme Team. I began to influence their operation by applying knowledge I'd picked up in South Jamaica—for instance, I had addicts give me the names of other addicts, which helped me to avoid selling to anyone I didn't know. My strategies paid off, and after sharing them with other hustlers, I helped bring the Ice Boys' arrest record down to zero. They'd often ask me, "How are you still here? You've lasted longer than anybody else."

I should have been in school, but I was responsible for holding down the noon-to-midnight shift on the block. I came home at one in the morning and left at eleven, just before lunch.

My mother knew what I was into, and I was driving her crazy. She would yell, "I'm your mother, and you need to listen to me!"

I loved her, and I could see that she was working hard to give me a good life. She'd raised Dawn, Emerald, and Chad in our tidy home, but the neighborhood had changed dramatically since they had been in school. King Crack now ruled the streets only a few blocks away, and those who dealt it were the lords of the land. I wanted all the trappings of money and power that I saw flaunted on the street. I wanted what my peers wanted, and I lived not for my family but for my new team.

One day, my mother brought me in and made me sit in front of her. "Dimas," she said, squaring her shoulders, "you need to stop hanging with those drug dealers. You need to study and work hard and get yourself straightened out. If you don't shape up and come in at a decent hour, I'm going to send you to military school."

I looked at her and shook my head. We'd had these talks before, and I knew that her threat sprang from desperation because she couldn't afford to send me to any kind of private school. I got up and left the room, knowing that she couldn't stop me from doing what I wanted.

And quitting wouldn't have been easy because Mick and Nick kept close tabs on their employees. One day I had the flu, so I didn't go to my block at noon. A couple of hours later, Mick and Nick roared up to my house on their motorcycles, knocked on the door, and asked why I wasn't working the block. Startled, I stammered out my excuse: "I'm sick." Then I closed the door and slid down the wall, alarmed by the fact that they knew where I lived. Those guys did their homework, and they knew more about me than I'd realized.

I didn't want to have to tell my mother that I'd stopped going to school, so I began to leave the house at 7 a.m., pretending to go to class. As soon as I turned the corner, though, I'd head to a weed spot that Rocco's best friend, Steve, had opened in an apartment above a Spanish bodega. Customers would get the address to the weed spot, climb the stairs, and knock on the door. Someone would open the door and complete the deal, and then the customer would walk out. I had taken to sleeping at Steve's weed spot until my shift started at noon.

Around that time, a serial killer who preyed on prostitutes surfaced. The cops knew that one particular prostitute, an addict named Punk Rock, would be a prime target for the killer. One morning two officers walked into the weed spot and asked if we knew her. Of course we did, so they asked us to warn her about the killer.

Then the cops did something unexpected—they said our new weed spot had hit the narcotics squad's radar, so we needed to be careful. We nodded at the warning, but when the cops left, I looked at Steve and lifted an eyebrow. In my gut I knew the Ice Boys had a lot more going on than met the eye. Though the police sometimes snatched up their workers, none of the bosses had ever seen the interior of a jail cell, and the workers faced only obligatory harassment now and then. I couldn't have proved it, but I suspected the Ice Boys of having some sort of agreement with the police. Only through a turncoat could the police have penetrated their operation.

The Ice Boys had no qualms about flaunting their success. Everyone on the team but me (I was too young) bought new cars. Though I had helped them protect and expand their operation, they saw me as a young buck. I saw myself as a hard worker who was being ripped off at three hundred dollars a week, but whenever I asked for more money, their enforcers rose up to threaten me. I had become trapped in their organization and couldn't see a way out.

Meanwhile, my mother had enlisted my father in an attempt to rescue me from the perils of the life I'd chosen. Thinking strategically, they put me in the car and drove me to Camp Kiwago to get me out of the city, but even as we drove away, my thoughts centered on the streets. All I could think about was my drug business and the opportunities I was missing back home.

The camp was a great experience, but the change of scenery did little to deter me from the path I'd chosen. As soon as the camp ended, I went home and got right back to work. The Ice Boys were happy to see me—while I'd been away, the cops had made several busts at our weed spot, so I needed to lay low until things cooled down.

During my forced vacation, I visited my friend Blaze to smoke weed. He had a beautiful girl with him, and she was smoking weed laced with cocaine. She took a puff off her blunt, a hollowed-out cigar filled with marijuana, and then invited me to place my lips on hers as she blew smoke into my mouth. I blinked as the high hit me hard, and I walked away vowing never to do that again. I left that potent mixture alone for a while, but her kiss had opened a gateway that would beckon to me again.

I had always avoided coke because I'd witnessed brutal beatings administered by the Ice Boys whenever one of their team members got high on anything stronger than weed. Drug dealers are well aware of one unassailable fact—drug addicts are not good drug dealers because they're either too wasted to sell or they're likely to smoke the inventory. Either alternative is bad for business.

Working for the Ice Boys was like walking a tightrope. My mom was constantly frustrated with me for coming in late and missing school, and I hated making her crazy . . . but I didn't hate it enough to stop hustling. I began to leave the block before the end of my shift to keep the peace at home. Of all the people in my life, my mother was the easiest to please, and I could make her happy by coming home in time to tell her good night.

I never got close to any of the guys in the crew. They had a habit of keeping everyone at arm's length because no one likes to beat up a close friend. Rocco and Tommy seemed to like me, but they always went missing on payday.

At that point my feelings were about as mixed as they could be. I hated the Ice Boys, yet I admired them tremendously. I hated disappointing my parents, but I enjoyed the prestige that went along with being down with the Ice Boys. I was addicted to the hustle and challenge of selling drugs, but I knew I could be robbed or arrested at any moment.

Out of the blue one day, a white customer started fussing and hollering at me. "Daylight is crap," she yelled. "He stole my money and gave me fake crack."

Like sharks smelling blood in the water, the crew surrounded me and shouted that I better not be guilty of doing something like that. I told them the woman was lying, but they promised that Mick and Nick would not hesitate to punish me if something like that ever happened again.

I was devastated to think that my faithfulness could be so easily overlooked if a white crackhead started to complain. I figured something was wrong with that woman, and something was wrong with the Ice Boys.

Two days later a man pulled up on a bike to buy drugs. I looked at him and shook my head. "I don't know you, and I don't have any drugs."

Then that same crazy white crackhead rolled down the tinted window of her car. "I know him. He's cool."

When I hesitated, another addict saw that I wasn't going to give in. "I'll sell to him," he said. "She knows him."

I walked away and dropped a crack capsule where the buyer on the bike couldn't see me. The addict picked it up, sold it to the guy, and then gave me the money.

After taking the cash, I ran to a hot dog stand to get rid of it, but an instant later, cops swarmed the area—the situation had been a setup. I tossed my wad of bills into the hot dog truck, but too late. The police arrested me and the addict who had made the sale. Even though they couldn't find any money or drugs on me, I was charged with directing drug traffic because I'd been present during the exchange.

At fifteen, I found myself sitting in the back of a police car, my hands cuffed behind my back, well aware that this time I could end up at New York City's Rikers Island—one of the toughest and most notorious jails in the nation. My hands were slick with sweat, my heart thumping with anxiety, but somehow I had sense enough to protect my mom from the dread that had overtaken me.

So that I wouldn't have to call her, I lied and said I was sixteen.

*   *   *

I was first arrested at thirteen. One group of kids from my neighborhood were stealing cars with a "pulley," a device that allowed us to steal Hondas and Toyotas by breaking in through the back window, inserting an object into the ignition, and then pulling the ignition device out of its holder. Once that was done, we could start the car with a screwdriver.

I tried to steal a car once and failed, but I had friends who were pros. Lance's father was a truck driver, and he'd taught Lance how to drive so the boy could move cars when the father needed to park a truck. Lance would steal a vehicle and take it to a chop shop; there they'd pay him three hundred dollars. Then they'd strip the car and earn thousands selling off the parts.

Lance, Trevor, and a guy from Manhattan came to me and said they'd found a Nissan Maxima. I was excited because my sister

Emerald's boyfriend had promised me three hundred dollars if I would bring him a car. So we stole the Maxima, and Lance drove us away.

We were cutting across a major New York street when a police car passed us. One of the officers did a double take when he spotted twelve-year-old Lance at the wheel, and they hit the siren. We abandoned the car and split. Lance and the guy from Manhattan took off, but Trevor and I hid and tried to wait out the police.

Five minutes later, a cop pointed his gun at us and told us it was over. We lifted our hands and came out; then we told the cops that a fictional guy named Bobby had pulled up to give us a ride in his mother's car. Lance was fast enough to get away, but Trevor and I got arrested.

That night was the longest of my life. My mother was upset, crying and wondering how she was going to be successful. She was both trying to make a good life for me and working to finish her master's degree—not easy when she kept having to get me out of trouble. I ended up in family court, where I got a paid lawyer who ended up working as my lawyer for years.

My attorney got the charges dropped because I wasn't the driver.

Now, sitting in the cop car after the drug bust, I began to prepare my mind for the worst—Rikers. From hearing others talk, I knew the Central Booking routine. That night I would be sleeping on a cold metal bench with nothing but a cheap roll of toilet tissue for a pillow. I'd be surrounded by other guys who'd been picked up for various crimes, and no one would be in a good mood.

That much I expected, but the unknown had my thoughts racing. Anything could happen if I landed behind Rikers' fortified walls.

Rikers Island is one of the most violent jails in the country, a scary place even for hardened criminals. The jail overflows with drug dealers and killers and their weapons—knives, razors, and jail-made shanks. In New York City you could often identify a former Rikers inmate by the long, dark scars on his face, slashes that marked a man like a tattoo.

My impending visit to Rikers occurred at the height of the crack wars in the mid-eighties. New York City had a reputation of being home to heinous crimes—from kidnapping to rape and murder.

Because my father had worked as a captain at Rikers before he retired, I knew that the complex held offenders who were awaiting trial and either couldn't afford bail or had been refused bail. Criminals who had been given sentences of one year or less were held there, along with those who had been sentenced to serve more than a year and were awaiting transfer to a prison. The jail could hold up to 15,000 inmates—more than the population of many towns.

On my way to Central Booking, I couldn't help thinking about the pain and humiliation I'd seen on my mother's face the last time I got arrested. I couldn't stand the thought of my mother being dragged through the court system yet again. I wanted to spare her further degradation, so I told myself that nothing Rikers threw at me could be worse than the shame and soul-crushing guilt of knowing I'd hurt my mother again.

The cops fingerprinted the crackhead dude and me, then sent us to different cells. The charge against me was so insignificant that I convinced myself I'd soon be walking out with a probation deal and a slap on the hand. As the sun set over Central Booking, I stretched out on the metal bench, pillowed my head on the roll of toilet paper, and fell asleep.

The next morning I went before a judge who set bail at five hundred dollars and sent me to Rikers. Fear consumed me as reality set in. The brave front I'd put on to spare my mother vanished as soon as the word *Rikers* rolled off of the judge's tongue.

"Hey, I'm only fifteen! I'm fifteen! I'm just fifteen years old!" I yelled.

The cops in the room laughed. "Too late! You're going to the big house now!"

I knew I'd have to get tough in a hurry. I was tall and skinny—hardly the image of a bodybuilder. I went into beast mode and summoned the courage to attack with everything I had if anyone even gave me a threatening look.

The events that followed seemed to play out in slow motion. The holding cells clanked open as the guards cuffed us prisoners together and marched us single file to the Rikers Island express bus. During the ride over the unmarked three-lane bridge, I sized up every prisoner on the bus, ready to strike with full force at a second's notice. We reached our destination in fifteen minutes, but it was the longest quarter hour of my life.

The bus halted before large gates that opened to massive barbed-wire fences. I tied my sneakers extra tight, bracing for the worst. The guards marched us out and announced that Rikers was overcrowded, so we would have no beds that night.

The guards divided us into groups: one for adults, one for adolescents, and one for people in protective custody. Protective custody was for offenders who either couldn't handle the pressure or whose cases had generated a storm of negative publicity.

I wouldn't say that any area of Rikers is beautiful, but the most degrading spot was the shower we had to use—a broken-down, moldy stall that looked like something straight out of *The Shawshank Redemption*. By the time I saw that shower, I was desperate for somebody to get me out of the mess I had made.

I was able to call my friend Lance a couple of times and send him to Jamaica Park to get bail money. During one call, he told me the Ice Boys were too busy placing bets on a basketball game to find five hundred dollars to pay my bail. My blood began to boil. Purposely or not, they were sending a message: I wasn't important enough to bother with.

On the fifth night, I finally heard an officer bark, "Dimas Cook? Anybody here named Dimas Cook?"

I leaped up, nearly having forgotten that I'd given a fake last name.

"Come with me," the officer said. "You just made bail."

I couldn't restrain a grin that stretched from ear to ear. I flashed a peace sign and called, "Peace out, fellas!"

I knew I had escaped hell by only a few hours—they were about to send me into the general population, where fellow inmates say hello by beating and robbing newcomers. I knew it was a brutal place, and I wanted no part of it.

A flood of emotions washed over me—bewilderment when I thought about why the Ice Boys had let me rot in Rikers for five days, and overwhelming gratitude that I was finally free.

That night I went home, apologized to my mother for causing her grief, and slept for two days, waking only to eat, drink, and go back to bed.

*   *   *

After getting out of jail, I realized the time had come for me to take my life into my own hands. I thought about it long and hard and came to understand two things. First, if my bosses weren't going to bail me out, I might as well work for myself. Second, I knew all of the Ice Boys' customers, and knowledge was power.

I called Black Sean and asked him if he wanted to go into business with me. He was ready to jump onboard, so we decided to meet up in a few days to discuss how our partnership would work.

Before meeting with Black Sean, I wanted to try my hand at an independent hustle. So I went to a dealer and bought seven grams of cocaine with the last $300 payday I got from the Ice Boys. Then I went to see Blaze and asked him for help in learning how to cook cocaine into crack. He took me to a psycho named Fat Rock, a man who cooked crack on the side. His full-time job was beating people up.

Fat Rock was big, fat, and known for stomping people flat. I was a little worried about working with him but too eager to turn back. I had to give Fat Rock some cocaine to sniff, but then he allowed me to watch his younger brother Larry cook it into crack.

I watched Larry like a hawk, soaking in every step so I'd be able to do it myself. He showed me everything, and I left feeling confident that I could do it. Fat Rock tried to bully me for some more cocaine, but I resisted. When I left, I was grateful I hadn't been robbed, though I barely made it out of there with a profit.

That night I went to a block party to get reacquainted with friends from the Hollis neighborhood. My friends were out in full force, dancing in the street and having a ball. I moved from group to group, exchanging hugs with dudes I hadn't seen in a while and smiling at all the beautiful girls. We swapped stories and gossip, and I told several guys about my time in Rikers. "I'm not in any hurry to go back there," I joked.

I saw my friend Bullwinkle on the other side of the crowd and tried to get to him, but by the time I'd made it over there, he'd already left the party. I shrugged and carried on, talking to as many people as I could.

Then, without warning, the gaiety of the party turned to shock and horror. Several people ran into the partying crowd screaming that Bullwinkle had just killed Baby Wise.

I could only stand and stare. I had just seen Bullwinkle, and who on earth was Baby Wise? I knew lots of dudes on the street called Wise, but which one was Baby Wise? Fresh from Rikers, I felt terrible that Bullwinkle had done something that would put him behind bars forever. I'd nearly gone crazy after being in jail for five days, so how would it feel to know you'd be in that environment for the rest of your life?

I looked around and saw with startling clarity that I was surrounded by a band of past, present, and future killers. They were everywhere in Hollis.

I didn't have much time to contemplate that startling truth. Blaze had witnessed Baby Wise's murder and stooped so low as to steal the dying man's gun and money. The neighborhood was outraged when they learned those details, and people began to search for Blaze with justice on their minds.

I hurried over to Blaze's house, hoping that a neighborhood posse wouldn't show up while I was there. Blaze was home and proudly showed me Baby Wise's nickel-plated .380 automatic pistol.

I stared at it in disbelief. All I could think about was getting away from the gun and away from Blaze.

In the next few days, I put thoughts of Baby Wise's murder aside and tried to focus on getting my drug business off the ground. I didn't have enough cash to buy a significant amount of drugs, and in one crazy attempt I bought twenty grams of cocaine and ruined it trying to cook crack. That was a huge loss, so I got with my friend Smokie and we came up with the idea of robbing a cab driver, but neither of us had a gun. So Smokie and I went to see Blaze and persuaded him to loan us the .380 that had belonged to Baby Wise.

That night Smokie and I walked at least three miles away from our hood so we could hail a cab in a different community. We debated where to stop, then finally went to a back road near a street with an alley we could use for a quick getaway. When a green taxi pulled up, we got into the cab and asked the driver to take us to an address in South Jamaica.

Silence filled the cab as we rode and watched storefronts, gas stations, and parking lots slide by. I desperately needed money, but I'd never threatened anyone with a gun. What if the driver didn't give us the money? But surely he would. Who wouldn't hand over his money with a gun pointed at his head?

By the time the cab was nearing Blaze's block, I had mustered enough courage to pull out the pistol.

"Hey, dude! Pull over now!"

The cab driver tossed one frightened look over his shoulder, shouted something in a foreign language, and then opened his door and slid out of the taxi while it was still moving. For a moment I felt pure panic, then the cab crashed into the curb. I was so terrified that I jumped out of the car, pointed the gun at the stunned driver's head, and pulled the trigger.

By some miracle, the gun jammed. Smokie and I ran off, and I hadn't gone ten yards before I began to thank God that I hadn't killed the man. I'd never had the slightest desire to kill anyone—I thought only crazy, ruthless people committed murder. But I had pulled the trigger. If that gun hadn't jammed . . .

We ran to Blaze's house and hid out for hours, pacing and peering out from behind the window blinds as we prayed the cops wouldn't find us. While hiding out, we realized that Baby Wise might have pulled the trigger on Bullwinkle and had the gun jam on him, too. Bullwinkle might have shot Baby Wise in self-defense.

Even now, the memory of that incident has the power to shock me. In one instant, in a millisecond, I could have killed an innocent man, ruined my life, and devastated my parents. Though I had committed countless crimes, I hadn't committed murder. The realization of how close I had come to killing an innocent man still makes me stop and thank God for not allowing that attempted robbery to become a homicide.

Yet so many of the guys I'd grown up with, boys who used to play football with me, were now ruthless killers . . . and I was walking the same path.

*   *   *

The next day I hooked up with Black Sean to make some money. Because he had some product, we went to the corner of 210th Street and Jamaica Avenue to begin our new business venture.

Things started off okay. Several former Jamaica Avenue customers came to me, and I was on a roll. Then a black Mercedes with thick tinted windows pulled up and a window slid down. Rocco of the Ice Boys was inside the car, and his hot gaze was trained on me.

"You dudes cannot set up shop on this block," he said, his voice like iron.

I leaned down to see him better. "Why not? There's a spot on 212th Street and Jamaica Avenue. This here is my block."

"No, 212th Street is run by Cap and Shane, and trust me—you ain't no Cap and Shane. Besides that, they know us."

"But you know me," I pointed out.

Rocco stared at me a long moment, then shook his head. "I'm not gonna warn you again."

Black Sean and I stood silently as Rocco drove off. When the car disappeared, I told Black Sean that we needed to build this block and hold it down, but Rocco's visit had rattled Black Sean. He glanced around as if someone might be watching, then lowered his voice. "Let's just leave now and talk about this later."

Since there was no sense in trying to talk to him then, I suggested that we go chill at a friend's house. We hunkered down in a quiet corner and talked. We knew we needed to beef up our crew if we were going to be serious contenders in the drug game. We'd have to start looking for workers.

No sooner had we walked out of the house than a couple of thirteen-year-olds, Ricky and Hector, rode up on their bikes to ask whether they could hustle for us. We couldn't believe the timing—it was like a hood miracle.

We agreed to let them join our crew and put them right to work. For young cats, they came up with a brilliant plan to hide the drugs. They pulled out switchblades and sliced one-inch slits in the hand-balls they were carrying. Then they stuffed the balls with crack capsules. Black Sean and I were impressed, but not for long.

Soon Ricky and Hector came running back to us screaming that they'd just been robbed by a white biker. A bunch of us bolted out of the house and ran down Jamaica Avenue toward a popular Harley-Davidson club located at 211th Place and Jamaica Avenue.

On the way, Ricky explained what had happened. "One of the bikers was walking his Doberman near the club, and the dog found one of the balls and then the other."

"Man, where'd you hide the balls?" I asked.

"In the grass. So the dog had both balls and took them to the biker dude. He was about to hand them back to us, but he musta heard something rattling inside. He opened them up and found the crack."

I had heard enough. We stalked toward the biker club and found half a dozen leather-clad guys standing around their bikes. "Hey," I called, "you got something that belongs to us."

One ZZ Top look-alike smiled at me. "I've got your crack and the cops are coming. So what are you gonna do about it?"

Another yelled, "You'd better get out of here now!"

I hesitated, but I couldn't afford to call their bluff, so I backed down and we took the loss.

The loss of all that crack was the straw that broke Black Sean's back. He took the unfortunate turn of events as a bad sign—clearly, we weren't supposed to be in business together. He told me he was going back to hustling for Abdul, but before leaving he gave me a stern warning. "That house where you're hanging is full of cocaine heads," he said, his eyes narrowing. "If you keep chillin' there, you're gonna become one too. Remember the South Jamaica rules, Dimas. Don't fall for the tricks of amateurs."

He gave me a hug and turned to walk away. He hadn't gone two steps when Blaze rolled up and said the Ice Boys were driving around looking for me and Black Sean.

That did it. I clenched my fist as my temper flared. My courage was born from pent-up anger, disappointment, and frustration with the bikers and the Ice Boys. Those guys had played me for the last time, and I wasn't going to take it anymore. My dreams of having my own enterprise had gotten off to a bad start with the loss of the drugs to the bikers, but now the Ice Boys were looking to put the beatdown on us for an operation that had barely gotten off the ground.

I told Black Sean and everyone with us that I refused to run. I was convinced that the Ice Boys owed me thousands of dollars from all the time I put in for them, so they weren't going to punk me. I was ready to fight any one of them or all of them.

Eight guys stood around me at that moment, and they all claimed to have my back.

Black Sean looked at me. "If you want to step to them, I'm with you."

With that said, we all got our Braveheart on and headed over to 202nd Street. As soon as we reached the block, muscle twins Mick and Nick stepped out of a store and spotted us. "You wanna dance?" Nick called.

I stepped forward. "You looking for me? I'm right here. What's up now?"

Then this new cat who'd been hired after I left the Ice Boys stepped out with a gun to keep my crew at bay. That left me to take on Mick and Nick by myself, but I was so amped up I didn't care. We started brawling and slugging it out. They landed two hard blows and knocked me to the ground. Next they charged Black Sean. After punching him a couple of times, the Ice Boys walked away.

I scrambled to my feet. "We ain't soft; 210th Street is our block. We ain't no punks, you hear me? That street belongs to us!"

I told my crew to come on and we all walked away, including Black Sean. He'd been punched just enough to realize he didn't want any further part in our venture. He had kept his word and stepped into the ring with me, but when we all got back to our hood, he told me he was out. I never saw him again.

We didn't exactly win the fight, but nobody had ever seen anyone stand up to the Ice Boys like that. Everyone patted me on the back as we walked back to our friend's house. "You ain't no joke, Slim." "Yo, Daylight, you got mad heart!"

My mouth was bleeding and my heart racing, but I felt like a gladiator. I had stood toe-to-toe with the infamous Mick and Nick. According to the crowd around me, it had looked like I was handling the two of them together.

Once we reached the house, I was ready to collapse but learned that someone had stolen one of the drug packages I had stashed in the backyard. My temper only boiled higher.

When my adrenaline level returned to normal, I realized that despite my short-lived victory over the Ice Boys, I had no real friends. Someone at the house where I'd been hanging out had stolen my drugs, and all those who'd been shouting during the fight had gone off to do their own thing. I couldn't name a single trustworthy person in my circle of so-called friends.

The next day, however, I learned that my fight against Mick and Nick had elevated my street cred. Seemed like everybody had heard about the skinny teenager who stepped up to the mighty Ice Boys and held his own against both of them. The story grew as it spread throughout the hood, and by the end of the week you'd have thought I'd nearly killed them both with the jawbone of a donkey.

But the truth was far simpler: I was hood-famous and almost broke. With no partner to back me up, I'd end up seriously injured or dead if I kept operating on 210th Street. It pained me to admit the truth, but something had to change.

I decided to take a serious look at 212th Street and sell where I could. I became a nomad, hustling to sell here and there with no home base. When I saw that a new pool hall had opened on Jamaica Avenue, I slipped inside to check it out. The pool hall, I learned, was only a front; once inside, I found Jamaican drug dealers operating in the open. I wandered, amazed, through the dudes and even managed to pop off a few sales without being noticed. Based on the hustlers operating there, I figured the pool hall was run by Cap and Shane.

While inside, I ran into a drug dealer I used to kick it with from time to time. Chris was a wild Jamaican who dripped with gold— gold teeth, gold bracelets, gold rings, and fat gold chains that flowed down his chest. Chris knew I was wandering from place to place with no set block, so he said we could work together. He told me to stop by the pool hall the next day so we could figure something out.

When I approached the pool hall twenty-four hours later, the place was swarming with cops. Someone had tortured Chris, burning the inside of his mouth with a blowtorch and then slitting his throat. When they pulled his body out of his apartment, his ankles and wrists were bound behind him with ropes.

Chris's gruesome death affected me deeply. He had been filled with life, personality, and joy and appeared to be on top of the world.

Then men who were pure evil set to work on him.

The hit on Chris was more hideous than most. I ran into a friend on Jamaica Avenue, and he whispered that he used to work for Cap . . . and Chris's murder sounded a lot like Cap's work.

My mother never found out about Chris's death—the story never even made the papers. Most of the neighborhood murders were never reported in the press, so it was as if those victims had never existed except in the hearts and minds of their families. Some drug dealers were psychopathic serial killers, and messed-up deals were just an excuse for them to take their pleasure in killing.

Years later I read about several bodies discovered on a Long Island beach—bodies that turned out to be women who worked as prostitutes from Jamaica Avenue in the 1990s. When I was growing up, we all knew someone was killing prostitutes. I might have met the killer on the street and sold him crack.

But in my teenage years, murder was a normal part of life. I saw it, heard about it, and learned that I'd better be careful so the same thing didn't happen to me. As young teens, we'd talk about killings, smoke our blunts, and move on to the next topic of conversation, never to think about those murders again unless we happened to walk past the spot where a killing had taken place. Then I'd remember and remind myself to be careful so I didn't end up dead too.

After Chris's murder, Cap and Shane disappeared, and we figured they were hiding from the police. Almost overnight, 212th Street became a free market, and every dealer I knew was eager to carve out a piece of turf.

I positioned myself nicely. I partnered up with a boss named Stretch, pushing his work and my own.

Though Chris's murder had opened up 212th Street to a slew of new hustlers, it also drew the attention of the police. I took frequent breaks from selling in an effort to keep the heat off. I'd visit Smokie or my friend Clive, and sometimes I'd use coke. The discipline and drive that had pushed me into the drug market eroded, and I went onto the block only when I felt like selling.

I knew I'd have to wait until the block cooled down before I could return to steady selling. I pulled out for a while, and in my downtime I would often sit and stare at the wall, my mind filling with images of Chris, alive and smiling.

CHAPTER THREE

How DID I END UP in Rikers at fifteen? Sometimes I wonder why I didn't end up there sooner.

Though I had good parents, I lived in a culture that respected toughness, flash, and power. Even as a preteen, I knew the rap groups that had come from my neighborhood, and I was familiar with their lyrics. Despite my good family, I had immersed myself in the culture of Queens.

We young kids would gather around the older kids in our neighborhood and listen to them talk. We picked up their attitudes, and we knew that the real money—which meant the real power—was held by the drug dealers. We learned who was good at fighting and who was good at robbing. We learned that power brought respect and respect enabled you to walk down the street without any hassles. We recognized the worker bees, and we knew who the main bosses were—the street gods who rarely showed their faces but wielded tremendous power.

The kids in my neighborhood were used to a steady stream of violence and murder. We didn't see murders on the block in Cambria Heights where I grew up, but we knew that people in the drug trade lived fast and died young. The hood's rumor mill buzzed anytime someone was killed as people speculated about who had probably done the job. We knew about hits and people who could be paid to carry one out.

The culture taught me what I'd have to do to be cool, and necessity taught me how to learn my lessons. Not only did I learn about the drug trade, I learned about burglary as well. To get money, my friends robbed homes throughout Cambria Heights, so I was breaking and entering while still in junior high school. Our ringleader was a guy named Jamaican Kev. Jamaican Kev's crew made so much money from home burglaries that down-and-out drug dealers would often join our team to make enough money to get back into dealing drugs. After all, you need cash to buy inventory.

In the late eighties, the two main drug blocks in our neighborhood were Murdock Avenue and Springfield Boulevard. When I was in middle school, Mr. McNally of the Top Guns waged war against the Jamaican family that controlled Murdock, and two-thirds of the Jamaican family's brothers ended up murdered. Mr. McNally's enforcer charged people rent to deal on Springfield.

*   *   *

I've had many nicknames in my lifetime—as a child, my parents called me "the elephant" because I had a good memory. My sister called me "Mikey" because, like the kid in the cereal commercial, I would eat anything. Some of my close friends called me "Dee." On the street I answered to "Slim" and "Running Man," but as a drug dealer, my street name was Daylight, a name I'd copied from a Jamaican dealer in Queens. I liked the name because it was unique, flashy, and strong. It also had a positive connotation—I wasn't a wicked dude, and I liked the positive ring that went along with it. Jamaican Daylight sold the best drugs in his territory, and I wanted my name, like his, to convey success.

Plus, girls liked the name. I could just imagine a girl smiling and saying, "I go out with Daylight."

One day when I was hanging out with my friend Blaze, he mentioned that a guy named Tank wanted to fight me. "He's such a good brawler—" Blaze shot me a lopsided grin—"that I'm sure he's gonna knock you out."

I knew Blaze loved to orchestrate drama, so I didn't panic. I didn't even know anyone named Tank. But neither did I ignore what Blaze said because you never knew who had painted a target on your back.

My pockets were full of crack capsules, ready to sell. Blaze hipped me to a hustler's paradise called Hempstead Avenue, a place booming with customers. Blaze always knew where the action was, but Hempstead Avenue looked like a danger zone to me. Cops drove by regularly, and I didn't know any of the clients. After working the street a while, I told Blaze we'd better leave before we both ended up in jail.

As we started to leave, a dude called Sach came by. He was called that after a character in the old Bowery Boys movies because he wore a pull-down hat and had a long nose, but unlike the fictional Sach, Queens Sach was always decked out in the flyest gear and gold chains. I was wary of him at first, but Blaze said Sach was his dude, and Sach knew all about Hempstead Avenue.

Sach, as it turned out, was also a cocaine dealer. In no time, he confirmed what I'd figured out intuitively—the heat was on Hempstead at the moment, and if we continued to stand out, we'd almost certainly be stopped and searched.

Sach seemed cool, so we took his advice and walked away from Hempstead. I made sure to file Sach's name in my list of helpful dudes, especially when Blaze said Sach was a guy who could hook us up with the money I needed to get my own drug business off the ground.

With Hempstead a no-go, Blaze convinced me to go with him to his hood, where we could meet Clive, another hustler. Clive had the 411 on a lot of the customers on 99th Avenue, right across the street from Blaze's and Clive's houses. I looked forward to meeting another guy who might be able to help me launch my dream of being a drug boss.

As we walked up to 99th Avenue, however, we heard the pop of gunfire and the screech of tires. Instinctively, we ducked behind a shrub and averted our eyes, obeying the law of the hood: Do not look at a shooter. Hit men were notorious for shooting not only their targets but also anyone who witnessed the event, even those who spotted the getaway vehicle.

Blaze and I laid low until quiet settled over the neighborhood. Then we lifted our heads and looked around. The getaway car was way down the block, too far away to be a danger, but in the middle of a scraggly lawn was an all-too-familiar sight—a couple of young guys sprawled motionless and bleeding on the ground.

Since I had drugs in my pockets, I knew I had to get off the block. I left to stash my drugs at Blaze's house, then returned to watch the fallout from the shooting.

Neighbors watched from their windows and the sidewalk, many of them shaking their heads in frustration and regret. Red and blue lights flashed from police vehicles while gloved paramedics loaded the two lifeless bodies onto gurneys, covered them with sheets, and slid them into ambulances.

I was pretty sure those boys weren't going to the hospital. They were heading to the morgue.

Meanwhile, the cops strung up crime tape and combed the area, investigating the crime. One of them took pictures of skid marks on the road. As I closed my eyes and remembered the image of those two dead boys, I kept hearing the whir of the camera shutter.

I opened my eyes, and Blaze and I looked at each other. Reality had dampened our enthusiasm for hustling.

We walked back to Blaze's house to pick up my package. Blaze suggested that we go see Clive, so we walked over to his house.

Clive lived in a dark, cold basement with his alcoholic uncle. He nodded when he met me, and something about the way his gaze kept darting from place to place made me uneasy. After a few minutes, he told us he was hiding out.

"I messed up," he said, sitting on the edge of an old chair. "Like an idiot, I messed up Fat Rock's money, and he's gonna be looking to beat me."

I knew about Fat Rock—the muscleman was a well-known enforcer in Queens, and he'd taught me how to make crack.

Blaze's eyes went wide. "You hidin' from Fat Rock?"

Clive shrugged. "I'm used to him beatin' on me. Just part of the business."

"Wow, man." Blaze cleared his throat. "You got any coke?"

Clive's face brightened. "Yeah. Y'all want some?"

I waved his offer away. "Naw man, I'm good."

"Come on, Dee." Blaze elbowed me. "It's not crack, it's coke."

I had avoided using cocaine because I believed it was highly addictive. Then I remembered the afternoon that pretty girl blew the smoke of a cocaine-laced blunt into my mouth. I didn't get addicted then, so why couldn't I dabble a bit now?

I caved like a New York pothole. After all of the heavy stuff we'd seen that day, sniffing a little coke didn't seem like such a bad idea. It might even make me feel better.

I nodded at Clive. "Okay. Just a little."

Clive leaned toward Blaze, his face twisting in a grin. They whispered back and forth, as if they'd just activated some devious master plan to clean out my pockets.

I didn't want any part of their sneaky little scheme, but it'd be okay to do a little coke and leave, right? Clive put on some reggae music, then poured the cocaine into neat lines and offered us a sniff.

I lowered my head and inhaled a line. The cocaine hit me and instantly made me paranoid. In a flash I realized I didn't really know Clive. I could be robbed or shot in his basement. He was in a tight spot and hungry for money to get back in Fat Rock's good graces.

Worried and suspicious, I jumped up. "I've gotta go. Here's ten dollars. I'm out."

I felt a rush of relief when I stepped out into fresh air and daylight, but the experience didn't turn me off to cocaine. Far from it.

Once I opened the door to coke, I seemed to become a human magnet for the stuff. The next day, two girls on my block told me that if I wanted to have sex with them, all I needed to do was rent a room at the local motel and give them fifty dollars' worth of cocaine. I told them I only had weed on me, and no cash for the motel.

We decided to chill out in a backyard and smoke the weed. Then one of the girls pulled out a cigarette laced with cocaine and offered me a pull. This time I didn't hesitate. The effects were significantly stronger than the last time I'd done that. Dazed, I kissed the girl and walked away.

When I came out of my stupor, I tried to justify my new drug of choice. Maybe, I told myself, cocaine was the new "it" thing, as in the movie *Scarface*. I gave myself a pass because I wasn't smoking crack; I was just using cocaine. Coke was elitist and socially acceptable, especially in club and party circles. Crack, on the other hand, was considered ghetto, gutter, and crazy.

I told myself that cocaine was the calling card of big-time drug dealers and the drug of choice for progressive, forward-thinking women.

I rewrote my personal rule against casual cocaine use. Then, like a fool, I called Blaze and told him I was coming over for more coke.

*   *   *

Cocaine became a steady habit, and my body craved it. I no longer shunned it, but sought it out. Not only did I crave the high, but I also was entranced by the lure of the cocaine culture. Popping into Clive's basement became part of my daily routine as I walked to Jamaica Avenue.

One day, however, the devil came to get his due. Clive's worst fears were realized when Fat Rock caught up with him. He pulverized Clive's face over the package of crack Clive hadn't paid for.

By the time Blaze and I made it to Clive's basement, his face was covered in bandages. To tell the truth, I didn't show him much sympathy because my thoughts were centered on the cocaine Clive had lined up on a mirror. That pure white line was calling my name, and it seemed like forever before Clive offered me a taste. I was practically salivating by then, so I jumped at the chance to sniff it up.

Just as I was settling into my high, someone kicked in Clive's door.

I straightened and felt adrenaline squirt through my bloodstream along with the coke. Fat Rock, the scariest-looking dude I had ever seen, walked into the basement and looked around. I knew he was a ruthless bully who enjoyed watching people squirm. Maybe the cocaine was playing tricks on me, but the thick gold chains over his mustard-yellow jacket made him look especially sinister.

I pressed my hands to my legs to stop them from trembling. My mouth went numb, partly from fear and partly from the coke. I had always thought Fat Rock respected me as a hustler, but seeing me zooted up on coke immediately downgraded my status from hustler to addict.

With fire in his eyes, Fat Rock turned from me and glared at Clive. "I should beat you up again!"

Clive cowered behind his bandages. "You already did that."

"Man, you got this young dude in here messing up."

As if to illustrate his point, Fat Rock yanked me out of my chair and flung me up against the wall. Blinking, I saw my life replay before my eyes. In that instant I was a coward with no fight in me. The cocaine had transformed me into a squeaky mouse.

Fat Rock narrowed his eyes and stepped toward me. "I'm going to beat this dude to death."

My face was too frozen to grimace, but I almost wet my pants. General Cocaine was commanding my emotions, and the feeling he pushed to the front line was complete and total terror.

Fat Rock grabbed a fistful of fabric at the neckline of my shirt, then he lifted me until I hung, helpless, with my heels drubbing the wall. I was a tall dude even back then, so lifting me was no small feat. The realization that Fat Rock could pull it off one-handed was enough to freeze my blood.

I tried to speak but couldn't find any words. I was a rag doll in the hands of a vicious street warrior, and I knew I was about to die.

Fat Rock's breath wafted over my face. "It's time you entered hell, punk."

I didn't even try to throw a punch. Instead I braced for the blows by covering my face with my arms and hands, like a girl.

Fat Rock burst out in a wicked laugh. "This dude's soft," he said, still laughing. "I wasn't going to hurt you, you skinny stick."

Blaze and Clive laughed too, though their laughter was a good deal more subdued than Fat Rock's. "Yeah, Dee," Clive said, "Fat Rock's just messin' with you."

But he wasn't. The street has its own psychology, and Fat Rock had just herbed me—caused me to back down out of fear and intimidation. He had added my name to the list of drug dealers he could threaten and intimidate. He probably felt like he'd just struck gold.

Clive, Blaze, and I sat with Fat Rock while he took a sniff of cocaine. Then, using the same words Abdul had once said to me, Fat Rock looked at Clive. "Dude, you know I've got love for you, but if you ever mess up my money again, I will seriously hurt you."

I looked from Clive to Fat Rock and wondered if all the Queens bosses had studied the same hustler's handbook.

Clive, who handled his cocaine high better than I did, smiled at Fat Rock through his bandages. "Yo, I ain't no punk. You know I won't do that. And if we need to, we will fight."

Fat Rock flashed his jacked-up gold teeth, repaired after many a brawl in the hood. "Clive, you sure ain't no punk like this dude."

Under normal circumstances I would have stood to defend my honor, but under the influence of cocaine, I was ready to bow before Fat Rock and crown him king.

I managed to crack a half-smile when Blaze stood up for me. "Fat Rock, chill. That's my dude, and if he wasn't high right now, he would've manned up."

Blaze saved face for me! Feeling my high beginning to wear off, I drew a deep breath and mustered up what strength I could. I stood. "I'm out."

"Naw, man," Blaze said, trying to ease my embarrassment. "Stay."

Then Fat Rock caught my eye. "I know you ain't soft, Slim, but you're too young to be up in here sniffing cocaine."

I nodded slowly. "True dat."

Blaze and I left the basement.

As we walked down the street, Blaze warned me to watch my back because Fat Rock was sure to play me in the future. By that time I felt like myself again and was raring to go. "Let him bring it, then. We'll just have to fight."

Blaze shook his head. "Naw, man. He will beat you down."

I hated how Blaze loved predicting the worst for someone—especially when that someone was me.

*　　*　　*

One day Blaze suggested that we pop by Sach's house. He gestured to a house around the corner, and I stared in surprise—I'd never known Sach lived there.

Like a lot of houses on the block, his house was big and had a huge backyard, but what distinguished it from the others was the sense of malevolence that seemed to seep out of the place. Blaze and I knocked on the side door. From the backyard, Sach yelled for us to come around.

Sach was the best-dressed guy I had ever met. He was so into clothes that he would sew his own stuff and even hook other people up with great threads. When we reached him, Sach was dressed fly as usual in the latest Polo gear and was smoking a Philly blunt. "What's up?" he asked, passing the blunt to Blaze.

Blaze took a pull and then passed the blunt to me, so I sat and took a drag too. But then I started coughing, which made Sach laugh. "This is that good Brooklyn stuff, not that whack Queens weed."

I handed the blunt back as the back door creaked and opened. When Sach's mother stuck her head out, I jumped up and leaned toward the gate, ready to run.

Sach noticed my sudden movement. "Chill, dude."

"You smoking back there?" his mom hollered.

Sach lowered his blunt and glanced over his shoulder. "What?"

"Eunace will be down in an hour," his mom answered. Eunace was known as Sach's aunt. The woman claimed to be a witch and would come downstairs growling and cursing at any of us kids who stood in her way. I've never heard anyone speak the way she did.

She scared us to death.

Sach shrugged in a cavalier manner. "Okay, Mom."

I couldn't believe he could sit there and keep smoking in front of his mom. My mother would never have stood for that.

Sach took another pull; then he gestured to me while he grinned at Blaze. "Man, this dude looks like he's ready to take off running."

I didn't care that he was poking fun. In my business, it paid to stay alert and vigilant.

Sach stood and invited us inside. We headed down to the basement, where Sach had his private pad. The basement room had been nicely laid out with a big TV, a king-size bed, and a sofa. Toya, Sach's little sister, and some of her friends were hanging out in the room.

Toya recognized me as soon as I entered. "How you doing?"

I grinned at her, happy that she'd acknowledged me. "Hey, what's up?"

Toya was the leader of a group of cool and pretty high school girls. I was happy just to bask in their attention.

After a while, Sach and Blaze decided to go out to the backyard to drink. They told me I could chill in the basement, which I was happy to do with so many fly girls around. A few minutes after my friends left, someone knocked on the basement door at the head of the stairs. Toya called up, "Come on down."

Even before I knew who had knocked, I felt an internal alarm begin to clang. The door opened, and then a guy came down the stairs and stepped into the light. I recognized him from school and remembered that he'd beaten a grown man on Halloween. I'd seen the fight, and as I'd walked away, I kept thinking that I never wanted to fight *that* guy.

Despite the ringing alarm bells, I stood and introduced myself. "Hey. I'm Dimas."

"I'm Tank."

The name sounded familiar . . . and after a second, I figured out why. According to Blaze, Tank was the guy who wanted to fight me. That foolishness with Fat Rock was still fresh in my mind, so I was down to fight with anyone who came at me.

For a long moment Tank and I stood there eyeing each other,

exuding a palpable tension. Toya came over and tried to break the strain with small talk. A couple of the other girls did the same by flirting with us—"Both of you guys are really cute!"

One girl came over and told us to sit down and relax. She handed us cups of eggnog spiked with alcohol.

I took a sip and started to chill. "This is a cool crib."

Tank nodded. "It is."

With the tension between us broken, we started talking.

When Blaze came back down, he saw us sitting together and his eyes widened. "Tank—" his brows lifted—"this is the Dimas you were talking about."

Tank looked up. "I know."

Blaze couldn't leave it alone. "So what's up, then?"

I couldn't believe Blaze would keep needling Tank. Was he really that bloodthirsty, or did he just enjoy watching a good fight?

Fed up with Blaze's garbage, I jumped up and yelled as loudly as I could: "*I am Dimas!*"

Then Tank stood and stepped up to Blaze, looking him square in the eye. "I know who he is, and we are chillin' and having a good time. Why do you keep askin' me questions?"

Aware that he was getting nowhere, Blaze laughed and retreated.

Tank and I talked and laughed with the girls until about 10 p.m. As everyone started to head out, I asked Tank where he lived and discovered that he lived on my street, Murdock Avenue. Later I would learn that his father was a pastor, but Tank and I didn't do any talking about God that night.

We ended up walking home together. Along the way, Tank pulled out a blunt, so we walked and smoked. He told me Blaze wanted us to fight, so I shouldn't trust Blaze. I told Tank I'd suspected as much—some dudes just liked to stir up trouble. I'd be more careful around Blaze from that point on.

We reached Tank's house first, and as we split, he told me to stop by the next day at three because he knew a great weed spot. I agreed, and on the rest of my walk home, I wondered whether he had really wanted to fight me or whether Blaze had egged him on until he made a threat. But at that point, it didn't matter.

When I met up with Tank the next day, he asked if I was ready to go get the best weed in New York City.

"Where's that?"

"Just a short ride away, in Brooklyn. Neighborhood called Brownsville."

My mother had always warned me about Brownsville, yet that was where Tank wanted to go. I hesitated for about half a second, but the thought of smoking the best weed in NYC was irresistible. So we hopped onto the subway and rode over to Brownsville.

We met up with about ten other teens at Tank's weed spot, which did not disappoint. We all walked around Brooklyn smoking this imported weed called Chocolate Thai. While we were hanging out, a car rolled by and slowed down. Over the blaring music I heard someone inside the car shout, "Is that him?"

I turned in time to see everyone in the vehicle pull out guns and point them in our direction. I caught my breath, but then someone else screamed, "It ain't him! It ain't him!"

Tank and I both stood as if we were rooted to the sidewalk. The guys inside the car laughed and told us they were the Woo Posse and they killed for hire. I laughed too, to mask my fear, but on the train ride back to Queens, I told Tank that no weed was good enough to die for.

*　　*　　*

My best friends at the time, Trevor and Lance, didn't smoke crack because they got such an adrenaline rush from robbing houses. The hottest girls on my block, however, sniffed cocaine, and my neighbors across the street smoked woolahs—weed mixed with crack—for a while. As I hustled weed on the block, I began to buy cocaine and crack, and the cocaine heightened my social status. Tank and I would regularly hook up to smoke weed and sniff cocaine.

One day I introduced Tank to my friend Macho. It didn't take Macho long to notice we all had something in common. "Can I be down?" he asked once. "I can see y'all are coked up."

I looked at Tank. Why not let him join us? He was cool.

So the three of us headed off to smoke cocaine and weed together. When all the coke was gone, Macho said he could crush the crack so fine it would be like cocaine. We rejected the idea at first because everybody knew crack was a short road to poverty. Crack addicts were scary—people would kill their mothers and grandmothers for crack. For five minutes, crack would give you a high that surpassed anything you could imagine, but after that you would crash to a point of deep depression. Then you'd want more. You smoked crack faster to keep that high, and that's why crack dealers made so much money. Once you came down, the depression and paranoia were so bad you would do almost anything to avoid those feelings. One more hit would lift a user out of that depression, and that's why people would sell their bodies and commit murder to get it.

Girls would have sex with four or five people to get crack—anything to keep their high. Cocaine, on the other hand, made you feel high and energized without sending you crashing into depression.

That crack/weed mixture was my downfall. It blasted me into the atmosphere, higher than any high I'd ever experienced. But a few minutes later I came crashing back to earth. The high didn't last long, but man, it was intense.

A typical woolah cost ten dollars, and in search of that high I smoked woolah after woolah. In no time I had gone through a hundred dollars of crack and weed, but I had to stop when the crack ran out. I had hundreds of dollars on me but wasn't going to buy a lot of crack on one block—far too risky.

Before I knew it, Tank, Macho, and I were smoking every day in my garage. We'd start off sniffing cocaine, move on to crack, and then top it off with weed. I always had fistfuls of cash from hustling, so when the crack ran out, I went onto the street to buy more.

Many months whizzed by. One day I looked around my garage and noticed that the concrete floor was covered with three inches of used Philly blunts and crack capsules. No wonder the entire community knew I'd become a crackhead. My mom knew I was using drugs, but she never went into the garage, so she had no idea how much I was using.

Though my addiction was obvious to anyone with eyes to see, I had a classic case of denial. I had fooled myself into thinking I wasn't a crackhead because I didn't smoke crack with a pipe. Yet my addiction shifted my priorities. Getting high and staying high were all I cared about. The dream of building my own drug empire faded until it was a distant memory. Such is the mind-set of an addict. All that matters is the next high, nothing else—not work, family, or even food.

Tank, Macho, and I each dropped more than thirty pounds over the next six months. I started shorting my customers out of their drugs to feed my own habit. A group of Jamaicans I'd shafted were looking for me, as well as old neighborhood friends and the Supreme Team.

Despite all those highs, I had never felt so low. My friend Smokie nicknamed me "Running Man" because whenever someone came around to hurt me—and that happened often—I'd take off running and escape most of the time.

One day Tank and I became so desperate to get high that we robbed his next-door neighbor's house. Talk about risky! I didn't care where I sold, as long as I had enough money to replenish my supply and enough crack for myself to smoke.

In fact, I was about to hit rock bottom.

CHAPTER FOUR

I KNEW I WAS DESPERATE when I went to sell drugs for Fat Rock. He had a horrible reputation, but I had burned too many bridges by messing up everywhere else.

Fat Rock worked for Dragon, a drug kingpin and millionaire who ran drug spots everywhere. Dragon sent me to a weed spot in South Jamaica known as the Hole. The Hole was a storefront that wasn't really a store. At the side was a wooden door. If you opened the door, you'd step into an area that looked like a living room that someone had divided with a wooden wall. A gigantic door stood in the wooden wall, secured with ten locks, several heavy chains, and a few deadbolts for good measure. Next to the door was a hole a little larger than a human eye. A customer would shove money into the hole, and out would come a bag of weed. Simple.

But it wasn't so simple for the kid working at the Hole. I found myself locked in the other side of that apartment, behind the wooden wall. The worker's area held a toilet and a tiny kitchen. The only piece of furniture was a bed with a bloodstained pillow. Clearly, someone had been shot in the head while lying on it.

When Dragon took me to the Hole for the first time, he pointed to the bloodstain and gave me a grim smile. "That's what happened to our last worker."

I swallowed hard, realizing that I'd become not only a crackhead but also a crackhead surrounded by killers.

Fat Rock explained that my job at the Hole was to sell bags of weed. "But look here," he said, dangling a full bag before me. "You'll see that these bags are fat, packed full. If you bring some empty bags with you, maybe you can skim a little off the top and fill up some bags of your own. Make a little extra profit."

So I picked up some little cellophane jewelry bags at a Queens bodega that carried all kinds of drug paraphernalia—crack capsules, jewelry bags, even syringes. And then I let them lock me into the Hole.

While locked inside, I thought about all those locks and chains and deadbolts, and I tried to find a way out. What if the building caught fire? A hole in the floorboards, cut for a pipe, was large enough to drop drugs into the building basement if the cops came, but no human would fit through the hole. After peering down into the trash-ridden, rat-infested darkness below, I wasn't sure anyone would want to.

The only means of escape I could see was a skylight. I'd have to perform some amazing maneuvers to even reach it, but if I slid open a window, I could probably manage.

Locked away in that small space, I found myself stone-cold sober for the first time in six months. My eyes filled with tears as I took a long look at myself and asked aloud, "How did I sink this low?"

*   *   *

When I was little, a crazy guy named William lived on the next block. He used to terrorize us younger kids—he'd walk up, look down on us with utter disdain, and say, "You little punk." Then he'd hit us, hard, and make us cry.

We hated William, mostly because we feared him. Then one day when I was ten, we heard that William had gotten himself saved. We couldn't believe the rumor, so a bunch of us walked over to the next block to see for ourselves.

We found William outside his house. I summoned up my courage and walked over to greet him. "Hey William!"

He looked at me and grinned. "Yeah?"

"Are you really saved?"

His grin broadened. "That's right. I'm saved, I'm in the Lord, and you should be too. Do you want to accept Jesus?"

William seemed happy enough, and Dawn had been happy with Jesus, so I nodded. "Sure."

"Okay, let's go."

While the other kids trailed behind, William walked me to a park, where he prayed what he called a prayer of salvation. I repeated the words after him, and afterward I thanked him for helping me. Nothing had really changed for me, but again, a seed was planted.

William kept the neighborhood tongues wagging when he started wearing suits every day. Did being saved mean you had to wear a suit? He went to a strict church, and the next thing I knew, William was standing in front of the grocery store passing out tracts to anyone who'd take one. His church met in an old theater, and we'd stand outside on Sundays and listen to the people singing.

I thought I'd figured it out. Saved people wore suits, sang, and passed out tracts. If that's what being saved meant, I didn't want to be saved. After that, I left William alone.

When I was in fifth grade, I met my friend Roger at school. Roger seemed upset, so I asked what was wrong.

"Yo, my girlfriend broke up with me."

"What happened, man?"

Roger released a dramatic sigh. "She got saved."

I blinked, trying to imagine Roger's girlfriend wearing suits and singing. "What does that have to do with anything?"

"'Cause when you get saved, you can't have a boyfriend anymore."

"Man." I stepped back, stunned by this new revelation. "That sounds horrible."

Not much later, I heard about an older kid called Man who lived with Blaze. When Blaze came by the house one day, he told me Man had gotten saved.

"Really?" I was with at least ten other kids who were looking for something to do. "Let's go see him."

So the group of us trooped over to Blaze's house, where we found Man standing inside the gate of the fenced front yard.

"Yo, Man," we called out. "Can you still hang with us?"

He shook his head. "No, I'm saved."

"Wow." We stared at him and then looked at each other. "This is weird."

"Can you have a girlfriend?" someone asked.

He shook his head again—a bit mournfully, it seemed to me. "No, I'm saved. I'm with Jesus now."

"So—you're not going to play with us anymore?"

"No, dudes. You guys aren't with Jesus, and I am."

"Well, okay." We looked around, and some of us kicked at the grass. "If you need anything, let us know."

"I'm good. I'm with Jesus."

As we walked away, one of the guys looked at me. "I knew another kid who got saved. Someone pushed him in the face, and the kid said, 'I'm going to turn so you can push me on the other side, 'cause I'm not gonna fight you.' The guy went to push him again, but then he just stopped."

I stared. "Really? He just stopped?"

The guy nodded. "Yeah. He didn't push him again."

I fell silent, a little awed by this powerful stuff. The guy actually invited the bully to push him on the other side of his face? He didn't fight back? I had never heard what Jesus said about turning the other cheek, but I wanted to meet that brave kid. I'd never heard about that kind of courage.

The kid telling the story looked at me again. "Yo, this dude—you could tell he could fight if he wanted to. But because of God, he wouldn't."

I nodded, admiring the unknown kid even more. "Wow."

"I think God stopped him."

"Like God saved that guy."

"Yo, when you get saved, it's serious, man. We should all do it."

Someone from the back of the group spoke up. "I'm going to do it before I die."

"Huh?" I turned to look at him. "How do you do that?"

The kid shrugged. "You live normal, but right before you die, you say, 'Jesus forgive me.' So if you get shot or something, remember to say, 'Jesus, please forgive me.' Then you'll be saved."

That might not have been the best theology, but I always thought about that story as I went about my drug deals. That recipe for forgiveness became my backup plan. If I ever got in over my head, I might get shot and die. But if I did, the last words on my lips would be "Jesus, please forgive me."

Lying on that bloody bed in the Hole, I thought a lot about dying. But I wasn't ready to call on Jesus yet.

*   *   *

The day after I got locked in the Hole, someone from the fire department knocked on the apartment door, and I yelled out an answer. From my voice and manner they could tell they'd found a drug spot and I was a minor. The fire captain called the landlord while I eavesdropped from inside my prison.

"I'm bringing the police now," I heard the fire captain saying, "and we are rescuing this kid."

My heart pounded in its skinny cage of ribs. What they considered a good deed wouldn't earn me any points with Dragon, so I scrambled onto the bed and struggled to reach the skylight. While they worked on getting into the locked inner room, I pulled myself up and ran across the roof; then I made my way down to the street. I jumped into a cab and went straight to the video store Dragon ran as a front for another of his drug operations.

Fat Rock was inside when I arrived. After recognizing me, he shot me a suspicious look. "What happened? What are you doin' here?"

"The cops are on their way to the Hole, man."

His eyes narrowed. "Did you grab the weed on your way out?"

"Yeah."

"Pull it out."

I reached into my pocket and pulled out about two thousand dollars' worth of marijuana.

Fat Rock nodded in satisfaction. "Good work. Go chill out in the basement for a while."

Snake, another of Dragon's workers, followed me to the basement of the video store. When Fat Rock came down a few minutes later, Snake watched as Fat Rock began to beat me up. He beat me so badly that blood poured out of my nose and both my eyes started to swell. As blood streamed down my face, he stole about five hundred dollars' worth of weed.

I looked at Snake, but he was as scared as I was. He didn't say or do anything to help.

When Dragon arrived, Fat Rock told him I'd tried to rob the Hole. Without a second thought, Dragon came downstairs and began to beat me, ignoring my screams and protests. When he stopped, I thought I'd finally gotten through to him, but then he pulled a 9mm handgun from his waistband and put it to my forehead.

This was the moment I always thought I'd pray, *Jesus, forgive me*, but my brain stuttered and I couldn't think at all.

At that instant a bell rang, signaling that a customer waited upstairs. Without a word, Dragon lowered the gun and trudged up the steps.

Bent over, trying to catch my breath, I looked at Fat Rock from beneath swollen eyelids. "Why are you doing this?"

His sinister laugh echoed amid the junk in the basement. "It's just business, stupid."

I was a naturally thin kid, but after losing so much weight because of the crack, I looked like a strung-out addict. Fat Rock hadn't hesitated to treat me like one.

When Dragon yelled for Fat Rock to come upstairs, Snake and I followed, not knowing if we'd face cops, rivals, or something else.

An innocent customer, a guy who looked like a lawyer or a corporate executive, had lost three VHS tapes and had stopped by to pay the overdue charges. Dragon looked at his computer and saw that the tapes had been missing for over a year. When he added up all the rental fees, the bill came to $1,300.

Then Dragon, a psycho dealer who couldn't seem to process situations rationally, called for Fat Rock and pulled his 9mm on the customer. In a gravelly voice, he ordered Fat Rock to take the guy to the basement.

Even though I was a crack-addicted woolah head, I understood that Dragon shouldn't be operating his video store the way he ran his drug empire. I stood near the basement door, dripping with blood and staring at a decent guy who'd come in to pay his rental bill. Why was Dragon treating him like someone who'd ratted him out?

The poor man dropped to his knees and pleaded, "Oh, no! Please don't do this!"

Holding the gun steady on the customer, Dragon glanced at Fat Rock. "Take him to the basement."

The man began to tremble. "I misplaced the tapes. All I did was misplace some videotapes!"

I shook my head, unable to believe what I was seeing. That customer could have been my sweet mother, who misplaced videotapes all the time. Whenever she found them, she returned them and paid a reasonable fine. No one had ever put her through this kind of torture.

These guys were crazy.

Dragon waved his gun in front of the customer's face. "You have one week to come up with my $1,300 or I'm coming to your house." He pulled out the guy's application card and held it before the man's eyes. "In case you don't believe me, I have your address right here."

Still shaking, the poor man stood. "Thank you, sir. Thank you! I'll be back with the money, and I will never lose a tape again."

I watched the man leave and wondered what would happen if Blockbuster operated the same way Dragon did. The idea was so bizarre I burst out laughing.

Dragon turned and frowned at me, not at all amused. "You're gonna work off your loss as well. Take him back to the Hole." He had made a few calls and found out it was safe to return.

Someone shoved me in the back of a Toyota Corolla. Then Freeze, Dragon's partner, drove me back to the weed spot. Freeze had a bad stutter, but he managed to warn me on our way to the apartment complex. "Y-y-you messed up, kid. We're go-go-gonna use you to send a message to all our workers."

When we pulled up to the Hole, Dragon was already waiting at the corner, his expression as dark as thunderclouds. He held a long-handled branch cutter, and for an instant I couldn't figure out why he wanted to trim bushes. Then he walked over to the car and grabbed my hand. "I'm takin' a finger."

"Man!" I screamed. "I'm only fifteen. Don't ruin my life like this!"

I'm not sure why, but the mention of my age snapped Dragon out of his rage. "Oh, shoot, you're fifteen?" He looked at Freeze. "Lock him back in the Hole."

A few minutes later, I was once again trapped in that hellhole. I cried on and off for three days, but I wasn't allowed out even for a minute. When I would sell out, Snake or someone else would come by to bring me more weed. Snake would often slap me just to make himself look tough.

Alone in that awful place, I cried out to God for help. I had sunk to the lowest point of my life—a fifteen-year-old crack addict with two black eyes and a bloodied shirt, locked away in the Hole. I wasn't sure if God would answer, but I had no one else to turn to. No one else could see me in that miserable place.

At the end of the third day, Dragon unlocked the door and looked at me. "Your replacement is here. You can go." He threw me a hundred-dollar bill. "Come back in a week."

I ran to Tank's house and told him about everything I'd been through. He felt bad for me, but what could he do? After that, I went home. My mother had been worried because, most times before, I had come home or at least called her to let her know I was alive and okay. She hugged me, and I knew she was torn between loving on me and fussing at me for causing her so much grief.

Unaware of just how deeply I was into drugs and how much danger I was in, my mother pleaded with me once again: "You're not like those guys you hang out with. God has a plan for your life." Part of me took notice. Could God really show me a way out? But my addiction had a far stronger pull on me than either of us realized.

As soon as Mom left for work the next day, Macho came over and we smoked woolahs. During that high, I went to my sister Emerald's room and stole her jewelry so we could buy more drugs. Then I made the room look as if there'd been a burglary. My sister was no fool, though, and she saw right through my charade.

I was disgusted with myself. *What did I do?* That's when I realized how low I'd fallen. Because I'd been smoking it with marijuana, I'd been rationalizing my use of crack. Once I'd stooped so low as to rob my own home, I could no longer deny that I was a hard-core crack addict. Embarrassed, I left the house, running away from the people I didn't want to disappoint anymore.

Walking through the neighborhood, I caught up with an old classmate. He sold drugs for Jamaican Stretch, and he, too, had recently run away from home, so he let me crash in a place he was renting.

After a couple of days, the two of us decided to work together. As we headed outside to sell crack on the block, a man walked up and pointed a machine gun at us. "Take off your coats," he said, wrapping his hands around the gun, "and walk away."

Standing there on the icy sidewalk, I stepped back, slipped, and fell, which only made the guy more nervous.

"Don't move!"

Slowly, I stood up. "You can have everything, man," we told him. "Just don't shoot."

We handed over our coats—with our drugs tucked inside the pockets—and the guy ran off. Now we had no money, no drugs, and no coats.

We couldn't handle any more frustration, so we decided to call the cops. They picked us up and gave each of us a ride home.

That night I confessed almost everything to my mother. I told her about being robbed and owing money to several friends. I confessed that I couldn't stop smoking crack and weed. I admitted I needed help.

And because my mom was a good mom, she helped me find a way out—she made arrangements for me to go live with my brother in North Carolina for a while. Coincidentally, Tank's dad shipped him down to North Carolina as well, but to a different city.

I didn't know where Tank was going. But at fifteen, I knew I couldn't live like an addict anymore.

CHAPTER FIVE

I HAD TO GO TO Raleigh, North Carolina, to find myself. I stayed with my brother, Chad, in his two-bedroom apartment, so I had to stay clean. We slept together in a king-size water bed, and each morning he would tell me how I'd beaten him up in my sleep.

One Friday night I asked if we could go to a club or something. He took me to a dance club, but I felt out of place because I didn't know anyone. At the end of the night, though, I met a girl and we exchanged numbers. Two days later I took her to the movies.

After the movie, Chad sat me down for a heart-to-heart talk. "Dee," he said, "how could you go into a club in North Carolina and date the worst-looking girl I've seen in this state?"

He wasn't trying to disrespect the girl. He was trying to help me see that I no longer had any self-esteem or self-confidence.

He was right. The drug life causes people to forget who they are.

They become whatever they need to be in order to get more drugs. Good girls become prostitutes, businessmen become thieves, and parents become people who don't care about their kids.

Chad arranged a self-esteem-building adventure for me. He worked for a major airline, so he could fly for free. He called his best friend and coworker, Miles, and they planned a Las Vegas trip. Chad took me to a tailor and told him to measure me from head to toe and fit me with a custom-made suit. "I want my brother to look like a million dollars," he said. "Throw in some new socks and shoes."

After that, he took me to get a fresh haircut. When we walked into the airport, he introduced me to everybody, inviting them to come meet his baby brother. He did it up!

With the rich and famous, we flew first-class to Las Vegas. We stayed in a beautiful hotel and walked around the city together. I gambled twice but decided that gambling wasn't my thing. Chad gave me a hundred dollars, so I decided to use that money to buy more clothes instead of feeding a slot machine.

I had forgotten that I liked to look good. The drugs had stolen so much of my identity that I had neglected to take care of myself.

Chad and I attracted attention everywhere we went, and that positive attention reminded me that I was not just an addict. I hadn't been raised to be an addict, and I was not going to end my life as an addict.

I will forever be indebted to my brother for loving me and helping me see that I was more than a craving for crack. My brother saved me from that addiction.

By the time we arrived back at Chad's house, I had become a man on a mission. My brother had a weight room, so I started listening to music and working out. I was determined to get my weight up and build some muscles.

After a month my mother called. She had the money to pay off my debts, she told me, and my brother thought I was strong enough to go back home.

I thank God for my mom. When I arrived back in New York, she met me with open arms and handed me the cash I needed to close the door on my past.

*   *   *

I promised myself I would never be an addict again. I was brimming over with strength, love, and confidence. I decided that if I used anything, it would be marijuana, not hard drugs.

After arriving home, I knocked on doors and paid people back the money I owed. No one called me Running Man anymore. I was only fifteen, but I'd been through a lot in my short lifetime—in many ways, I had the mind-set of a much older man.

But my old life was not finished with me—not yet.

One afternoon I opened my dresser drawer and found two crack capsules . . . and the old me took over. I called Tank and learned that he'd just come back home clean too. I told him I was coming over, and on my way to his house I bought some weed. I rolled up a blunt and we smoked it. Then I told him about the capsules, and he agreed to smoke the crack with me.

We dumped the crack into a new blunt and, man, did we want it. I fired up the blunt and took a pull. Then I passed it to Tank. After he pulled, we looked at each other and both said, "This ain't worth it. Let's sell crack but not use it." We flushed that blunt down the toilet; then we started lifting weights. Physical exertion took the edge off our craving.

Girls in the neighborhood began to take notice of our new physiques. Tank had two neighbors who were popular girls and who flirted with us every day, and their attention built up our self-esteem like nothing else. Without the drugs clouding our senses, we were more focused and clear about what we wanted to do. We had our minds on our money and our money on our minds. We strategized how to set up shop and realized we needed more cash and a band of brothers to be down with our crew.

Tank wasn't afraid of violence, so he naturally attracted violent people. I attracted hustlers like me.

One day I approached Twin, an old childhood friend. Twin wanted to be down but was obsessed with having Kareem in on the partnership. Kareem was a psycho, a gun-slinging stickup kid who had once robbed me at gunpoint. No one messed with Kareem because he had a reputation for stabbing people and robbing drug dealers. I didn't want anything to do with Kareem, but Twin was determined to bail him out of jail and then bring him aboard. Reluctantly, I agreed to go forward with the business.

Twin and I were earning serious money when Kareem got out of jail. I didn't know how things were going to work out, but Tank and Kareem clicked almost instantly. Tank started hustling for Kareem, and I kept running my own enterprise.

Though some people can put the past behind them, I knew that Kareem and I were never going to be friends. He went to a cheaper place to get his supply, and his stuff wasn't as good as what I sold. He paid less, so his quality suffered. On the other hand, I had the purest, fattest, and cheapest capsules around, and I worked hard and was more skilled at hustling. Consequently, I ruled the block in sales.

But while hard work may help you get ahead in some areas, on the street it gets you noticed by guys who would stab you for your territory. Kareem hated me, and so did Kirk Green, a Top Guns boss who worked Springfield Boulevard.

I was on my way to becoming the street god I'd always wanted to be, but I knew there were lots of dudes who wanted to take my place.

CHAPTER SIX

I CAUGHT MY GROOVE as an independent hustler on Hollis Avenue. Using crack was totally behind me. The money on 207th Street and Hollis Avenue was unbelievable.

Hollis and 207th was a historic block in the drug game, and not everyone was savvy enough to work there. Before I showed up, the other dealers on the block didn't have a clue about who was working for whom. Once I began to dominate the block, however, that confusion dissipated, and I began to attract jealous attention from several competitors, including Kirk Green and Kareem. Though I was young, most dealers recognized that I could run an operation alone better than most of them together.

As my business thrived, I hungered to expand. My dream of commanding the street was strong, alive, and on its way to becoming reality.

I also began to check out the block bordered by 203rd Street and Hollis Avenue. To have any chance of taking that territory, I needed to form a solid team. A boy named Trey started showing up to work for me when he was only eleven, so I put him on that block. Because his dad was a user, Trey was tough and wise to the streets. Fat Dre was another of my workers. He was my age and lived in the target zone on 203rd Street.

Enlarging my crew proved to be lucrative, and we moved packages of crack faster every day. Fat Dre made hundreds of dollars while Trey and I made thousands. In a short time, the business on my block was as lucrative as on the Ice Boys' block. In fact, some of the Ice Boys' most loyal customers started buying from my crew.

I knew things couldn't keep growing at that brisk pace—there wasn't enough room for two large operations. A drug war was inevitable, so I was always considering my next step.

One afternoon a Toyota Cressida pulled up to the curb on the block where I was working. Jamaican Stretch, who had started to occasionally sell drugs for us, was behind the wheel. When I stopped to talk to him, he told me the most amazing stories about drug deals in Washington, DC. He gassed me up, telling me that in the District I could turn over fifty thousand dollars' worth of drugs every few days.

My operation in Hollis was picking up steam, but I could feel tension in the air. All my competitors were extremely dangerous. They arranged hits and waged bloody turf wars with the Supreme Team. During one drive-by shooting, a pregnant girl was murdered in South Jamaica, and three Top Guns had been arrested over that hit, so those three were in Rikers.

Kirk Green and Kareem were the main reason Hollis Avenue hadn't been overtaken by one crew. With their muscle, they were able to keep turf wars off the block, but the warring factions kept looking for an opening into the territory. I kept feeling the spotlight of their attention on me.

With so much tension in New York, DC began to look like a drug dealer's Disneyland. I finally told Stretch I was down with going to DC for a few weeks to make a twenty-thousand-dollar profit. That would be enough to get my feet wet out there before returning to Hollis Avenue. I knew I needed to be purchasing at kilo level—buying one thousand grams, or 2.2 pounds of cocaine—to run a better operation. That kind of money would allow me to move into the big leagues.

Stretch agreed to fly Trey and me to DC to infiltrate and work the community. Like a family, we planned everything together—getting new fake IDs, arranging the flights, and dreaming big dreams. The plan worked . . . at first.

The drug game in the District was fast and fascinating. Money moved so fast there that people became millionaires in no time at all. Our NYC dime packages, which sold for ten dollars, were worth twenty dollars in DC, and our New York twenty-dollar packages sold for fifty. I could not wait to hit my block at 14th and Spring Streets NW.

Trey and I sold ten thousand dollars' worth of drugs in three days. I was able to pocket a profit of five hundred dollars through the old trick of repacking the weed and selling extra bags, but I knew we should be clearing several thousand dollars. After I handed in all the money Stretch expected from my sales, he told me that I did well and that he would pay me six hundred dollars. What?

Taking advantage of our youth, Stretch flipped the script once he had us in DC. I told him I wasn't a worker—I was a boss. Then he slipped into his thick Jamaican accent, screamed at me, and showed me his gun. That gun was a great silencer—my voice dropped to a whisper. I shook my head and told him that his game was messed up but I had no problem with it.

The truth about our situation didn't remain a mystery for long. Through rumors on the street, we learned that Stretch worked for another drug boss and that we had been brought out to be Stretch's workers. I had left my own thriving business in NYC to become the prisoner of a gun-wielding Jamaican underling.

To ease our frustrations and take the edge off, Trey and I began to smoke a lot more weed. The weed in DC was good and convenient. I wore my NY swag and sported a mouthful of gold teeth, so the girls in DC were all over me. Needless to say, we attracted attention, and that's not always a good thing.

Word got out that two kids from NYC, Daylight and Trey, were infringing on established turf and making a lot of money. A sixteen-year-old hustler named Rob didn't look like much of a drug boss—he was short and young and well dressed—but he controlled a large territory and wasn't shy about defending it.

One afternoon Rob walked up to me. "The next time I see you out here," he said, "I'm gonna shoot you in the head."

I knew Rob wasn't fronting. A crackhead had schooled me to Rob when we first arrived and told me that Rob had already killed a lot of people. I knew the dude meant what he said.

I looked him in the eye and put up my hands in a "don't shoot" pose. "I don't want any problems with you, man."

"It's finished," he said, dead serious. "The next time I see you, be ready to die."

My thoughts started spinning. I didn't want to die, so I had to change my plans. All I wanted to do was sell my stash and go back to New York City.

I was selling out of a sleazebag motel, so I stationed myself at one of the street-level windows and started hustling through addicts. I made sure Rob didn't see me selling.

The next day, Trey and I eased back out to the block. This time, the hood was in an uproar because they'd heard I had an eleven-year-old boy selling drugs. Store owners started tsk-ing and shaking their heads when Trey and I walked by. I felt as if I were living in a small town where all the neighbors had joined together to take a stand against evil. We could feel the tension in the environment, so Trey and I gave our drugs to a female crackhead to sell for us.

I went into a liquor store and bought a bottle of Cisco, aka "liquid crack," to calm my nerves. When I came out, a heavyset cop ordered Trey and me to put up our hands. Apparently he had been watching us for a while because he asked the crackhead for the drugs. As soon as she handed over the packages, I took off running. I didn't know DC well, but I got a good lead on the chunky officer. The Running Man was off again.

The situation shifted from bad to worse, however, when I ran out of options. I couldn't run to the crack house where we were living because a kilo of drugs was stashed there. I had no family and no friends in the District, so I couldn't run to anyone else's house. Though I scrambled like mad, I had nowhere to hide.

The cops shone a flashlight down an alley and spotted me crouching behind a garbage can. I was trapped, so I put up my hands and surrendered. The fat cop who'd had to chase me punched me so hard in the stomach that I vomited in his police car.

DC didn't feel like Disneyland anymore. At fifteen, I was headed to a jail in the murder capital of the United States.

*   *   *

Going to jail in DC rattled me more than going to Rikers because I didn't know anything about the system. In DC I had no problem telling the authorities I was only fifteen, so I was remanded to Cedar Knoll, a juvenile facility. The cops were entertained by young Trey and lit into him hard, but he didn't crack. When they asked who we were running drugs for, we both snitched on Kenny, a fictitious character we invented. But Kenny was really Stretch.

The courtroom in DC was even more imposing than the one in New York City. Both the judge and our court-appointed lawyer were forthright about not believing we were from the District. Trey and I knew we couldn't fabricate a background from the area, so we changed our story and blamed the fictitious Kenny for bringing us to DC to sell crack. Even though I made up a lot of the story, my frustration over our situation spilled over and helped convince the judge and the lawyer to believe at least part of our fiction. I couldn't stop shaking my head at how stupid I'd been to leave my own operation in New York.

The judge set a court date for twenty days out—and twenty days is a long time when you're in jail. They separated Trey and me. I knew I would have to wait out those twenty days, but I wasn't sure what would happen to Trey. Later I learned that he had family in Maryland, so they drove to DC and bailed him out.

For a juvenile detention center, Cedar Knoll was not easy. When I first arrived, I was placed in a cell on lockdown for twenty-three hours a day, let out only to eat and exercise for an hour. I paced back and forth in the small space, doing push-ups and chair dips, preparing myself to fight at any moment. After a week, I was placed in the general population so I could attend the Cedar Knoll version of school.

I was also given a little green Bible to keep in my cell. During my twenty days in Cedar Knoll, I read the New Testament several times front to back.

Oddly enough, a female guard knocked on my cell door one morning. "I never saw someone read the Bible as intently as you," she said. "You're different from the rest here. Keep reading. God is going to do something through your life. I am a follower of Jesus, and I can see that you belong to him. I can see it in the way you look at the Bible."

I couldn't explain why, but I loved that little Bible and could not put it down. But I didn't understand how it could apply to my life. I stood in awe of Jesus and the disciples, but what did they have to do with me? I couldn't see myself ever becoming a "church boy." To me, church was filled with whack people who wore stiff suits, sang their heads off, and listened to a preacher who yelled while spitting and flinging sweat onto the people in the front rows. So even though I believed in God, I had no idea what he might want from me.

As the days passed, however, I had an epiphany in that jail cell—I became convinced that God had put me in Cedar Knoll to keep me from being murdered on the street. If I hadn't been in jail, I would have been out on those DC blocks, and Rob would have seen me. He would have opened fire, and as fast as I was, I still couldn't outrun a bullet.

God saved my life by putting me in jail. I didn't understand why he would *want* to save my life, but I was glad he had.

*   *   *

As a preschooler I wasn't allowed to go many places on my own, but I had been given free rein to play in my backyard. Our house had a Bradford pear tree out back: a tall, flowering specimen.

I loved climbing the pear tree, which might have been anywhere from thirty to fifty feet tall. As a little kid, I would have described it as "ginormous," and I loved the challenge of climbing it with my friends Trevor and Robert.

One day I went into the backyard to climb the pear tree. I left Mom washing dishes at the kitchen sink, and I knew she wouldn't worry as long as I stayed within our fenced yard. The chain-link fence was secure, and the only gate was topped with sharp aluminum spikes.

Since I was alone that day, I decided to climb to the very top of the tree, which would lift me even higher than our house. Very few leaves remained on the tree at that time of year, so I had a clear view of the neighborhood stretching out before me.

I was about halfway up when I was overcome by a strong sense that I needed to go back down. I didn't know why, but I obeyed my gut instinct and swung around the tree to begin the climb down. I placed my foot on a branch, then transferred my weight—and the branch broke. I felt myself falling, saw the ground rushing up toward me, and heard the snap and crackle of smaller branches as they cracked beneath my weight. Then I saw the spikes on the gate. I was heading right toward them, so I closed my eyes and let out a scream, then felt the pressure of metal hitting my stomach. The impact seemed to bounce me off the gate, and I landed on the ground in the backyard.

Like a dog that'd been hit by a car, I leapt up and began to run around, confused and terrified and certain I'd been mortally wounded. I expected to be hit by a wave of pain and then die, but finally my terror expended itself. I stopped, drew a deep, shuddering breath, and lifted my shirt, expecting to see blood and gaping wounds.

I saw no wounds at all. Only a one-inch scratch. *What?*

I glanced over at the gate. My head and chest had been heading for our neighbor's yard, and my legs had been aimed at our backyard. That gate should have sliced me in half, or at least impaled me, so how could I have missed it?

I hadn't. I saw clear evidence of impact—the sharp aluminum spikes had been bent by the blow. There they were, bent backward like some giant hand had come down and pressed on them.

I ran into the house to tell my mother what had happened. I was a little surprised she hadn't already come out; surely she'd heard me scream or glimpsed my fall from the kitchen window. She always became hysterical when I got hurt, so I knew this would send her over the edge. She'd probably want to rush me to the emergency room for doctors and X-rays and experts to tell her I was truly okay.

"Ma!" I yelled, opening the back door. "I fell outta the tree and landed on the spikes; they should have stabbed me, but they bent back."

Without even lifting an eyebrow, my mother turned from the kitchen sink and answered me in the most detached voice I'd ever heard from her. Without even a trace of hysteria, she looked at me and said, "Son, God has a plan for your life." Then she turned and went back to washing the dishes.

From that moment, whatever happened, I knew that God had something for me to do. If someone talked about God, I wanted to hear what was being said. But God himself had preserved my life . . . or maybe he had arranged for that branch to break so I'd realize his power. I don't know, but my young mind had been mightily impressed with what God could do.

While at Cedar Knoll, I wondered whether my mother had been right . . . and whether God still had a plan for me.

*   *   *

Just as I was settling into Cedar Knoll, a corrections officer told me I was going to be moved to a maximum-security facility. My court date was only two days away. I scouted out my location and decided that if my case didn't go well, the Running Man would be taking off.

My court date arrived, and my mother arrived with it. She came down from New York, and the corrections officers at Cedar Knoll released me to her because, as a minor, I was seen as a victim of a nefarious drug lord. Little did they know . . .

The train ride with my mother was hard to bear. As we headed home, she tried talking some sense into me, but she might as well have been speaking to a rock. I was committed to the drug world and would not listen. While she talked, I kept thinking about my operations on Hollis Avenue. I had to get back to work before my space on both blocks got snatched up by someone else. I didn't want to think about anything else.

CHAPTER SEVEN

On the train ride home, I made a list of all the people who owed me money, and I thought of the people who'd be happy to buy some drugs from the package I'd hidden in my bedroom at home. As soon as Mom and I reached Queens, I headed back to the block. My clients had missed me and were glad to see me.

I was happy to hear that some of my competitors in NYC had gone to jail while I was incarcerated in DC, a development that kept dudes off my block. Unfortunately, Kareem was not one of them. That predator's operation remained in full swing. He was hungry and acted as if he felt invincible.

Tank was still working for Kareem, who told Tank he wanted to kill me. Tank told him to chill out, but every time Kareem got drunk, he would rant and rave about getting me off the block. His were not idle threats. That psycho wanted to shut me down, and murder was the best way he knew to do it.

I had weapons, but my measly arsenal couldn't hold a candle to Kareem's. At the time I had just two guns—a .32 pistol and a little pen gun that could fire only one shot. I wasn't even sure the pen gun worked, and I was too scared to try it lest I blow off my hand. Clearly, I was no match for the notorious gunslinger Kareem.

Yet a showdown between me and Kareem appeared inevitable because I wasn't about to give up or move on. I had an indefatigable work ethic and outhustled most of the lazy drug dealers on the block. A lot of drug dealers beat up their clients and even robbed them to show how tough they were. My reputation for nonviolence boosted my sales because people felt safe spending their money with me. Most of my clients were Queens homeowners who had important jobs in the community. Others were functioning addicts who were willing to pay for some semblance of peace along with their product.

One day, my crew and I heard about two separate shootings: Kirk Green had been shot in South Jamaica, and Tommy from the Ice Boys had shot Vinny, a dealer from Murdock Avenue. Nobody knew who'd shot Kirk. Since he had a knack for ticking people off, the police must have had a long list of suspects.

My house-robbing friends asked me to go with them to the hospital to check on Vinny. While we were there, I ran into Kirk's girlfriend, and she told me he was in a room down the hall. Even though we were vying for the same drug block, I'd grown up with Kirk and most of the drug dealers around the area. We had history, so I went to check on Kirk as well. He seemed to appreciate my visit but remained a little distant. I got the impression that he liked me but he liked his money more. So I wished him well and left.

Keeping your enemies close was good hood politics.

*   *   *

As a first-time business operator, I got greedy and made two rookie mistakes.

First, I put workers out on the block and practically advertised that I was a serious competitor. There's nothing wrong with a little ambition, but in the illegal drug trade there's no faster way to get a bull's-eye painted on your back.

Kareem attacked first. I was out hustling when I saw him jump out of a car in full predator mode—a glint in his eye, his hands jammed in his pockets, and determination in his step. He was coming straight for me, so I slipped into a backyard and waited about ten minutes. I hid my stash and a roll of bills and kept out forty dollars in dummy money, knowing I was certain to lose it.

When I stepped back out onto the street, Kareem leapt on me like a lion taking down a gazelle. I gave him the forty dollars, but he made me empty out my pockets and take off my sneakers to be sure I wasn't hiding anything else. After he pocketed the money, I watched him go. I was pretty sure he didn't have a gun, but he wasn't the kind of guy you test.

Kareem took off with his get-high partner, and I went back to work. Getting jacked was beginning to feel so normal that I considered it a street tax and carried on with business. I understood the stickup kids. Tank and I had robbed people, too, but only to intimidate the competition or to get back on our feet after a big loss.

My second mistake was double-dipping. Kirk had a one-eyed worker who used crack but had a lot of clients. He wanted to work for me because I sold a superior product—I invested in quality and packaged it well. But when I gave One-Eye a try, he smoked up my drugs and made me so mad that I robbed him at gunpoint, taking his stash of Kirk's drugs.

When another of Kirk's business partners, a guy called Billy, pulled up in his BMW 535, One-Eye told him that I'd robbed him. He then called Kirk, who was out of the hospital, while I told Billy what had happened. Billy told me to follow him to speak to Kirk. I had my gun, so I was okay with that, but I also brought a friend along.

At Campus Magnet High School, Kirk stepped out with a guy from the Top Guns and yelled, "This is war! I do not care who you get, but do not show up on 207th Street."

My friend and I got in a cab and rode off. We assessed our weapons and realized we didn't have enough firepower to go against those guys. So we decided to launch a new block, 205th Street. Better safe than dead, right?

I moved the operation the next day, but 205th was nowhere near as active as 207th. It was a slower block that didn't have the steady clients of 207th. I hated the move, but I had to stay alive, so I decided to make it work. I met Zara, a pretty girl who lived on 205th, and Little Simone, and I employed both of them right away. The next day I recruited Tank to work for me. He was wild and didn't respect the drug culture, but he could and would take on anyone. Our operation began to move forward as we snatched up new clients and brought back old ones. Within two weeks, business started to pick up.

I was on my way to realizing my lifelong dream of being a street god. At the age of sixteen, I had become a boss and politician in the drug world. Building up a dead block and running it felt like second nature to me.

My life picked up romantically, too. Zara, who had been with Fat Dre, broke up with him and began to show interest in me. I thought it would be great if we became a get-money couple. She made it clear she did not want to be broke. Ever. She had a great work ethic and was from a family of third-generation drug dealers. If I became part of her family, I would inherit street cred and muscle. Zara was fast, unpredictable, and violent, but I was willing to take her on because her family offered significant perks. If anyone messed with her, her crazy cousins and uncles would beat them up.

One day a drunk wandered onto 205th Street and tried to beat Tank up for his drugs. Tank pulled out a gun and began to pistol-whip the guy. From windows and sidewalks, dozens of people watched Tank take down a grown man. I fired my gun in the air to let everyone know we were armed and dangerous, but in a neighborhood where the residents were sick of drugs and violence, firing a weapon was a stupid thing to do.

The next day, Tank and I went to sell on 205th. I told Tank to hide the drugs outside the park at 205th Street and Hollis and get what he needed after each sale. I bought a bottle of Cisco so we could drink and be merry, but the action on 205th Street began to pick up.

While we were drinking, police surrounded the park. A resident had called about the gunshot the day before, so the cops were on high alert. When we spotted them, I told Tank to be cool and relax, but he shouted, "The drugs are right next to me!"

I stared at him, not believing what I'd just heard. The cops came forward and found the drugs, referring to the park as "crack jack heaven." They were talking to someone on walkie-talkies, then I heard a crackle as an order came through: "Arrest the tall one." I took off running, but I'd been drinking, so I slipped and fell.

As the cops cuffed my hands behind my back, I had a hard time controlling my anger at Tank. I'd told him to keep the drugs out of the park. Because he got lazy, I got arrested.

The cops put me in a van, then drove around picking up other drug dealers. As we rode in the back, one guy near me scraped off his fingerprints with the sharp edge of a soda-can pull tab that he'd hidden. The sight of his bloodied fingertips disturbed me, and I knew he had to be wanted for something like rape or murder. Why else would he sit there and mutilate himself?

Once again I faced the very real prospect of going back to Rikers Island, but this time I had no Ice Boys to bail me out. I was on my own.

That night I pillowed my head on a roll of toilet tissue at Central Booking, and the next morning I went to court. After the judge set my bail at seven hundred dollars, I climbed aboard the van for the ride back to Rikers yet again. I realized that some of my confiscated drugs had disappeared overnight—if they'd all been presented as evidence, my bail would have been thousands of dollars. Only the arresting cops know where those drugs went.

At Rikers, the CO (corrections officer) assigned me to module seven, a dormitory-type space run by a psycho named King Tito. He kept order with a knife, and right after I entered, he had twenty dudes press me up against the wall and put a knife to my throat because he wanted my army jacket. I took off the jacket, but my blood boiled.

As I began to plan my revenge, a cop called my name. My brother, Chad, had sent seven hundred dollars to bail me out.

Later I learned that King Tito was one of the founders of a notorious street gang. If I'd attempted any kind of revenge, the odds wouldn't have been in my favor.

Once I was free again, I went back to the 205th Street block and picked up where I'd left off. Tank apologized for not putting the crack where I'd told him to put it. Small comfort, but at least he made the effort.

One morning I left Zara's house and walked toward our block. I felt my nerves tighten when a couple of cops approached and told me to stand with my hands against the wall. I wasn't too worried, though, because I didn't have any drugs with me.

But while I stood there, hands in the air, they put a package of crack on me, then made a big deal out of finding it. "That's it, Daylight," one of them said. "You're going down this time."

I couldn't believe it. I'd been set up, and I wasn't sure who was responsible. The cops released another drug dealer in their custody and took me instead. Later I learned that they had also arrested Tank on robbery charges.

Off I went to Rikers Island, and this time it looked as if I would be there a while.

*   *   *

My bail was set at $2,200, a lot higher than before. Zara had only drugs and no money, so she couldn't bail me out, and her cousin had stolen my cash. My workers, who carried my drug inventory, conveniently disappeared, and Zara wasn't able to come through with cash from a hustle. I knew my brother had just given me seven hundred dollars, so I didn't expect anything else from him.

Cops ushered me and some other prisoners into a cell with twenty people, just like before. A CO said we'd be taken to general population in an hour. Some of the guys got bailed out before that happened, but I knew better than to hope for a last-minute ticket out of jail.

When the hour was up, the cell doors opened, and the guards took us around to several modules. Some of the dudes were jittery with nerves, but I knew what to expect and I was ready to fight if necessary.

I found myself in Mod 10 Upper, a crowded area on the second floor. The module held three rows of sixteen beds, with a couple of extra beds in the row next to the bathroom. Three concrete walls surrounded us, while the fourth wall held the "bubble," the office where the corrections officers worked and observed. The bathroom contained ten toilets and five showers. Each man was assigned a bed and a small dresser for his personal belongings.

If we stood and stared through the bubble, we could see the module opposite ours, but that was all. No sky, no windows, no sunshine. Nothing but forty-nine other men and rows of beds.

When I walked in, the guard pointed to an empty bed, a stack of

STREET GOD

sheets, and a wool blanket that smelled like wet dog. I looked around and saw forty-nine guys staring back at me. I knew one of them from the neighborhood—his name was Country. I could tell he recognized me, but he didn't say anything. Later I found out why—he was claiming to be from Manhattan, which was an outright lie.

Where you were from mattered a great deal in Rikers. People from Harlem were considered tough; people from Queens were assumed to be soft because Queens was a civil, middle-class community. But the stereotype of Queens' weakness didn't always hold true—lots of Queens residents learned how to fight out of necessity, and the boxing champion of the Elmira Correctional Facility was from Queens.

If you were fighting a man from Brooklyn or Harlem, you could assume that he might stab or shoot you instead of settling things with words or fists. So I never bragged about being from Queens while in Rikers, but I never denied it, either. We Queens men had pride.

All the modules had a leader or leaders and a system of governance. Ten Upper was run by guys from Brooklyn and Manhattan. I kept quiet and tried to blend in, not feeling any ambition to reign in Rikers. In jail, power plays usually centered around the phone, the television, and the front-of-the-line position. Every inmate was supposed to be allowed six minutes on the phone, but the guys who ran the house talked for thirty minutes or an entire hour. I noticed that a skinny kid in jail for murder got an hour on the phone, but he was from Brooklyn, so he had favor with the leaders. Country had an hour too, but he acted like such a stranger that I kept my distance. He was fronting as a dude from Manhattan, so I let him carry out his little masquerade.

The most dangerous and ugly-looking guy was named Scarface—one of several Scarfaces I would meet in Rikers. As you might expect, a long, dark scar marked his face: the result of being slashed with a razor blade.

My first week was fairly uneventful. My mother came to visit, and I told her what I needed. Inmates don't wear uniforms at Rikers, so new clothes helped with status in jail. My lawyer came to see me and told me to keep low because we couldn't beat this charge. He said I had so many drug arrests that I would blow trial and get years behind bars. He advised me not to bail out but to earn time for good behavior so he could get me into a program called Shock Intervention. If I completed that program, he said, I could be home in six months.

On my way back to the cell, a guard told me I had a package. My mother had sent me T-shirts and pants. I called Zara and told her to keep the money for my bail; I needed to get some jail time under my belt.

That night wasn't as uneventful as the others. A fight broke out in 10 Upper when a guy who wanted phone time came in and started making demands. The Brooklyn inmates jumped him, so the guards had to remove him from the house.

Scarface didn't join in that fight, but he wanted people to know he was tough, so he began to randomly dis people with insults and taunts. Jail is a dog-eat-dog world, and only big, violent dogs can reign supreme. Scarface wanted to maintain his position, so throughout the night he strutted around threatening people.

On the way to breakfast the next day, I ran into some dudes from Hollis and Springfield Gardens, two Queens neighborhoods. They gave me props by yelling out that I was a boss and that people better not "front on Daylight." On my way back from breakfast, Scarface taunted me, yelling that dudes from Queens were suckers. I figured he was trying to prove himself to his Brooklyn squad, who were wondering why he hadn't joined in the fight the night before. I kept quiet and minded my own business.

By the time we went out for lunch, things were calmer. My Top Guns friends were in Rikers fighting a murder case. I spoke with a dude who had been in the car with the shooters who had killed the pregnant girl in South Jamaica. The whole hood knew he wasn't the type to kill, though he wouldn't think twice about fighting. He did a good job of representing Queens and had props on Rikers. He told me that Mod 8 was a Queens house on both sides.

On our way back to the cell, Scarface started up with his mouth again. Country, the only guy who even came close to being a friend to me, stayed quiet. When Scarface got back to the house, he turned and yelled, "What are you looking at, Slim?" and put his hands up in my face.

I looked at him without speaking.

"Just like I thought," he said, snorting in derision. "A punk."

I went on inside and waited. After a couple of minutes, I saw Scarface heading to the bathroom. Seizing my chance to end what was certain to be escalating tension, I walked up behind him and punched him in the face when he turned. I had the advantage of surprise, so I was able to hit him about ten times before the guards came and pulled me off him. They called me the aggressor and moved me from 10 Upper to a tougher place, 10 Lower.

When I reached 10 Lower, I found myself staring at a group of psycho cats. When I stepped inside, they tried to surround me in the old intimidation move, just like inmates had on my last visit to Rikers. This time I stared them down and dared whoever wanted to approach to bring his best. One by one, they walked away, leaving me alone to move in and look around.

After a few weeks, a new arrival pulled a razor on me because he wanted my phone time. I fought him with a towel to avoid getting cut, then the corrections officers pulled me out of that house and put me on the opposite side of 10 Lower.

In 10 Lower, Scarface—a different Scarface—and a guy from Brooklyn had the most respect and clout.

While I was in 10 Lower, a Dominican guy called Pablo challenged me. I fought him four times and lost every time, but my pride got hurt more than my body. I connected with Scarface, and he put me in his troublemaking army—I became his soldier. One day he called on me to create a riot on the way to lunch. With no choice but to obey, I stepped into Mod 9 and challenged anyone who wanted to fight. The entire module remained silent except for the leader. When I led the charge and punched him, he hit the ground and 10 Lower began to beat up Mod 9.

As the riot progressed, a couple of COs grabbed me and pulled me out of the fray. I faced a punishment of ninety days in isolation, but the disciplinary officer gave me a break because she used to date my father. When I returned to 10 Lower, a young man who couldn't form a sensible sentence came up behind me and choked me until I passed out. Then he took a razor and sliced my face twice.

I've never felt so helpless in my life—being choked, unable to snatch a breath, watching the world grow dim, and then waking up with blood all over my face. I imagined the worst and went for help.

The officers rushed me to the doctor, and by God's grace the wounds weren't too bad. The guy's razor was so dull I didn't even need stitches. The wounds healed, and I learned that the guy who'd jumped me was a close friend of the leader in Mod 9.

The corrections officers packed me up and moved me to Mod 9, but when I walked in I recognized a guy I'd beaten up in high school, so I knew I was in trouble. I dropped my bag and crossed my arms, waiting for the rumble to begin. I had challenged the entire house two days before, and I had a personal problem with a guy pretending to be from anywhere but Queens, so the odds were definitely against me.

After about an hour of watching and waiting, I rapped on the officers' window. "I can't sleep here," I told them. "Something bad is going to happen if I do."

So they moved me and my bag to the next house, Mod 8.

A kid named Corey presided over Mod 8. Corey looked like a

bodybuilder and had a reputation for being a great fighter. He was a reasonable leader and ran the house well. One of Zara's cousins was in Mod 8, so I had backup if anything went down.

I started to smoke cigarettes in jail, but Corey told me smoking was dumb. The next day I found a workout partner, and we did push-ups to prepare for the Shock Intervention Program. When I got back to the module after lunch, my cigarettes had disappeared. Someone had gone into my locker and taken them.

My workout buddy pointed to the thief, so I went to Corey, but he smirked when I complained. "This is jail, so it's going to happen. Handle it."

Handle it? Okay.

I walked over to the kid who'd taken my cigarettes and hit him in the face.

As always, I got transferred, this time back to Mod 10 Upper, only this time I was on the side run by a dude named Miami. When I walked in, the atmosphere was different from what I remembered. Guys looked at me and whispered, "That's Big Slim." Without trying to, I'd built a reputation for fighting. People knew I hit fast and hard.

I didn't realize that I'd gained a reputation for trouble. "Big Slim is crazy," the word went around. "You don't want to mix it up with him." I hadn't won all the fights I'd participated in, but because I fought big names, the mantra became "Don't mess with Slim."

My reputation had grown far bigger than I deserved. I didn't have the self-confidence to believe it myself, but I began to see the results: "Go ahead, Slim, use the phone thirty minutes. You don't have to fight with us." They gave me phone time before I even asked for it. Nobody challenged me, and no one wanted problems with me.

Then I made the mistake of believing in my own myth. I was getting a load of respect and love from people, and I'd hear them say, "If you got a problem, you need to talk to Slim or Miami." I started to get a big head, which filled me with chutzpah. One night I decided to rob the entire house.

Everyone was asleep, except for two or three dudes. "Watch this," I whispered to one of the guys, then got out of bed and went from dresser to dresser, robbing people of their food stockpiles: chips and crackers and candy bars. I put all the stolen food in my dresser and my bag, then went to sleep.

The next morning people woke up and realized they'd been robbed. They went to Miami, who was a fair guy who upheld justice, and he couldn't believe anyone had the guts to rob the whole house. The entire day passed, and no one solved the crime until one of the witnesses told a CO that I'd done it.

The CO came inside and called me over. "You had it good here, but you robbed these people, so now you're transferring out. Come on, Slim, let's go."

When the house heard that, all forty-nine other prisoners came toward me with their fists lifted. I had picked up my bag, ready to follow the CO; but when everyone came toward me, I wasn't sure I could make it out alive. The situation was crazy—because it was nighttime, we were in a darkened room and could barely see. Someone threw the first punch, and I ducked. Someone else threw another punch and made contact, but he'd hit another guy, not me. Pretty soon the place went nuts as all the other guys beat each other up. I slipped down to the floor and picked up my bag—heavy with all the stolen food—while the cop pulled out his nightstick and began to beat the others away from me. I made it out of there without a scratch *and* with all my stolen loot.

"Okay," the CO said when he came out. He was sweaty and tired, and he looked exasperated. "Slim, it's time you learned a lesson. We're putting you in Mod 3 Lower."

I'd heard about that particular module. It was rumored to be the worst hellhole in Rikers, and it was home to adolescents who looked like muscle-bound thirty-year-olds. The violent side of Mod 3 Lower regularly experienced slashings, robberies, and violence. Only the strong had power in there, and my reputation was about as big as a gnat compared to those of the giants in that place.

When I walked in, I was told to go see Moosey, a tough kid from Brooklyn who had power over the entire island. No one had ever beaten him in a fight. Moosey asked where I was from, and I told him the truth: "Queens." Moosey's mouth curved in a twisted smile, revealing a mouthful of gold between the long scars on his face. As my stomach churned, Moosey told me he owned both phones and the whole house.

"Good," I said.

His smile broadened. "Relax, Slim. Get some rest."

Thinking that maybe I'd be okay as long as I didn't get into trouble, I sat down and dozed off, my head on my folded arms. I woke to find a razor at my throat. My bag of stolen food was gone, but I didn't say anything, so I got out of that situation without being cut. Stolen property never lasts, and I got what I deserved as far as that goes. Since I was a thief, it seemed only fair that in Rikers I was robbed every time I turned around.

I could handle being robbed, but I couldn't handle not being able to close my eyes for fear that someone would slit my throat. The tension in Mod 3 Lower was so thick that I could practically cut it with a knife, and everyone kept looking at me like I was a juicy bone and they were starving dogs. At one point during the night, I picked up a wringer mop and held it by my side, prepared to beat off anyone who wanted to attack me.

That's when I knew I would never last in Mod 3 Lower. I was a fighter, but I wasn't a killer.

The next morning I went to the COs and told them I wasn't going to make it in that module. Content that I'd learned my lesson, the COs moved me to the other side of Mod 3 Lower.

A smart and well-respected Puerto Rican kid presided over the other side. He had an army behind him, and while his side wasn't exactly peaceful, it wasn't as violent as Moosey's side.

Everything was going well for me until another Scarface entered the picture—the third Scarface I'd dealt with in Rikers. This guy was from Brooklyn and had a huge slice down his face. Everyone disliked him, but he was cool with Moosey, who'd known him in Brooklyn. To show off for Moosey, Scarface the third pushed my head while I was on my way back from lunch. When I turned around, an officer stood right beside me: "Keep cool, Salaberrios."

I turned around in time to see Scarface III smile at Moosey and say, "They know who's boss."

The whole house had become fed up with Scarface III destroying the peace, so when he got comfortable in his bed that night, I hit him in the face and punched him eight or nine times. He stood up, bleeding, and another guy named Harlem stepped forward.

"Fight him," Harlem told Scarface.

Then the strangest thing happened—Harlem decided to take on Scarface himself. You have to understand that there's something primal about the pecking order in a jail. In the same way that younger lions will challenge an older lion once he begins to weaken, men will challenge a leader if they perceive that he's become vulnerable. When the men around me saw Scarface bleeding, they realized he was weak. Their focus shifted from me to him.

Scarface pulled out a shank, and Harlem did the same. I stepped back and watched those guys stab and punch each other until the COs came in and intervened. I was covered in blood from punching Scarface, so they placed all three of us in waiting rooms.

When the cops asked me if I wanted to go anywhere in particular, I said, "One Lower," because I'd heard that Tank was there with a broken arm. I thought I might be able to help him.

The COs decided to place me in protective custody in 7 Upper, an adolescent house on the other side of Rikers Island. I didn't want to be away from my friends, so I pretended to be suicidal and wrapped a sheet around my neck. When they did the head count that night, they took one look at me and came rushing in. In the medical unit I told them I was lonely and that the only friend I had was in Mod 1 Lower.

They transferred me in record time. I guess the last thing they wanted was a former CO's son being dead on arrival for his transfer. Even though my dad had retired by the time I was incarcerated in Rikers, a lot of the COs either remembered him or knew his name.

A couple of times I was supposed to go to the Bing unit (the Central Punitive Segregation Unit—that is, solitary confinement), but plans would change and I wouldn't have to go. Later I heard that an old friend of my father's had prevented my transfer.

Being locked up in Bing meant being in a small individual cell for up to twenty-three hours a day while surrounded by the screams, wails, and insults of the psychos who'd been locked up for thirty days, sixty days, or even longer. Inmates in Bing mess with the new arrivals and call out threats such as "When I see you in the yard, I'm going to break every bone in your body." No one could relax during the single hour they were released to wander in the yard because they never knew who or what sort of person was about to attack them.

Believe me, I was grateful when I realized some of my dad's friends had protected me.

When I arrived in 1 Lower I found Tank and Bullet, who had once robbed me. The guy who had shot the pregnant lady in South Jamaica ran the house with a crew from Brooklyn, using Tank and Bullet as backup in case a Brooklyn/Queens battle ever broke out.

I was in a sweet spot. I had no ambitions in the house but was happy to be with my friend and some dudes from around the way.

CHAPTER EIGHT

My way out of jail came through the Shock Intervention Program, designed for inmates sentenced to more than ninety days for nonviolent offenses. My lawyer had put my name in for the program. When my turn came, I listened to the spiel with interest: I would enter a military-style boot camp program in which I would receive strict disciplinary guidance, intensive physical activity, military precision drills, substance-abuse treatment, and educational classes. I would be transferred to a camp in Butler, New York, and live in a barracks. I thought it sounded like a great fit for me.

After being in Rikers for six months, I thought the physical drills, counseling, and substance-abuse treatment were a refreshing change. I loved the military lifestyle, and I even liked my drill instructor. We'd get up at 6 a.m. and exercise, then go on a long run or a march in military fatigues. Having a strict schedule suited my personality, and the six months flew by. At the end of the program, we had a graduation ceremony—the only one I'd ever participated in—and my family came up to see me receive my certificate. I felt as if I had accomplished something significant.

I went to see my mother, who was eager to help me get a job and start a new life. I had learned a lot in the Shock program, and I wanted to change. Mom hooked me up with an employment agency, but their attempts to find me a job failed miserably—my street skills didn't match up with what companies wanted.

I told my mother and my new parole officer that I was going to concentrate on my education, so I went to Queensborough Community College and took its GED preparation classes, thinking I might go on to college. Oddly enough, my old nemesis Kirk Green was attending classes there too. I rode to Bayside with him in his black Jetta, but our times together were awkward. Instead of talking about education, we talked about a business model in which we could work together selling drugs. He also told me about the time he ran through fifty thousand dollars in two months.

"Yo, man, that's beautiful what you're doin', goin' to school and all," Kirk said.

The counselors at Shock had arranged construction jobs for everyone coming out of the program, but the job paid minimum wage. At the end of each hard workday, our employers would give each of us a check for twenty-four dollars. I worked at those jobs for about a week, but I couldn't shake the feeling that my work was worth more than twenty-four dollars a day. Pride crept into my heart, and I began to think about how I could get back into the drug game without getting caught.

I still wanted to be a street god in my world and the kingpin of the New York drug world, so I went back to 205th, my block. A new dealer had moved in, and I didn't even care at first. Then Zara told me the block was being controlled by two guys, City and Rome. Apparently my return from jail had alarmed them.

One day Kirk dropped me off in the neighborhood. As I walked toward Zara's house, a crack addict came up and said City had been arrested—the cops had found his stash in a billboard sign. I wasn't surprised because even I knew where City kept his stash.

I told Zara the news, and then she said she wanted to go smoke some blunts. She told me about a new weed spot near the Ice Boys' block.

"Let's go," I told her. I didn't worry about having marijuana show up in my parole officer's drug test because I was a serious believer in goldenseal, an herbal pill that supposedly masked illegal drugs in urine. Zara got her purse, and we began to walk down 205th Street.

When we turned the corner, I saw a girl who used to hang with the Ice Boys and a guy who looked like my friend Paul. I lengthened my stride and called, "What's up, Paul?" then realized I'd made a mistake—the guy wasn't Paul.

"Yo," I said, backing away, "I thought you were someone else."

The guy got in my face, but I wasn't going to be intimidated. "Do you know who I am?" I asked.

I brushed on by, and Zara took my arm. "Let's go," she said, hurrying me along.

As we walked away, I heard someone yell, "What's up *now?*"

When I turned around to check things out, I saw a gun pointed at us. "Run!"

I put Zara in front of me so I could shield her, and then we heard the pop of gunshots. We ran toward the safety of a corner, but I felt something pinch my leg before we made it.

Once we were around the corner, I asked Zara if she was okay. "I'm fine," she said, looking at me. "Are you?"

I ran my hand over the back of my leg, and it came away bloody. "I'm hit," I told her. "I'm bleeding pretty good."

We waved down a dollar cab—a taxi that travels down a major street loading people up for a dollar per person—and when I got in I told the driver I'd been shot. "Cover the wound," he said before stopping to get a towel from his trunk. My heart raced as I peered out the back window—what if the shooter came around the corner to finish the job?

When the cab driver gave me the towel, I told him to hurry to the hospital. The towel he gave me was too filthy to put on an open wound, so I took off my shirt and used it to apply pressure to my leg.

The drive to the hospital seemed to take forever. Every traffic light seemed to be against us, and the traffic was heavy and slow. I gritted my teeth against the pain, but my imagination kept making things worse. What if the wound got infected? What if the hospital reported I'd been in a shooting? What if the bullet traveled up my leg and reached my heart? *What if, what if, what if?*

When we made it to the hospital, I limped into the emergency room and yelled, "I'm shot!" To my amazement and consternation, they had me sit and fill out a stack of forms. When I'd finished, another man called me into his office and said the law required him to call the police for any shooting victim. I grabbed my paperwork and told him my girlfriend needed to notify my mother.

I grabbed Zara, and we headed toward the exit. The last thing I needed was police involvement. The cops would call my parole officer, and she'd watch me even more closely.

We caught a cab at the hospital and told the driver to take us to Zara's house. Once there, I cleaned my wound with rubbing alcohol and staunched the bleeding with Band-Aids. Zara told me that since my parole officer might stop by my house, I needed to go home. She was right, so I went home in another cab.

At home, Mom noticed my limp, but I told her I'd cut my leg. I went to my room and begged God to help me. Then I fell asleep. When I woke up, I found that I could walk almost normally. Later,

I saw both an entrance and an exit wound, so I knew the bullet was no longer in my leg. I thanked God for his help. I was thrilled to be alive.

I took a cab to Zara's house, and her family was happy to see me—they slapped me on the back and said I was a really tough guy. Zara's uncle had nosed around and learned that the guy who shot me was from Brooklyn and that he'd had a fight with Paul earlier in the day. When I had called him Paul, he'd thought I was messing with him. Plus, the girl he had been talking to remembered that I'd once worked for the Ice Boys, which was why he responded so forcefully.

I thought things would cool down, but a few hours later, City got shot. The hood buzzed with the story of City and Daylight both getting shot, and everyone wondered whether there was any connection.

No one wondered more than I did.

*   *   *

The next morning I walked down to 205th Street and saw City and Rome in a restaurant. I walked in and overheard them talking about how to move forward—what could a dude do after he'd been shot? I studied City carefully, but his gunshot wound must have been like mine: scary but not life threatening.

I nodded as I walked forward. "City, I heard what happened. If I can help, I'm here."

"I'm out." Rome shook his head. "I am not hustling on this block."

"You gonna leave me now?" City gave his partner an indignant look. "What do you think you're gonna do?"

"I don't know, but I'm out."

I'd never had a better opening. "City—" I looked him in the eye—"I'll be your new partner. I have guns and I'm ready."

City looked at Rome again, then nodded at me. "All right. I'll meet you here at 6 a.m."

"I'll be here."

Rome stood and hugged City, and then he walked out.

What a punk dude—bailing after his partner got shot. I'd been shot myself, but I wasn't about to give up my dream.

I slid into the seat Rome had vacated. "What happened to you, man?"

City shook his head. "A guy came into the store where I was getting a drink, pulled out a gun, and said, 'Give me your money.' I grabbed his gun and punched him in the face, but the gun went off and hit me in the leg. I threw the guy out of the store and he ran off. He got the shock of his life when he tried to stick me up."

I chuckled. I knew people would rally around City because he'd fought back. He would never be an easy victim.

Zara and I were excited about this new opportunity. I was going to set up business again on 205th Street, and it would be nice to establish my drug spots peacefully. Zara and I went out and bought product, then packaged it in ten-dollar capsules. After we bagged up fifty capsules, I went to sleep at Zara's house.

The next morning the alarm went off, and I jumped up like someone had yelled in my ear. I wasn't used to getting up in the dark, but you'd be surprised how many people are on the streets at 6 a.m. I made my way through the darkened streets and saw City walking toward me, right on time.

Everyone in the drug world knows about the 6 a.m. rush, though most dealers don't understand why so many customers are eager to buy so early in the morning. As a former addict, I knew from personal experience that the sun had tended to sober my high. At six in the morning, the skies are still dark and people are eager to get their last fix before sunrise.

City and I started selling. He had his regulars, and he was surprised by how many people yelled, "Yo, Daylight is back!" My product was superior to his, and he couldn't understand why. The answer was simple: Most drug dealers bought their supply from whomever the other dealers recommended. I didn't ask other dealers—I asked addicts. I figured that if anyone would know who had the best stuff, they would.

This time I was determined not to get caught.

Within a couple of days we heard that YB, a thug who worked for Mr. McNally, wanted to close down every block but his from 9 p.m. onward. The news sounded like a Mafia-type move to corner the market, and I felt trapped.

City laughed when the news hit our block. "I ain't changing nothing," he said. "I'm staying."

The next morning I stepped into a corner store for a minute and Muscle Greg, one of Mr. McNally's enforcers, walked in on me. He stood in front of me, looking as broad as a barn door, then he said what he'd been sent to say: "Daylight, you cannot hustle out here."

My heart went to my throat for a second, then I remembered my motto: *If you're going to fight, always throw the first punch.*

I hit Greg and knocked him into the groceries. Then I leaped on him and beat him bloody. He managed to get up, but I grabbed him and threw him across the store.

"I'm sorry, man," he said, wiping blood from his nose. "You won."

I went outside. "Come on; we're not done."

Greg lifted his hands. "I quit. This is your block. I was just playin'."

I was a little surprised I'd won the fight so easily, but then I remembered the Shock Intervention Program. I was thin from all that running, but I'd also developed muscles I didn't realize I had. Muscle Greg was big, but he was no match for a guy who could run ten miles and do 100 push-ups without stopping.

The word went out—Daylight would beat you down if you messed with him.

*   *   *

After my fight with Greg, City was all smiles, telling anyone who'd listen that his partner was no joke. City was tough, but he seemed confident that I could hold my own with other gangsters. After all, Greg was known for beating down dudes, and I took his heart. Kirk and his team faced trouble somewhere else that night too, so they backed off 205th Street.

After that, City opened my eyes to the world of Def Jam, the leading hip-hop record label. City and his friend Rome knew all the heads of Def Jam. In fact, City always wore Adidas running shoes, and I'd heard that Run-D.M.C. copied their Adidas style from him.

City offered to take me to a Def Jam party. Before the party, however, he prepped me like an anxious mother preparing her son for his first day at school. "Dress fly," he instructed. "And bring everything you need—don't be asking to borrow from anyone else."

The party was hosted by Rick Rubin, a cofounder of Def Jam, and he'd paid $75,000 to screen *Hellraiser III* in a private showing. I hung out with Q-Tip from the hip-hop group A Tribe Called Quest, and I met several other artists. I was cordial to everyone and careful not to ask for anything. The atmosphere was pure NYC Hollywood— bright lights, fancy foods, fly girls, and thumping music. I loved it.

At the party, I learned that Run-D.M.C. had bought this dude Garfield a BMW 535i, which had the best sound system I had ever heard—strong bass, crystal clear sound, real power. That system would wake me up at night, and I'd know without looking that Garfield had just driven by my house.

When I met Garfield, I asked if he would ever sell his car—and if he would, what the right amount of thousands would be. His girlfriend was tight with City, and she said, "He wants to sell it. Bring him five thousand cash and he'll make the deal. He's scheming on a new car, and he needs five thousand more. That man is all about his image."

A few days later I was getting ready to buy his car when all kinds of drama broke out. As 9 p.m. rolled around, Zara and I went down to the block to finish selling. I hadn't paid much attention to YB's nine o'clock curfew, but at the appointed hour one of his lieutenants came down the street with his crew. The lieutenant, a guy named B who happened to be YB's son, had always looked suspiciously at me, and there he was, coming straight toward me, along with about twenty of his crew.

Though I didn't have a gun with me, everyone knew I owned guns, so I put my hand in my pocket as if I were holding a weapon. I took Zara's arm with my free hand, and we started to walk right through their group.

"Chill," one of B's guys called out. "He's strapped."

I clenched my jaw and walked a little more confidently, as if I wasn't worried. But clearly, they'd come down to start a fight over that stupid curfew.

*   *   *

Though I had never been issued a driver's license, the next day I jumped into my mother's car and drove to Hollis Avenue. When I saw one of B's team members, I pulled over to confront him about what had happened the night before. "Daylight—" he put up his hands and backed away—"I had nothing to do with it. B wanted to start a beef with you."

Hearing my suspicions confirmed, I grabbed my gun. "He wants a beef? He's about to get a war."

I called in my crew and set up to work on Murdock Avenue and Colfax Street, as well as Linden Avenue and 200th Street, where I'd worked before. Tiny, whom I'd hired, had my gun, and I told him to fire if the other crews approached him.

Later, as I was driving, I saw B, YB's son, on 204th Street. I pulled up and said, "What's up; you want beef?"

He put up his hands to fight, but I pulled out my gun. I pointed the weapon at him but shifted it up and to the side to fire a warning shot into the air. B ran for his life, and as I watched him go, I realized that I just had started a war with YB and the Top Guns. Unfortunately, I hadn't realized how connected those teams were.

While I worked with the team at Murdock and Colfax, I saw Homicide ride by and look at me. I knew he was cool with YB, but I kept thinking of him as I'd known him in my younger days. Back then, he'd beaten up Macho and I'd considered working for him.

A small building on Murdock Avenue housed a pool-hall numbers spot—a place that also ran an underground lotto. I was selling drugs and playing pool in the spot, and as I took my shots I noticed that they'd propped the back door open—a first, as far as I knew. But the weather was hot, so maybe they just wanted to let in some air.

I had just finished sinking a ball when Tiny ran in. "They got us," he said, his eyes wide.

Before I could respond, Homicide, YB, and E—three no-nonsense, vicious dudes—walked in the front door. After one glance, I sprinted out the back door and ran for my life.

I hid out at a crack house, where Tiny finally found me. He seemed a great deal more relaxed than he'd been in the pool hall. "They just wanted to talk," he told me.

I snorted. "They're liars. I shot at a Top Guns dude, and you can't do that and get away with it."

Tiny shook his head. "Naw, man. They said they were coming to discuss territories for Mr. McNally."

"That was a hit squad, Tiny. They wanted to take me out."

I called City, and he told me to come to the block because he'd spoken to YB. Later that night City saw E and identified him as the man who'd shot him in the store.

I was starting to feel claustrophobic. Zara and I had had a fight, I'd fired a warning shot in B's direction, and a hit team had come after me.

Tiny and I made up our minds to gun it out on 205th Street. I bought a war car for five hundred dollars, intending to use it for a drive-by, if necessary.

We drove the war car to support City and hold down our block.

I pulled up a block away and parked the car, then we walked to 205th Street. When we reached it, I saw City and YB talking. I didn't know what to do first—shoot or talk some more.

"Come over here, Daylight," City called.

YB agreed. "We fight with hands first," he said. "Then we shoot if necessary."

I drew a deep breath and approached them, bracing for whatever might happen next.

"Look," YB said, "my son has ambitions, but you shouldn't have tried to kill him."

"He came here with twenty dudes to fight," I answered, "so I fired into the air to let him know 205th Street is not to be taken by anyone."

YB rubbed his chin. "The beef is squashed. You and City hustle all day, and let us have the night shift from 9 p.m. to 6 a.m. You guys keep the days; we'll take the nights."

I looked at City, then nodded. "No problem."

"Done," City agreed.

We parted in peace, but I didn't believe a word YB had said. Experience had taught me that you could only trust other dealers so far, and you could never, ever let your guard down.

I began to plan for a slow exit from 205th Street.

*   *   *

While sitting around and thinking about what I should do, I had a flashback to a time my brother, Chad, had taken me to a barbecue in Winston-Salem, North Carolina, about a hundred miles away from his home in Raleigh. I met a cousin there who smoked weed, so I went for a ride with him. During the ride, he pointed out a line of forty cars stretching around the block. "They're waitin'," he told me.

"Waitin' for what?"

"To buy weed. Or crack."

At the barbecue, I saw a guy with a big bag of crack capsules. I asked how much they sold for, and he told me they were twenty dollars. *What?* That same capsule would have sold for five dollars in NYC.

The more I thought about it, the more lucrative and welcoming North Carolina seemed. I wasn't going to risk my life in a drug war over one slow block in New York.

I took my idea to Stretch and suggested we open up a business in North Carolina. This wouldn't be like DC. This time we'd be our own bosses—I'd bring my drugs, he'd bring his, and we'd be equal. He agreed, so we arranged an exploratory visit to Winston-Salem.

Stretch and I flew down to Raleigh, where my brother picked us up. Chad had no idea we had flown in with packages of crack and weed. He grabbed our bags and welcomed us. He seemed genuinely glad to see us and introduced us to everyone he worked with. All the while, I hoped we wouldn't run across a drug-sniffing dog.

We got into my brother's car and went to his apartment. Stretch and I were excited about the possibility of setting up a more profitable business away from the dangers of New York.

When my brother finally dropped us in Winston-Salem, we met a guy at a barbecue. We pulled him aside and said that we had crack and wanted to make some money. He quickly began to bring others who wanted to buy our stuff. He brought one guy, Troy, who bought almost everything we had.

Sales were absolutely no problem in Winston-Salem. One dude, Money Smith, was younger than Stretch and me, but he had one of the baddest cars around. He wore lots of big chains, flashing everything he owned. I thought he was nice but foolish. New York had taught me that a dealer has to maintain a low profile—those who flash their stuff go to jail. But flamboyant Money came in, threw four thousand dollars on the table, and bought everything we had left.

We made a nice profit but not nearly as much as we'd have made if we'd sold to individual customers. I was happy, but Stretch was upset we didn't make more.

We flew back to New York with visions of money and drugs dancing in our heads.

*   *   *

I kept running my operation in Queens but barely spent any time on 205th Street. It was great to be away from the dangers of the street for a while, but the beef with the Top Guns and YB wasn't over, so I was a little anxious about that. I knew I'd have to keep looking over my shoulder anytime I ventured out to sell. Plus, I had an appointment with my parole officer on Jamaica Avenue.

The visit with my parole officer should have been routine. She didn't know I'd recently expanded my operation into another state. She thought I was enrolled in a program to get my GED, but I'd only agreed to that to keep her off my back. I wanted to get my GED, sure, but I cared a lot more about expanding my operation.

Once inside the building that housed the parole office, I walked past a line of criminals—one guy I knew was crying because they were sending him back to jail. He had acted hard and tough back in the day, but there he stood, cuffed and weeping like a baby. I also recognized a guy who ran with Kareem.

When the parole officer called me into her office, I dropped into the chair facing her. She asked how I was doing, and I shrugged. "Fine."

She gave me a hard look. "I just got your report, and you've had three dirty tests for cocaine. You're going to jail."

I blinked in surprise as she came out from behind her desk to handcuff me. What—how could that be right? I hadn't used cocaine in years.

Then understanding dawned. For the last several months I'd been cooking crack. My job was to heat the cocaine over boiling water until it turned into a liquid. Then I let it harden until it could be broken up into chunks and sold. I never wore gloves when working, and that was my mistake. The cocaine must have been absorbed through my skin into my bloodstream. That oversight was about to launch me into the hellish New York City prison system.

As I stood and the cold metal cuffs slid around my wrists, I relived the six months of torture I'd already endured at Rikers. Thirty-two fights in all, mostly because some guys in Rikers didn't like dudes from Queens. Beatings and slashings and constantly being on guard, afraid for my life—no way was I signing on for another stint at Rikers. But how could I get out of it?

I heard the snap of the cuffs as they closed, and then my parole officer said, "I'll be right back." In that instant, I knew I had to take the only chance I would have to escape.

I'd always been physically flexible, and break dancing with my friends had maintained my flexibility to the point that some of my friends called me Flex Master. I could shift my linked hands from behind my back to the front, and that ability paid off in my parole officer's cluttered office. Quick as a flash, I brought my hands down, stepped through them, and sat again, acting as though I had nothing more on my mind than a nice bus ride out to the jail.

My parole officer walked back in and sat at her desk. The minute she planted herself on her chair, I leapt up, opened the door, and ran with all the determination I could muster. I made it to the steps, then leaped over the staircase, avoiding the steps completely. *Boom!* After crashing on the pavement at the end of the flight, I hurled myself over the next set of steps, and the next, doing anything that would get me to the ground floor before my pursuers. I was in a race for my life. I could hear the pounding of feet on the stairs behind me, but the element of surprise had given me a formidable head start.

My heart felt like it was going to pound right out of my chest. I was scared but far too committed to turn back and surrender. When I reached the first floor, I looked for the security guard who usually stood at the door, but he had disappeared, probably stepping into the restroom or going outside for a smoke. I didn't stop to wait for him; I just barreled through the door and kept running.

No one was more surprised than I was when I landed on the sidewalk. I was on Jamaica Avenue and in the middle of a shopping district that was always packed. I dove into the crowds of shoppers, yelling, "Look out! Excuse me! Coming through!" After a few steps, I felt a smile creep across my face—I was like the star of an action movie, except that this was real life. If I messed this up, there'd be no "take two." Word on the street was that if you escaped from Rikers or police custody, you'd automatically be facing whatever jail time you'd earned plus seven years.

Still, for the moment I was in the clear, and I had friends who worked on Jamaica Avenue. I took a quick left and headed into a crowded mall, looking for the barbershop. Two well-known barbers worked there—one would soon become a lead artist for a popular rap group; the other, my friend Wiz, was legendary for his appeal to women from Queens.

When I found the barbershop, I ducked into a back room and heard someone in the front say, "Yo, the cops are chasing some guy through the mall!"

Right after that, a guy opened the door to my little hiding place, spotted me, and said, "Oh, shoot."

I lifted my cuffed hands and looked him in the eye. "Call Wiz. I need to get out of here."

He nodded in agreement. "Stay quiet. The cops are everywhere."

When he closed the door, I prayed the hood's most frequently recited prayer: "Lord, if you get me out of this, I promise I will do good."

A few minutes later, Wiz opened the door and gave me a head-to-toe glance. Spotting the handcuffs, he nodded and promised to come right back with some help.

Wiz was big on jewelry and always wore good stuff, lots of original pieces, so he knew the jeweler in the mall. He stayed away for a few minutes and then returned with a small saw designed to cut metal. He sawed the chain holding the cuffs together, freeing my hands, but I still wore those shiny silver bracelets.

Knowing the cops were looking for a guy in a blue shirt, I grabbed a beige shirt from a shelf in the back room, then asked Wiz to put me in a barber's chair facing the wall. "Give me a unique haircut with weird sideburns," I said, my brain working at warp speed.

Wiz put me in the chair. As he worked on my head, I pulled the long sleeves over the cuffs and kept moving my hands, knowing the police would be looking for a guy sitting quiet and still, not a guy who acted as though he'd never been cuffed before.

One of the barbers, a brave dude, said, "I'll drive him away and get him outta here." He looked at me. "When I pull up, come out to my car."

I didn't know the guy, but when he pulled up a few minutes later, I walked out the front door with a new look, a new shirt, and two shiny silver bracelets. I walked with bent knees to make myself look shorter. As I got into the car, I nearly melted in relief.

But my escape was far from being a done deal. The police would be looking for me at my home, my girlfriend's house, and all the spots where I liked to hang out. So I had to get out of town, and I had to do it fast.

And I had to get out of those stinkin' handcuffs.

I knew that all kinds of guys escaped, went to their girlfriends' houses, and ended up getting busted there. But that was because they hung around, and I had no intention of staying more than a few minutes. New York agencies moved slowly, and cops met before making a decision to move on a suspect's location. So I figured I had at least thirty minutes to grab my belongings, my drugs, and some money before heading out.

Once at Zara's house, I decided to call around to see if I could bribe someone to get my cuffs off. I called the barber who'd driven me away, and almost immediately he said, "I have a guy who can do it." I told him to bring the guy to Zara's house and I'd meet them there.

A few minutes later, my driver walked in with a distinguished-looking black man. I gave the guy fifty bucks, and he unlocked my cuffs with a universal key. "Who do you work for?" I asked, curious.

He stood and put the key back in his pocket. "I'm a parole officer."

At that exact moment, his eyes went as round as dinner plates. I'm sure he'd just realized I was the guy his coworkers were searching for, yet he'd just received fifty bucks for setting me free. But what could he do? He was on my turf.

The minute he left the house, I bolted out the back door and ran through yard after yard until I put ten blocks between me and Zara's house. I found out later that within fifteen minutes the cops' special task force raided my girlfriend's home.

For the moment I had managed to escape, but I still had to leave the city before I could rest.

CHAPTER NINE

After leaving Zara's house, I knew my chief goals would be selling my remaining drugs, using the cash to buy a large amount of powdered cocaine, and getting to North Carolina. Certain that the police would be searching for me at my usual haunts, I bounced from place to place, sleeping in a different spot each night and staying on the move. Some of my friends were drivers for limousine services, so every night I would go to a location and lie down on the backseat floor of a friend's car. My nerves were strung as tight as violin strings because I knew there could be no turning back. I had earned a trip to Rikers and then some.

Within two days, I managed to sell the rest of my drugs and borrow a couple thousand dollars from loan sharks—enough to get a lot of cocaine so that I'd have plenty of inventory in North Carolina. When I finally obtained my coke, I considered how to travel south.

I didn't have a car, and the airport was too risky. That left the bus—too long a trip—and the train.

I was a little worried the cops might have posted my picture somewhere at the train station, but I got lucky. I went to the depot on Halloween night, and lots of people were walking around in costumes. I had strapped packets of cocaine all over my body, then asked Zara to dress me like a woman. She bought me a wig and even did my nails. I put on women's shoes, a blouse, and pants. I know I looked odd—at six feet six inches, I wasn't exactly a demure-looking female, but Zara and I got on an Amtrak train to Greensboro, North Carolina, without anyone stopping us. I didn't care if I looked foolish—my only concern was getting out of town.

As we boarded the train, I asked God to get me down to North Carolina unnoticed. As we rolled through Virginia or thereabouts, a guy looked at me and shook his head as if to ask, *What would make a young man go transgender?* Others looked at me like—well, if looks could kill, I'd have been dead on arrival in Greensboro.

After two days of running on adrenaline in New York, I relished the opportunity to rest for a while. I slept most of the trip, and when we stepped off the train in Greensboro and caught a cab, I realized I'd pulled it off. I'd managed a clean escape from New York's finest.

To my mixed-up way of thinking, God had shown me grace and mercy. I was sure someone would have killed me if I'd stayed in New York. Too many people wanted my business and my territory, and it was only a matter of time before one of the Top Guns decided to shoot me for it.

The cemetery held far too many competitors in the drug business.

In hindsight, I know that God didn't bless my crime, but he *did* show me more mercy and grace than I realized. He got me to North Carolina, where someone was waiting to tell me about Jesus. God had a bigger agenda for my life than I did, and I needed to be in a different situation to see it.

*   *   *

With a pound of marijuana and several ounces of cocaine, Zara and I got off the train and caught a cab to a cousin's beautiful house in the suburbs of Winston-Salem. My cousin opened the door with a grin but stopped short when he saw me dressed in women's clothing. "Why you dressed like that?"

"I just escaped, man. Long story."

My cousin told us we could stay, but only for a week.

He took us to a barbecue, where connections opened before my eyes. Some people I met there advised me to go to the Winston-Salem neighborhood called the Boston Projects, where another cousin lived. They said I'd be able to sell everything there.

Zara had to go back to New York to take care of her son, so she left on a bus. I hooked up with my cousin who lived in the Boston Projects, aka the BDP, or "Boogie Down Projects." He took me to a house where two addicts, Tori and Faye, lived. We hit it off from the start. For two days I hung out at their place and sold all my crack. The weed I sold in one shot.

Stretch was at some guy's house in Winston-Salem, so I called him and told him to come to the Boston Projects. He did and sold his inventory in a day. Flush with cash and a feeling of accomplishment, Stretch rented a car and we left for New York City. On the ride up we laughed, smoked weed, and talked about the gold mine we'd discovered.

Stretch had a car in the city, so once we arrived he let me take the rental to pick up Zara and some more drugs. That night, I pulled up on my block at 205th Street and Hollis Avenue and hooked up with MD, another dealer I'd met while working on 205th. He told me the cops were looking for me everywhere and grabbing anyone over six foot four.

MD was smart, and I admired his business mind. While everyone else was selling crack bottles for five dollars, he was selling them for three. As an advanced thinker, he was ready to leave Hollis Avenue, so I asked if he and the rest of my old crew might want to join me in North Carolina. City wouldn't leave the area. Tiny, my lieutenant, was being held in juvenile custody.

I was dismayed to hear that my empire had disintegrated, but the business part of my brain knew that this small piece of territory was nothing compared to what I'd found in Winston-Salem.

I was relieved when MD said he was ready to go. He brought his driver and a different car. MD taught us an ingenious transport trick—we put the drugs in cookie bags. Soon we were off and running. We talked business all the way to North Carolina, and I was glad we got to spend some time together. Tank and I used to rob MD's workers, so we needed to bond.

MD was an expert with maps and enjoyed creating routes to keep us away from the highway patrol. During the crack boom, everyone knew drugs moved out of NYC and Miami, so highway patrolmen would randomly profile and pull over African American drivers. We, however, got to Winston-Salem without a problem.

Stretch didn't like the look of the Boston Projects, so he went to a place called Happy Hill Gardens, a neighborhood that didn't live up to its name. The place was rough and had a stickup element. I didn't want to mess with it.

We met up with Big Jay, a client who had once cleared us out of inventory. MD clicked with him, so they decided to partner. I loved my spot in the Boston Projects, where I knew I could rent a room from Faye and move product quickly.

I caught on that Southern dealers played the game well. Most NYC dudes behaved as if they were smarter than Southern guys because people talk slow and soft in the South. MD and I respected each dealer we met and didn't underestimate anyone. Stretch thought

Southerners were dumb until he got robbed. That was our first warning—from then on, we were wiser about where we set up shop.

Hearing about Stretch being robbed made me nervous. I bought two guns that same day and stayed strapped during all transactions of over three hundred dollars. The temptation to rip someone off was too great for some of the kids to ignore. I didn't want to shoot anybody, but I did want them to know I was armed.

I chose to sell weight instead of messing with the small packages. I sold wholesale to other dealers and sold small pieces only in my Boston Projects spot. Then I got reacquainted with Troy, a guy from a long line of drug dealers whom I'd met on my last visit to North Carolina. Troy had one problem—he used crack. He also loved marijuana, so he could hang during the day, but at night he wanted crack cocaine. I was pretty good at working with addicts, so I used him to introduce me to clients who wanted weight. We went everywhere together.

But I wanted Troy clean so that he could be a better businessman. He became my mission, and boy, did I work hard to break him of his crack addiction. Beating an addiction isn't easy, though. I'd beaten an addiction to crack, but I couldn't seem to shake my craving for success and power.

*   *   *

Troy had a distant cousin named Biggie, a huge guy who was all Southern-born muscle. He went around Winston-Salem using his size and power to rob people, often slapping his victims and launching them across the room before robbing them. Word was out that Biggie and a guy named Tech 9 were partners in their robbery trade.

Troy told me about a female drug dealer who bought a lot of weight, so I went to see her, strapped with my 9mm handgun. That was a good thing, since Biggie was with her. As I was about to close the sale, Biggie said, "Wait, let me look at it," and my stomach twisted. He squinted at me as if he might want to try something. Then I caught Troy shaping his fingers like a gun, signaling to Biggie that I was armed.

Biggie got the message. "I don't want it," he said, and walked out.

I looked at Troy, my irritation rising. Biggie hadn't come to buy; he'd come to steal, and only my gun had prevented that from happening. I said as much, but Troy shrugged. "Naw, man, that's just Biggie."

"I should shoot him now." I tensed my jaw. "That dude was going to try something—"

"Chill," Troy interrupted. "My cousin's just trippin' out on cocaine."

I was still furious, but I let it go.

We went up the block, and I sold out of packages. I called MD to see how he was doing, and he'd sold out as well. So we prepared for another trip to NYC.

Then MD called to tell me we could save time by going to Atlanta and buying weight there. Not knowing anyone in Atlanta, I hated the idea, but off we went. On the way, MD told me about Flood, a Hollis dealer who lived in Augusta, Georgia.

"What?" I glared at him. "I thought you said Atlanta."

"Sorry, man. It's Augusta."

During our trip, MD explained that the change meant we'd pay a little more for these drugs, but we'd save money on gas and tolls. "It comes out about the same," he kept saying, "but we'll get better drugs than those from Miami, and we don't have to ride on I-95. You know that place is full of people who do random searches."

I wanted to get away, so I agreed. When we reached Flood's spot, we saw that he was a flashy dealer, with nice cars and tons of gold jewelry. He had a group of dudes with him, and I wasn't surprised to hear he was a target of a federal investigation. Anyone *that* flashy was inviting trouble. My paranoia kicked in big-time.

I was hoping to do a deal and get out of there, and fortunately, everything went well. We got good product, and MD was thrilled with the deal. We drove back to Winston-Salem without a care in the world, laughing and talking the entire way.

We went straight to work. I sold the new product but didn't make as much money because my profit margins had been cut. I was irritated by the realization that we'd gone through a lot of travel and danger for a new supplier, yet I'd only made a thousand-dollar profit after five large sales. I told Flood I needed to make five to ten thousand off every trip.

Most people don't understand how risky the drug business is. Product gets stolen, lost, and confiscated by the cops. Plus, a dealer risks his neck every time he ventures onto the street to make a sale.

Troy introduced us to his cousin, who rented a house in a cul-de-sac near the Boston Projects, and she let us use an apartment in that building. The owner was a working addict who was rarely there, so Troy's cousin gave us a set of keys to the place. As a casual user, she wasn't interested in robbing us, and when large clients called, we could serve them at a different apartment down the street.

The setup worked well for about a month, but then a drug dealer borrowed our rented car and got arrested because he didn't know how to drive a stick shift. I told MD that my scale was in the trunk and had cocaine on it, so we'd have to shut down our operation. I knew that dealer would rat us out, and he did. The next day the cops raided the house, only to find a couple of kids doing their homework in it.

Being cautious, we left that drug dealer alone, and MD split away from me and found another place to stay. I went back to the crack house in the Boogie Down Projects. Sometimes I'd move around and sleep at hotels. When we sold out of our inventory, Zara and Stretch left for New York to pick up more drugs. Zara had to stay in Queens for a week to help with her son, and Stretch decided to visit his son too.

After spending some time with their kids, Zara and Stretch decided to bring some weight to North Carolina. At the time, Amtrak was a great way to travel with drugs, so I told Zara to keep the drugs in her panties and she'd be fine. The Amtrak team often searched our bags, I explained, but they weren't allowed to search people. Stretch convinced Zara to carry his drugs, too.

I drove to Greensboro to pick them up, but when the train arrived, I couldn't find them. My pulse quickened as I searched through the arrivals, but I tried to remain calm and not look like I was searching for someone who didn't arrive. I opened the door to the Amtrak depot and asked for a bathroom, and that's when I noticed officers looking at me—probably wondering, rightfully, whether I was the pickup guy.

After using the bathroom, I walked out and asked a departing passenger if a recent arrival was the train from New York. When he said it was, I went outside and got in the car where MD waited.

"They got busted," I told him, breathing fast because I was mad, paranoid, and scared.

MD shook his head. "Man, I'm sorry. I know that was your girl."

I sat motionless a moment longer, and then MD looked at me again. "Get her a paid lawyer and get her out."

MD started the car and we left, but I was upset all the way back to Winston-Salem. A good portion of my supply was sitting in some police evidence room, and Zara was in jail. So was Stretch, probably.

MD dropped me off at the crack house. "Don't forget to get her a lawyer," he said, "so she don't snitch you out."

"Man, she is not a rat." I straightened my spine. "She wouldn't do that to me."

The next day, Zara called and told me what had happened. As hardheaded and independent as ever, she hadn't listened to my advice about hiding the drugs on her body. The cops rolled on her when she got off the train, and they searched the bag inside my new Timberlands and found the crack. They knew Zara wasn't alone, so they searched for Stretch, who had eluded them by hiding on the train until the next stop. They caught him in High Point.

I had taken a great loss with their arrests, and for a while MD was the wealthiest guy on our team.

I was nearly broke.

*   *   *

MD had to pay for the next drug trip, and I tagged along for the ride. He rented a car from a woman he'd met, and he loaded the vehicle with college textbooks.

I didn't trust the woman because the car situation felt like a setup. Our driver, Blue, was a tall African American who looked white. He became our product driver. He was amazing and could drive for ten hours without even getting drowsy.

My concern wasn't with Blue; it was with the woman who owned the car—she didn't add up. Why did she appear out of nowhere and offer her vehicle? Who did that kind of thing?

As we passed through New Jersey, a rookie cop pulled us over only a few miles from New York City.

Blue rolled down the window and looked at the cop, waiting for an explanation.

"I pulled you over," the officer said, "for driving too slow."

It was the lamest excuse I had ever heard.

The officer walked back to his squad car, but on his walkie-talkie I could hear someone reprimanding him for stopping our car prematurely. Something clicked in my brain. I knew that woman was bad news! The car was being tracked and we'd been set up, but the rookie cop had moved too soon. Their plan must have been to catch us *after* we had picked up our drugs in New York, not now.

Blue didn't get a ticket, and the cop didn't see anything in our car. Later, I told MD what I'd heard over the walkie-talkie, and he smiled. "I have a trick for them." We drove into Harlem and parked the car several blocks away from my pickup spot. Then we went to a grocery store and bought the specific items on MD's list: crackers, Pepperidge Farm cookies, chips, drinks, and Krazy Glue.

After we'd bought those items, we went to see Marco, our supplier. Marco seemed nervous about Blue and kept wondering aloud if he might be a cop. "Don't worry," I reassured Marco. "I got him covered."

Thankfully, Marco trusted me enough to allow me to purchase what I needed. Then MD carefully opened the Pepperidge Farm cookies, took out a fancy cookie, put the drugs inside, and then put the cookie back on top. Using the Krazy Glue, he resealed the package so no one could tell the package had been opened.

When we got back to the car, I told MD I needed to go through Harlem to buy some angel dust. I smoked some, and as a result became as paranoid as a cat in a room filled with rocking chairs. When a couple of narcotics cops pulled us over as we drove through New Jersey, I was high and paranoid.

One of those officers was the same rookie cop who'd pulled us over for driving too slow. They thought they had us, but we had the upper hand. We told them we were on a college tour. MD, who'd always been well-spoken, told them what he was studying. "I'm checking out Penn State," he said, "to see if it's for me." He was even wearing a Penn State hat.

I was so paranoid and nervous that I almost fell as I got out of the car.

We stood by the side of the road and watched as officers searched the car from top to bottom. They checked out the tires and pulled up the seats. They went through the groceries, opening the box of crackers and dumping out a bag of chips. Then they gave up on the groceries and left the cookies untouched.

When they were finished, they exchanged glances of frustration, then told us we could go. "Sorry, boys, we were misled," one of them said. With a final "drive safe," they allowed us to drive away.

We thought the car might be bugged, so from that point we wrote notes to each other. Clearly, the cops had provided that shady car back in North Carolina. When we stopped to eat, we gathered around the restaurant table to regroup. MD said, "From now on, let's talk about the woman as Harvard and Winston-Salem as Penn State."

So we laughed and called Harvard all kinds of swearwords, then we dumped the car and told the woman cop where to pick it up. Word got out that the cops had tried to trap us, but we'd beaten them. When we discussed the woman cop, we realized no one had ever seen her get high, so she couldn't have been an addict.

Because she was more familiar with MD's operation than mine, MD had to find new drug spots again. To help him, he brought in two guys from New York City, Royal and Mental—both of whom I'd known in school.

*   *   *

After that experience, I decided to drop anchor and make BDP my main selling spot—I'd hustle alongside the dudes from the projects. But Royal and Mental began to crowd my operation, and they were flashy, which made the situation dangerous. Mental was especially loud, bold, and violent. One Saturday morning I heard him yelling, "Forget everybody out here. I don't care about any of these down-south punks."

I stepped out of my crack spot. "Calm down, man. You don't want to start a war out here."

"Oh, yeah?" He glared at me. "I'll punch you in the face too." He waited while I stared at him. "Say something, Daylight."

I wish I could have let it go, but as a boss I had to fight him. I went straight at him and we fought, then he got under me and slammed me and I broke my finger.

Royal came running to break up the fight. I stood, my finger hanging limply, and I knew what I had to say in order to maintain my status: "Now you know."

Mental charged me again, and I stopped him with a solid punch to the face. He tried to wrestle me to the ground, but I didn't let him get ahold of me.

After the fight, I couldn't go to a doctor because of my status as an escapee, so I self-medicated with weed. My cousin in the BDP had a girlfriend named Renee, and she helped me wrap my hand.

His girl became a valuable friend. She knew the community, and she seemed to like me. My cousin assured me that he and Renee weren't serious, so I began to spend a lot of time with her. She knew Winston-Salem, and she knew who had the drugs. She proved to be my gateway to wealth.

My clientele tripled overnight. I became prosperous and felt I was on my way to becoming a top drug lord.

Word got out, however, that Mental had set up a crack spot across from some Harlem dudes who were gunslingers. I caught Mental and tried to help him out. "Hey," I told him, "you need to leave that area alone. Those dudes are bad news."

"Those guys are soft," Mental argued. "And I don't care, anyway."

"But we don't need a war, man. Let's just chill."

He backed off and jerked his chin at me. "I got this."

That evening Mental came down the block, and I invited him into the apartment where I was smoking weed with some girls. When we ran out of cigar papers to roll up the marijuana, Mental volunteered to pick up some more.

"Sure, man, you go." I grinned at the young women with me. "I'll stay here and keep these girls company."

Mental stepped out the door, and in the next second we heard a flurry of gunfire. I pulled out my gun and told the girls to hit the floor. The sounds of gunfire popped for at least two minutes.

We remained facedown on a dirty apartment floor until the shooting stopped. One of the girls lifted her head. "Mental is out there."

After several minutes, during which all I could hear was the whooshing of blood in my ears, someone knocked on the door. One of the girls ran to answer it, and Mental stepped back into the room.

"They tried to kill me," he said, perspiration shining on his brow. "They came from everywhere, all of them shooting at me. They came out from behind bushes and buildings, and I had to run right past one of the shooters."

"Who was it?" I asked.

"Those Harlem dudes."

I took a deep breath and said the first thought that came to my mind: "Mental, you're bad for business."

We all sat up and brushed ourselves off. I gritted my teeth every time I looked at Mental—he was a magnet for trouble. Selling in the Harlem dudes' backyard was greedy and unnecessary.

I called Royal, and he came over to my spot. We spoke alone, and I reminded him that a drug war would land all of us in jail. "The best solution," I said, "is to send Mental packing. Give him some cash and get him back to NYC. After things cool off, we can bring him back to Winston-Salem."

Royal agreed, and he drove Mental back to New York.

The next morning a cocaine dealer named Vic rode up to me on a bike. "Hey," he said, narrowing his eyes, "we all know you want to retaliate."

I was armed, and for a moment I thought about shooting him in the back. But I didn't.

"We're not trying to go to war," I told him, "and Mental is back in NYC." That statement didn't seem to carry much weight with him, so I pressed my point. "How dumb is it for two groups from New York City to have shoot-outs in the South? It's gotta stop, or we'll all end up in jail."

He nodded.

"Mental went against our judgment," I concluded, "and that's why he's gone. He's been sanctioned for not listening."

That seemed to satisfy Vic, so he rode away to carry the news back to his Harlem crew. That group also consisted of Bumpy, the leader; Cameo, who was young and crazy; and Bumpy's girlfriend, Rose, a girl from Winston-Salem. Together they sold weed and crack. I liked Bumpy, but Cameo was a total loose cannon. I'd met all of them while buying weed from their spot in Rose's apartment.

Soon after my talk with Vic, I saw Cameo while on my way to the store with a local guy. After going to the store and a weed spot, we drove back down Trade Street. Cameo saw me and yelled, "It's on!"

I sighed. Mental was still causing trouble, and he wasn't even with us anymore.

When I drove up to our spot, Royal was with a dude from New York named Sheldon. When I told them what Cameo had said, we went into war mode. Because Sheldon and I had guns, we positioned ourselves for a gun battle while Royal went out to get another pistol.

Sheldon and I had waited about five minutes when we saw seven armed guys walking around our area like commandos. They peered around corners and checked out all sides of the building. We stayed quiet, knowing we were outnumbered. Those guys walked around our perimeter for at least four minutes before they regrouped and walked back down the hill toward their spot.

When they were a good distance away, Sheldon and I stepped out where they could see us. "Yo, Bumpy," I yelled, "we do not want a beef with you guys. Y'all stay down there, and we'll stay up here." I put up my hands, and I saw him nod in agreement. We let them know we'd seen them and did not open fire even though they were only a few feet away. "No beef from us," I yelled again, just to make things clear.

Then Sheldon and I ran to the crack house that was serving as my drug spot, and Sheldon banged on the door. To our complete shock, a football-shaped Southern stranger opened the door. What was he doing here? He must have been a paranoid crackhead because, once he saw Sheldon's gun, he wrestled it out of Sheldon's hands.

"Stop!" I yelled. "I live here!"

The stranger didn't listen. He put his other hand on my gun and was bringing Sheldon's gun around to fire at me. I left my gun behind and ran, hoping that I wouldn't feel a bullet blasting my back.

I ran toward an apartment across the street, and Sheldon followed. We crouched behind the safety of a concrete divider, breathless, and watched as all kinds of confusion broke loose across the street. The cops came and cuffed the crackhead, and then I saw them pointing to my drug spot. That addict was singing like an opera star, so I knew we'd have to close that location.

Sheldon and I went around the back way and ran through the woods until we came out on a different street. I called Royal, and he came to pick us up. Royal laughed about our ordeal for a good month, while Sheldon went back to New York. At times I wondered if I ought to do the same, but my dream of being the top dog kept me hungry . . . and in North Carolina.

CHAPTER TEN

AFTER THE DUSTUP WITH the Harlem dudes, I let things die down by moving for a week. MD found me and asked me to go with him on a trip to buy from Flood in Augusta. After a successful buy, MD told me to lie low. "It's too bad some guys from Harlem wanna get violent," he said. "I don't get involved, and you shouldn't either."

I did stay quiet—for a while. I took all my cash and bought a bunch of guns, planning to sell them in Queens. I hid them in my hiding spot and stayed on the move to avoid attracting too much attention.

The supply of drugs had dried up by the time MD and I returned, so instead of working my new spot, I went to the other side of the projects and sold where people were desperate and their usual suppliers were empty-handed. When MD and I had both sold out, we connected. MD wanted to make a run up to NYC, but I hung back.

While I waited, Renee and I lay low in a hotel. I didn't want to get shot by one of the Harlem dudes who wanted to pick up where things had left off.

MD returned from New York with good and bad news. "The bad news," he said, "is there's no coke. The good news is I found heroin."

I made a face. I had never dealt heroin and never wanted to deal it. Heroin meant three years in prison per bag, and I didn't like being around dope addicts.

I exploded. "Why didn't you wait until the coke arrived? Instead you pick up stupid heroin?"

"I did wait two days," MD answered. "But dope was $130 a bag, and I know a dope spot in Winston where I can move the heroin."

I forced myself to calm down and went with MD to the dope block. The place was nasty, with dope fiends all over the place. Vic ran a spot there, and he was cool with us being around. He sold cocaine and said the heroin fiends liked to shoot cocaine with their dope.

Then one of the fiends tried our heroin and said it was bad.

Frustrated, I went into a dope spot to try to sell it. Vagabondish, raggedy-looking men and women crowded the run-down apartment, several of them lying on a bed covered by a blood-streaked sheet. Looking around, I saw spoons, lights, needles in arms, and people who nodded vacantly as spit drooled over their chins. The scene was straight out of a horror movie. Those lifeless, senseless people looked half dead, but every time a police car drove by, like zombies they sat up and yelled, "Cops!"

After two hours without selling a single bag, I looked at the spilled blood and the needles and thought about HIV and AIDS. I had enough bags with me to earn sixty years in prison, and for what? For *this*?

"I'm out," I announced to anyone listening.

Vic looked at me. "Are you guys going to take my spot?"

I shook my head. "No, we got stuck with this mess."

I went back to MD and told him to keep the dope and give me

whatever, but I couldn't sell heroin. When I returned to my spot in the projects, I learned that a home-invasion crew from Brooklyn had robbed my spot. All my guns had vanished.

I'd gone from having over $100,000 in goods to having almost nothing. Zara's lawyer got a chunk of my profit, thieves got my guns, and MD got a load of bad dope, leaving me crushed and in the middle of a drug war.

*   *   *

I was completely frustrated. How could I stay on the run in North Carolina with no money? I used to be a drug boss with my own crew, but now I was back to hustling on the street, trying to find a sucker dumb enough to give me money for fake crack.

I knew I had to come up with a quick answer. Renee was upset that I'd hit a streak of bad luck, so she offered to talk to her connections to get some weight in drugs. I told her to hold off until I could build up some cash, and then I went back outside and looked for someone to hustle. Soda, a basketball player and a bona fide celebrity in Winston-Salem, came over to see me and brought some weed to smoke. I told him I was low on cash and product, and Soda said that he'd hit hard times too.

At that moment Groove walked up. Well into his forties, Groove dressed like an addict despite being the wealthiest dealer in town. But I didn't know that then.

Soda greeted Groove with a grin. "Hey, what's going on?"

Groove grinned back. "Not much."

Soda glanced at me, then looked back at Groove. "We need to buy some weight, but we don't have much cash."

Without hesitation, Groove pulled an ounce of crack from his pocket. "You need a thousand dollars."

"Only have two hundred," Soda said.

"I have two hundred too," I added.

Groove tilted his head, considering us, then he nodded. "Here's half an ounce and you owe me a hundred dollars."

Soda and I split the crack and started hustling. In an hour we had turned our seed money into fifteen hundred bucks. Crack addicts would come up to Groove, and he would point them to me or Soda. I loved the feeling of hustling and turning nothing into something.

After an hour, we gave the fifteen hundred to Groove, who then gave us two ounces. "Now you guys owe me five hundred."

That night we sold another two thousand dollars' worth of crack, pocketed a thousand each, and had enough left over to buy two more ounces. I had never turned crack into money so fast. Before the night was done, we started selling weight, pocketing six hundred dollars off each ounce by selling one-hundred-dollar pieces to drug dealers.

Groove was not a gangster, and Soda and I were gentlemen, not thugs. Groove loved us, and no wonder. Everyone loved coming to us because we didn't scare or intimidate them.

When Soda and I quit around 1 a.m., we smiled at each other and decided to form a partnership. In one night we each went from only two hundred dollars to over four thousand dollars and the ability to buy eight ounces. We worked four weeks for Groove and were able to buy weight from him—and you need serious weight if you want to move an impressive amount of product.

After a month, I remembered an old saying: *What happens in New York happens everywhere.* In New York City, the people with big money and less stress were the dudes who owned weed spots. Crack attracted trouble—murderers, police busts, and robberies. So why was I still messing around with it?

*   *   *

After getting back on my feet, I thought about shifting my business model for peace and longevity, primarily selling marijuana and just dipping and dabbling in crack and gun sales. I went to Renee and asked who might sell me a pound of weed, and she told me about a guy named Boots—so named because his feet were unusually large. I went to see him, bought the pound of weed, and started a weed spot at a house where a girl named Jessica lived. Word of our spot got out around the same time two nomadic weed spots closed, making ours the most accessible. From my time in NYC, I'd learned that it paid to have a key location near the street action, plus it helped to be generous with fat bags and lots of change. We did service with a smile and hooked up all kinds of people with weed.

Money from all the Southern drug dealers came pouring in, and I soon needed a new connection because I sold more bags than Boots could supply. Then Little Darryl came along and sold pounds at sixteen hundred dollars a pound, five hundred dollars cheaper than Boots. The larger quantity enabled me to sell by the ounce to small dealers. Every day I went through pounds of weed and made two thousand dollars in profit.

Everything was sweet until someone murdered Little Darryl. I was heartbroken. Wasn't the weed business supposed to be safer than dealing crack or heroin?

Then someone told me Fisher wanted to meet me.

"Who's Fisher?"

"The man who supplies Boots."

I learned that Fisher was a drug dealer from Queens, so we had that in common. A Jamaican, Fisher sported a designer haircut and drove a slamming Jeep Cherokee. I loved his style.

Fisher sold me a pound of weed at twelve hundred a pound, then gave me two extra pounds. "You work for King Fisher now."

At that price I would work for anyone. I started selling Fisher's product, selling at one hundred dollars an ounce and undercutting my competitors. Soon all the weed customers in Winston-Salem came to me.

Boots hated me for dropping the price, but we became equals

when we both bought from Fisher at the same rate. But because Boots didn't stop selling crack, he was caught in a big bust and picked up by the feds. With Boots out of the picture, my weed business went through the roof. Everyone loved Daylight, the marijuana street god. The crack dealers were happy I'd quit the business, and the Harlem dudes felt less threatened because I'd left Trade Street and moved to Derry Street. Everyone was happy—for a while.

My successful strategy involved moving the weed spot every six months, from Derry Street to Trade Street and then back again. Why? Because traffic drew attention, and after two cops watched a spot for a while, it took them about six months to arrange a strike. As long as we stuck to my plan, we stayed ahead of the bust.

After six months at Jessica's house on Derry Street, we moved to Trade. A month later, Jessica's house was raided and the cops found nothing. We laughed about it, and the cops never returned to the Derry Street house.

My drug enterprise was now thriving and wildly successful. It had been a long journey, but I'd finally made it. Money was coming through faster than the crack. It seemed as if every weed-using teenager, young adult, and sports lover in the Winston-Salem area drove to BDP to buy weed, and I controlled the entire operation. My reach extended far beyond the BDP, in fact. Almost every weed spot in Winston-Salem was connected to us. I supplied users with dime bags and dealers with weight.

Now I was living the street god life I had fantasized about. So much money was pouring in that I took to stuffing big water cooler bottles full of fifty- and one-hundred-dollar bills. My workers were buying cars and running the club scene. I was hanging out with all the celebrities in town. Whenever I heard people on the street complain about not being able to buy weed anywhere, I had to chuckle. I knew it was because I was waiting for my next delivery. Fisher brought in the big shipments, but my operation was the means for it getting to the streets. Because the crack epidemic was so bad at the time, weed dealing seemed to have fallen off the radar of most law enforcement agencies.

Being hood fabulous had its perks. I'd round up the hood and fly us all to out of town to Rap Fest and other concerts or to popular clubs, which I'd buy out for the night. I'd rent a fleet of cars for the team to get around and hole us up in hotels. Throwing away $10,000 at a time on the team was no issue.

I was positioned right where I wanted to be, with all roads leading to Daylight. Even my enemies couldn't escape my reach. Jealous and not wanting to further fatten my pockets, they'd buy from other bosses, unaware that those bosses worked for me too.

After all that work I'd put in to reach top-dog status, it felt great to be able to roll big for once. Everybody loved Daylight, or so I thought.

Even so, once I moved our spot to Trade Street, I anticipated problems with the Harlem crew, so I was carrying a big .44 Magnum nickel-plated handgun like the piece Clint Eastwood carried in *Dirty Harry* and *Magnum Force*. When Cameo and his friend stopped me, I pulled out my gun before I saw he wanted weed, not trouble. Even though I kept the gun pointed down, the threat upset my potential customer. Cameo and his friend walked away.

I let them go, but I suspected there'd be trouble, so I moved across the street to watch for Cameo. Three minutes later I heard a shotgun blast and hit the floor. I pulled out my .44, but I couldn't see anyone. Three more shots followed, and I stayed down. Then I picked up my gun, ready to knock Cameo to his knees. But I didn't see him or anyone else.

The next day I put the incident behind me and went out to do business.

Word got out that the dumb Harlem boys, led by Bumpy, shot up the end of Trade Street. A few days later, a guy who'd shot Bumpy years before came walking down Trade Street. Bumpy and five guys from his

Harlem crew approached him, but he kept walking, shaking his head as if to say everything was cool between them. People sitting out on their porches stood and walked to their hedges for a closer look—you could almost hear them murmuring, "That's the guy who shot Bumpy."

When they neared my spot, one of the Harlem guys opened fire and shot that dude six times in the back with a .45 pistol. The guy slumped to the ground as his blood pooled on the asphalt.

"Why'd he come walking down Bumpy's block?" someone asked, and I wondered the same thing. What was the guy thinking?

The cops and detectives showed up, and an ambulance took the guy away. Seeing so many ragged bullet holes in his body, we thought he was dead, but later we learned that he'd survived.

When all the officials were gone, kids rode their bikes to the spot and pointed at the bloodstains in the road. Trade Street had provided them with a legacy of blood and violence.

Everyone shook their heads, sorry about what had happened and wondering why it had happened at all. I could only come up with one answer: Bumpy and his crew hadn't forgotten, and they hadn't forgiven. They'd taken their revenge, and that was the end of it. The Harlem crew went back to business as usual.

Shortly after that, word on the street was that Bumpy sold out and his crew drove back to New York City in five cars. When they returned with new inventory, the cops raided them. The police found kilos and guns, and Bumpy was busted with all the loot.

Cameo managed to get away and tried to make peace with me soon after. I told him I hoped the war was over and his team was okay. Mostly, I hoped I never had to see those dumb hustlers again.

Then Vic, the guy who ran their cocaine spot, got picked up for murdering Little Darryl. I was stunned when I heard the news, and then I realized that my adversaries were disappearing one by one.

Though some people left the area, others returned. Royal and Mental came back from NYC, and Mental brought a dude named

Jah with him. I didn't want any new guys around. I'd hit bottom and recovered while Royal and Mental were away, and I didn't want people I didn't know working in my business.

Jah proved to be trouble. Royal loved notorious people, and Jah wanted to be infamous. He took a liking to Renee, and she began to braid his hair for money. I knew nothing good would come out of that.

Royal also brought news from New York. Kirk Green, my old adversary, had been home with his mother when someone knocked on the door. His mother recognized the visitor and let him in. Then she called Kirk. As Kirk came downstairs, the guy pulled out a gun and shot him several times in the head.

The story so shocked and upset me that I drove to NYC to attend his funeral. I looked in the casket, but his head was so swollen that the body inside didn't resemble the guy I'd known. What a terrible end to a life. Despite our differences, my heart twisted in sorrow. No one should have to die the way he did.

*   *   *

Before going back to North Carolina, I decided to buy some NYC weed, put it in my tires, and drive it to North Carolina. I was high when I came up with the idea, and I should have taken that fact into consideration. When I reached North Carolina and opened the tire, I discovered that the weed had been ruined by rotating at eighty miles per hour. I lost three thousand dollars on that stupid notion, but I didn't care. I swallowed the loss and kept making enormous amounts of money. Then I spent it on things like paying a DJ to shout out my name in a club, as well as on guns to sell on my next trip to New York.

Settling into North Carolina, I encountered pockets of superstition and learned that witchcraft isn't uncommon—people could hire someone to work roots or spells on people. Blass, another drug dealer, began to date a woman who called herself a witch, and other people kept their distance from both of them. An aura of darkness surrounded that woman, an almost tangible evil.

Some of Renee's friends didn't know about the woman's profession and hung out with her. After a week, several of them had mental breakdowns, and two had to go to the hospital. Renee warned me not to stare at or talk to that woman because she meant us harm. I wasn't sure about that, but I knew the woman drove a green Honda Accord and was always trying to get my attention.

Meanwhile, I had begun to get homesick for New York. I arranged a quiet trip for me and Renee. I hired Troy, who had a little hatchback, to drive us, so one night we loaded the car with guns and took off.

Listening to the hum of the tires on asphalt, Renee and I fell asleep in the backseat. About an hour into the trip, I woke up because a car kept honking. I sat up, and Troy caught my eye in the rearview mirror. "The car behind us keeps honking," he said. "Do you know who that is?"

I turned and peered at the headlights. It was hard to see in the dark, but in a cone of light from a street lamp I realized the car behind us was a green Honda Accord. Blass's girlfriend.

I woke Renee and gestured at the vehicle behind us. "It's her."

At that moment the car changed lanes and pulled alongside us, and the woman smiled at Renee and me. Just a simple smile, but it was enough to thrust a dagger of fear into my heart. Then the Honda sped off.

Renee caught my gaze. "How'd she see us?"

"She didn't," Troy said. "This car has tinted windows, and you guys were lying low in the backseat. She couldn't see you."

"But she knew," I pointed out. "She knew we were in the car."

"How'd she even know about this trip?" Renee looked from me to Troy, then leaned toward the front seat. "Did you tell her?"

Troy shook his head. "I didn't tell anybody."

Renee settled back, but I could see a shadow in her eyes. "She can't hurt us. Jesus is stronger," she said.

I tilted my head. I'd never heard Renee talk about Jesus before, and my surprise must have shown on my face.

"My mama taught me about Jesus," she said, almost defensively. "I'm backslidden now, but I know all about him."

Backslidden? What did she mean?

We smoked some weed and went back to sleep. Whenever we woke, we'd turn to see whether the Honda was behind us, but we didn't see anything. Finally Renee said, "I am done worrying about this. Let's drop it and change the subject." So we did.

New York City is home to more than eight million people—that's over double the population of Los Angeles, and three times the population of Chicago. You can meet a friend on the street in New York and never see him again because the city is so densely populated.

I pulled into Harlem to buy some weed. The streets were packed, so I got out to walk, and then out of nowhere the woman with the green Accord grabbed my arm. I whirled, not knowing who or what to expect, and she did some weird thing with her hand against mine. I jerked my hand away.

I turned and walked away, more than a little spooked.

I bought the weed and went back to meet Renee. I told her what had happened, and she began to swear at the evil woman. Then she narrowed her eyes. "Did she touch you?"

"Yeah."

Renee nodded with conviction. "She's trying to work a root on you."

We smoked some weed, but instead of feeling mellow, I began to feel morbidly paranoid, more wary than I had ever felt before.

I dropped Renee at my mother's house and didn't worry about the police finding me. Mom had moved twice since I had escaped from my parole officer, and I was sure the police weren't savvy enough to keep track of those kinds of details. Since I hadn't killed anyone, my case was probably cold.

I sold the guns, but not without complications. Troy drove me to one place where I traded three 9mm pistols for a pound of weed, but I had to wait an hour in the back of a weed spot. I was beginning to wonder if I'd stumbled into a setup, so I told the owner Troy had a gun in his car that would level a house. Right after that, the pound of weed miraculously appeared.

At another sale, a Jamaican Rastafarian kept asking for bullets and telling me to wait for his friend. I realized the guy had no money and wanted to rob me. He got angry when I took the gun and forced my way past him. After selling that gun to someone else, I vowed never to sell guns again.

I picked up a friend named Bree and found my old driver Blue, who was also in town. He was willing to drive my drugs back with Bree. This time I knew better than to place the weed in a rotating tire, so I hid the weed inside the spare in the trunk. Before leaving New York, I bought a bag of Crazy Eddie—angel-dust weed soaked in embalming fluid—from a dealer at 116th and Park. I tucked it away for our trip back to Winston-Salem.

I had money, my own business, and a girlfriend. But I also had a self-described witch on my tail.

*   *   *

It should have been a nice trip. Renee was happy I had sold all the guns and turned a tidy profit, even though I didn't need it. She knew that this trip had been an attempt to ease my homesickness, and she was okay with that. I'd just wanted to walk my hometown streets and see my mom.

For some reason, though, as soon as we hit the North Carolina border, I began to freak out. I became paranoid, yelling that the cops were coming. Renee kept telling me to calm down, but I couldn't. The best I could manage was to stay quiet.

"That root is taking him," Troy called from the front seat. "I've seen this before." Troy and Renee clearly believed that Blass's girlfriend had put some sort of curse on me.

When we arrived in Winston-Salem, Royal met us. "Bree is here," he said, "and they had a problem. You'd better go see them."

When I found Blue and Bree, they told me they'd had a flat and had to drive on the spare tire, which is where they'd hidden the weed. Blue knew what had happened the last time, and sure enough, it happened again. Because the weed was ruined, I snapped.

I screamed at Bree and Blue, calling them thieves and bums. They were capable of conspiring against me, and I believed they had worked together to rob me.

When I got back to my place, I pulled out the bag of Crazy Eddie angel dust and smoked it, but my mood worsened. Paranoia consumed me as I walked toward my weed spot. Otis, my marijuana supplier's brother, was waiting for me with a pistol in his hand. He shook his head and told me that Fisher had been killed.

I was so high that I barely understood the significance of what he was saying. I blew off the news about Fisher's death and asked to see my stash. I knew I had crack left over from my last purchase, and I had to know whether I had been ripped off.

Royal was in my apartment when I arrived. I greeted him, but then my body slipped out of my control, and my mind turned to mush. I had no idea what was happening, but everything in my field of vision was tinted the color of blood. My body moved as if it had a mind of its own. I kept yelling, "Give me the gun!" while I tore up the apartment looking for a gun to shoot myself.

Meanwhile, my mind kept trying to stop my body. I felt like a little kid trapped in a runaway vehicle that I couldn't stop. The kid kept yelling, "Stop, please!" but that runaway vehicle was intent on crashing and burning.

Somehow I found my gun. I was about to pick it up, but Royal grabbed it and pushed me away. I tried to take it from him, but he was strong. Enraged, I went to the kitchen sink and began punching glassware and smashing plates and glasses with my fists. Blood streamed from my knuckles and the back of my hand while broken glass spangled the floor.

Even Royal was astounded at my behavior. He turned and ran from the room, as bewildered as I was.

I whirled and found myself standing alone in a field of broken dishes and blood. Terrified by what I'd done, I sprinted out of the house and looked around, finally spotting an open door next to a gleaming porch light. I ran to it, stepped inside, and found myself in a stranger's house. The people inside screamed and I kept running, running through their house, out their back door, and through their backyard.

I ran farther until I finally recognized Renee's house. When I reached it, she let me in. Her mother took one look at me, then went to work.

As Renee held my arms, her mother pulled off my bloody shirt. Renee then took a different shirt, one that had "Jesus, the New Generation" printed on the front and back.

After cleaning me up, Renee exhaled a deep breath and smiled. "You need some weed to calm you down."

I sat with her and smoked some, then chilled. Renee squeezed my arm. "Let's go to a club and sell this last bit of crack."

We went to a club that catered to dudes and girls who lived at the BDP. We hustled there, selling some crack. Then we sat to chill out. A friend of Renee's told us about an episode in which she'd had dealings with Blass's girlfriend. She described the same things I had experienced, from the red-tinted vision to the suicide attempt. Then she admitted that she'd ended up in a hospital for several weeks.

She got up to get a drink while Renee and I looked at each other. The coincidences between our stories were striking. Maybe I'd smoked some bad weed, but her story made me wonder.

While we were talking, a guy came over and took the girl's seat. I told him to get up, but he only looked at me.

In a flash, I leaped on him, knocked him down, and beat him on the floor. While blood poured from his nose and mouth, a beastly urge overcame me. I crouched over him and bit his face like a wolf, ripping flesh from his face.

While onlookers screamed, I looked up, my smile red and bloody, and someone yelled at me to leave the club. Renee didn't hesitate. She ran to me, lifted me up, and rushed me out of there.

Blood covered my Jesus T-shirt. Renee took me to her house, cleaned me up, and cried, telling me that I had turned into an animal.

Desperate, I called my mother. "Ma, I need help. I feel like I'm losing my mind."

She told me that I had a cousin in Winston-Salem who was the pastor of a church, so I should go there.

"I need real help! Not some church." I slammed down the phone and fumed, angry and frustrated at her response.

I didn't know it then, but after my call my mother phoned all my siblings and told them to prepare themselves for bad news—she didn't think I'd survive much longer. Then she went to church and put my name on a prayer card, begging people to pray for her son.

Back in the projects, the story spread like a contagion—Daylight, who had a *lot* of guns, had lost his mind. When I stepped back onto the drug block, about thirty people from Winston-Salem skittered away from me like rats before a fire.

I didn't know what to do. By now I was convinced that something more than bad weed or crack had a grip on me, and I didn't know how to break free. One person told me to burn the clothes I had been

wearing when the woman who called herself a witch had touched me.
I burned the clothes, yet I still wasn't myself.

To make matters worse, my mind kept playing tricks on me.
I began to believe that I was Moses and that I should walk barefoot
in certain areas. I heard about a baby born in the projects and became
convinced the child was baby Jesus, born to save the world.

My delusions became so strong that Renee told her mother that
I had gone off the deep end. Her mother fetched two of her friends,
and the three of them came back and asked Renee if they could pray
for me.

I agreed, so Renee took me to her house and the prayer meeting
began. When I walked in, those three ladies called on Jesus, then
came toward me. I think they recognized that, while demon possession is not regularly acknowledged in our country, as it is in other
parts of the world, I had made myself a prime candidate for it because
of my lifestyle.

The three women saw that and went right to work. "I bind this
demon up in the name of Jesus," Renee's mother said. "Loose him,
Satan! Come *out*!"

As they called on Jesus over and over again, it felt as if something
threw my body to the floor. The women anointed me with oil while
commanding the demon to come out in Jesus' name. I writhed like a
snake, but they kept praying. I spat up fluid, and they kept praying.
For three hours those little old ladies toiled for my deliverance.

Then Renee opened the door and looked at me. "Oh, dear God!"
she cried. "His neck—look at his neck!"

I couldn't see what was happening with my neck; I only knew I
felt sick and confused and in dire need of help.

One of the women told Renee to get out, so Renee left and slammed
the door behind her. That's when I began to vomit into the garbage
can. My neck expanded and something came out of me; then I lay
back and felt tingly all over—a peace that surpassed understanding.

What I encountered in that moment was much more than a feeling. I tangibly sensed the Lord's presence within me. It was like nothing I had ever experienced.

God, are you serious? I silently asked. *I've always believed you exist somewhere, but I never knew you were this good or this real.*

That peace was so relaxing and bright . . . I'd never experienced anything like it. I felt clean and pure for the first time in my life. My entire body felt new. I knew this change came from Jesus, and I was happy to surrender to him.

Lying on the floor, I welcomed Jesus into my life. My heart had been changed, though I didn't understand why or how. When I got up, I left my past on the floor and devoted what was left of my life to Jesus.

I didn't have the theological knowledge to explain what had happened to me; I didn't understand sanctification, justification, or regeneration. But I did understand that my allegiance to the world was gone and that I had joined with God in a new way.

That night, I emptied the crack out of my pockets and threw it in that garbage bin. I went outside and looked up to the heavens. I said, "Lord, I will never sell crack again . . . only weed because it's natural."

*   *   *

I left Renee's house with a newfound faith.

I knew I needed to be surrounded by people who had given their lives to God as I had, but I didn't know where to start looking for them. I remembered my sister Dawn—she went to church. I would find God's people in church. Days earlier, my mother had urged me to go to church, and I had refused. Now I *wanted* to be in church; I *longed* to be with God's children. I needed them, and I knew it.

Those three elderly women didn't forget me either. They were my biggest cheerleaders early on. "Hold on to your faith," one of the women would say whenever she saw me on the block. "I'm proud of you," Renee's mother would tell me. She also gave me a warning that sticks with me even today: "Woe unto you if you go back." I knew what she meant: God had rescued me from nearly certain death, but I might not get another chance if I turned my back on him.

I stopped eating as I felt an irresistible urge to fast and pray. I'm embarrassed to admit I would eat an occasional bite of a tree leaf when no one was looking, but I felt as though the Holy Spirit was purifying me to serve him completely and without reservation—to rid my body of my old desires and habits in order to make way for something new.

My dreams and ambitions changed overnight. I no longer wanted to be a street god. I wanted to be a man who followed Jesus.

CHAPTER ELEVEN

A FEW DAYS LATER, I rolled out of bed in a nondescript, two-story brick apartment building that looked like all the others in that North Carolina housing project. The unit I was staying in was part of my marijuana empire—a sprawling thirty-unit distribution center of weed spots that sold dime bags, ounces, pounds, and weight, moving half a million dollars' worth of product every quarter. We stored the goods elsewhere so no passersby would spot any signs of dope or paraphernalia.

Renee and I had lived in this unit for about six months and had been in the area even longer, moving between apartments to avoid police detection. I had founded the operation eighteen months earlier but had become a Christian who loved Jesus and longed to abandon the money machine and blood sport I'd created. Ruthless wars waged over respect and dealers' real estate had claimed thirty of my team-mates' lives.

How could I escape the life I'd created?

There I was, a New York City drug dealer, waking up in a weed house in the Boogie Down Projects, one of the toughest neighbor-hoods in Winston-Salem. But on that day I was different, and I had a new Lord over my soul. Despite my newfound faith and a sincere desire to change my lifestyle, I still had to deal with the mess I'd made, and much of my situation hadn't changed.

I had the same face—one wanted by the police in New York—and the same vehicle. I was the same felon on the run, even though I had a peace that surpassed my highest highs and a joy that topped my most intoxicated moments. The web of my sin was thick, and I was ensnared in it. Some people from the drug game still wanted to kill me, and the cops were still watching my every move. I carried lots of heavy baggage that didn't vanish just because I had accepted Christ.

The hood didn't know what to make of the rumors about me becoming a Christian, but they loved me as a drug lord. My friends were tough guys who devoured leaders who showed even the slightest sign of weakness. I knew everyone would be watching to see if my change of heart would make me weaker and more vulnerable.

Most people in the hood viewed church as an institution that required tough guys to abandon their masculinity and become as soft as the blue-eyed, fair-skinned, dainty Jesus in old European paint-ings. There was no way I was going to become effeminate, but I knew someone would test my armor to see if Jesus had made me less of a man. It was only a matter of time before one of the local stickup kids approached to see if I had become an easy victim.

Oddly enough, I felt more like a man than ever. I felt stronger, more focused, and not at all afraid of the future, for a change. I was convinced that no matter what it looked like, my destiny resided in Christ Jesus.

Knowing that I needed to learn more about Jesus, I found a little Baptist church and started attending services. A visiting minister, Reverend Newton, arrived at the church about a month after I started attending and told the people, "I'm new to Winston-Salem. My wife and I just moved here. I'm a painter, I'm a minister, and I want to serve here and help out." He was a statuesque man—tall, with a goatee, glasses, and a big ol' smile.

Reverend Newton and I hit it off right away. After we met, he invited me to his studio so he could show me the sort of art he created. He was famous for painting beautiful pictures of angels, and he gave me a Bible and a book on success by Robert Schuller. I'd never read a book for pleasure in my life, but I read that one. I also spent a lot of time reading the Bible.

When I wasn't working at my weed spot, I was down at the church, trying to learn something new about how to follow Jesus. One afternoon Reverend Newton gave me an appraising look. "Dimas," he said, "you have charisma."

"What's that?"

"It means people will follow you anywhere. You have a quality that draws people to you."

"Really?"

"Yes, and you have to use that for Christ."

I nodded, grateful that someone had seen something positive in me.

Buoyed by the reverend's encouragement, I asked the church to bring me a van every Sunday morning at ten. I would get up at nine and start knocking on doors in the projects. "Get up, get dressed, we're going to church," I'd tell them, and people would come. They'd pile out, all sleepy-eyed, and I'd pack ten to twelve folks in the van. Every Sunday, four or five people from that van would get saved.

I was loving church, loving the Christian life, and loving the challenge of telling other people about Jesus. The trouble was, I'd never really gone to church before, so I didn't know how things were done. I had no idea that church had a particular etiquette.

In the Shock program, I'd been taught that if you were in a meeting and started to feel drowsy, you should get up and go stand in the back of the room. That way you would show the speaker proper respect and not fall asleep during his talk.

So every Sunday, as the building warmed and I sat on a crowded church pew, I'd start to feel drowsy. Rather than nod off, I'd get up and go stand in the back. I did it out of respect for the pastor, but after a while people started to turn and stare at me, wondering what in the world I was doing in the back of the church.

At other times I'd be sitting in church, hearing the Word, and I'd feel the Lord speak to my heart and tell me to share a certain verse with the pastor. Since I thought I was supposed to share this guidance from the Lord immediately, I'd stand up with my Bible and walk down front, then catch the pastor's attention and show him the verse. "The Lord," I'd whisper, "wanted me to share this verse with you."

The first time it happened the pastor just looked at me with a surprised expression on his face; after that, he'd nod and get right back to his preaching.

And during the invitation, when the pastor would address those who had a spiritual problem, he always seemed to personally invite me to go down and pray at the altar. He'd call those who wanted to come to Jesus, which I'd already done. Then he'd call out to those who had a problem with cursing, and if I'd been struggling with my tongue, I'd go down to pray. Once I got that under control, I'd hear him call out to those who were struggling with impure sexual thoughts, so I'd have to go down and pray about that. No matter how many things I got a handle on, it seemed as if there was always something else I needed to pray about.

One morning a woman pulled me aside. "It don't take all that," she said, gesturing toward the altar where I'd been praying. "Go down there once and be done."

"Maybe that works for you," I answered, "but not for me. I'm going to keep trusting to do better. When I don't feel I have to go, I won't." So I kept going to the altar until the day I didn't have to go anymore.

My unconventional behavior upset the deacons, but the pastor said, "You leave that boy alone. He's growing in Jesus the only way he knows how."

He was absolutely right.

*   *   *

As a new Christian, I was filled with such enthusiasm and joy that I couldn't help expressing it. Every once in a while, though, I'd stop to think about all the things I'd done, and regret would fill me with sadness. I was particularly bothered by the memory of the low point when I robbed my sister Emerald's room. The jewelry I stole from her had been worth $178 (I knew this because after I'd stolen it, Emerald's boyfriend had wasted no time calling to tell me that was how much I owed her). That figure loomed in my mind as a debt I needed to repay.

One Sunday, my church leaders announced a new class on baptism. I attended the class and within minutes was saying, "Let's do it!" After listening to my testimony and observing my growth in Christ, the leaders agreed to baptize me. So they gave me a date, and I prepared for the big day.

I knew baptism was supposed to be a public event, a way to symbolize dying to the old life and being raised to walk in a new life. I showed up at church that morning in a great mood, ready to show the world that I had become a new person. I'd grabbed a change of clothes from my closet, not even looking to see if the pants and shirt matched, and my heart pounded like a kettle drum when the pastor led me down to the little pool in the front of the church.

"Have you, Dimas—" he said, placing one hand behind my back—"accepted Jesus Christ as your Savior?"

"I have."

"Then I baptize you, my brother, in the name of the Father, the Son, and the Holy Ghost."

He tipped me backward, and I felt those cool waters flow over me. Then he lifted me, and when I broke the surface of the water I wanted to shout for joy! I felt new, clean, and thoroughly different.

I went into a little side room to change out of my wet clothes, and I slipped into the shirt and pants I'd grabbed from the closet. As I fastened the pants, I felt something in the pockets and pulled out a wad of cash—exactly $178. I shrugged and put the money back in the pocket, checked my appearance in a mirror, and then headed out to find a seat in church.

As I walked down the aisle, I spied a familiar face and stopped in my tracks. Emerald—my sister, who was visiting all the way from New York and who hadn't even known that I was attending that church— was sitting in a pew looking at me, her face streaked with tears.

And I knew what I had to do. I pulled that wad of money from my pocket, walked over, and pressed it into her hand. Then I hugged her and whispered, "Sorry about the jewelry."

My heart soared with the knowledge that God had arranged things so I could right one of my wrongs. I hadn't asked Emerald to come, and I hadn't been aware of the money in my pocket until after I came out of the baptismal waters. But God knew.

*   *   *

Since deciding to follow Jesus, I was determined to sell marijuana only. I knew the evils of crack, but weed seemed mild. It was, after all, a natural plant—or so I thought at the time. My weed empire was booming and vast. I would visit a different weed spot every day, reading my Bible as my workers and I waited for customers.

Wouldn't you know, the more I tried to read my Bible, the more customers showed up. I'd be a couple of verses into Matthew and someone would knock on the door wanting an ounce of weed. I'd make the deal, pick up my Bible and read a couple more verses, and then I'd hear another knock, someone wanting three ounces. I was making more money selling weed than I'd ever made selling crack. I was almost convinced that all that Bible reading was bringing customers to my door.

I had also learned that people gave offerings at church, so every week I'd try to sit next to the prettiest girl I could find. Then I'd pull a big stack of money from my pocket and put it in the plate as it passed by. That always won a smile from the girl, so I really was what you might call a *cheerful* giver.

Then I noticed the big brown box at the front of the church. During one portion of the service, people would walk up there and put envelopes in the big box, so I asked a man what they were doing. "They're giving their tithes," he said. "That's the tithe box. You take 10 percent of whatever money you made that week and put it in the box."

"Are you serious?" I asked, delighted. "This is great!"

I came up with a new plan for giving. Each week I'd make ten or twenty grand, always in cash, so every Sunday I'd take 10 percent of my earnings and put the cash into little white envelopes. Then I'd go down front and stuff the envelopes into the tithe box, thrilled that I was able to do it.

Not many weeks later, the pastor climbed into the pulpit and smiled at the congregation. "I'm happy to announce we're starting a building fund," he said, gripping the sides of his pulpit, "because tithes over the last two months have tripled!"

The congregation burst into applause. I clapped along with them, but I had no idea that other people weren't dropping thousands of dollars into the tithe box. I thought everyone cheerfully gave lots of money.

The church was thriving, and soon they started a Sunday school class before the worship service. "Are you *serious*?" I said when I heard the news. "More time in church? This is great!"

So I started getting up earlier and going to Sunday school. About that time I bought a BMW, a gorgeous, fully loaded sports car, and I was as proud of it as a dad with a new baby. I drove it to church, hoping that one of the girls I liked would notice it—and me, of course.

In Sunday school one morning, Sister Boston, a wonderful woman, stood to give a testimony. Excitement sparkled in her eyes and vibrated in her voice as she shared that she'd run out of money at the end of the month and needed eighty dollars to pay her light bill. "I was thinkin' I'd soon be sitting in the dark," she said, looking around the class, "but then God provided the money I needed. Praise the Lord!"

Sister Boston was jumping for joy and everyone was clapping, but I stared at them, bewildered. This woman was jumping up and down over eighty dollars? That was a pitiful testimony. If they wanted to hear about God's blessing . . .

I stood. "I have a testimony too," I said. "God has been blessing me and my business. Outside in the parking lot I have a new BMW 535i, fully loaded. Say amen, somebody!"

For some reason, nobody clapped. Everybody sort of looked at each other, and then Sister Boston spoke from the back of the room. "Will somebody *please* talk to this man? This ain't right, and somebody's gotta tell him the truth."

I was taken aback. Was she jealous? Who cared about her puny light-bill story when I had a beautiful BMW 535i?

When church was over, I drove back to the projects. Not long after that, Tech 9—a guy who weighed at least 250 pounds—asked me to sell him an ounce of weed. When I showed up, he jerked his chin at me. "Let me smell that, man."

I handed over the bag and watched him open it and inhale deeply. After a minute, he said, "It's mine."

The look in his eye tipped me off—he wanted more than weed.

He wanted to rob me. He moved toward me and I pushed him away. "You can keep that."

I hurried home and asked Renee for my gun. "Jah has it again," she said, giving me a fake little smile. I put on my running shoes and went back out, finally locating Tech 9 at a girl's house.

I stood on the sidewalk and called him out. "Come on out and fight, you punk."

Tech 9 came out to meet me, and I threw the first punch, a quick blow to the face. Big as he was, Tech 9 couldn't box, but he could wrestle, so he kept trying to grab me while I kept trying to punch him. Finally we went down and were wrestling on the ground. We were evenly matched then, but Tech 9 got up and went to his car, then came right back.

As I prepared to throw another punch, I heard the Holy Spirit speak to my heart: *It's over.*

Tech 9 walked up and I lowered my fists. "We fought," I said. "You have the weed, and it's finished."

He looked at me, then nodded and walked away. When he was out of earshot, several people ran to me, buzzing with alarm. "He had a gun behind his back," one man said. "Good thing you didn't hit him a second time."

Good thing? *God thing.*

Still seething with frustration and anger, I went to Faye's house. She had recently come to Jesus, and she started crying when she saw me coming up the sidewalk. "What's wrong?" I asked, bewildered. I held out my hands to show her I hadn't been hurt in the fight with Tech 9. "Everything's okay. I'm fine."

A flare of anger sparked in her eyes. "It's not that. It's *you*, Daylight. You cannot do this. You cannot walk with the Bible and sell weed, too. You can't sell drugs and walk with Jesus. You've gotta stop!" She started weeping in frustration. "You can't do this. You can't *do this*!"

Her words pierced my heart so powerfully that I broke down and began to weep right along with her. The truth that rang in her words set me free.

"Faye, you're right."

I called up Otis, my weed supplier, and told him to meet me at Faye's in twenty minutes. After hanging up, I went to Renee's and grabbed all the weed I had left. When I met up with Otis, I gave it to him and told him he could do whatever he wanted with it. I was out. He kept asking, "Are you sure?"

"Yeah, I'm sure. I'm serving God now and want to follow him all the way."

Otis asked one more time if I was sure; then he flipped and started cursing me out. I stared at him—I thought I could at least expect a measure of gratitude for my generosity. Instead, he hurled invectives at me, distraught at the loss of business he was going to experience because I was stepping out of the game.

Later, I had to smile at the irony: Who would have thought that the very crack house where I started selling in Winston-Salem would also be the place where I stopped selling drugs altogether?

Not long afterward, the church youth pastor, Anthony Coles, explained that the word *sorcery* in Galatians 5:19-21 comes from the Greek word *pharmakeia*, from which we get the word *pharmacy*. "Witchcraft is associated with drug use," he said, "because the magicians would use potions to work their magic and affect people's minds. *Pharmakeia* is associated with demon worship and idolatry, too."

That lesson—combined with words from Faye and others—seriously messed up the church building fund. I write that with a smile, because I was happy to obey when the Spirit of God convicted me about selling marijuana. I wouldn't be able to tithe drug money anymore, but that was okay.

I called my team together and announced that I was finished selling drugs, period. Renee assumed my position as boss.

I considered myself retired from the drug business, but Jah and Mental had other plans. Unfortunately, those plans involved me.

*   *   *

A few days after I'd shut down my drug business, I woke early and got up to read my Bible. At the time, Renee and I were living at Jessica's. Renee was still asleep, and everyone else in the house was quiet.

A few minutes later I startled at the sound of someone pounding on the front door—an unexpected sound at nine o'clock in the morning.

I riffled through a mental checklist—was it the cops, the feds, or a hit man? One thing I knew for sure—whoever stood on the other side of that door wasn't bringing presents or candy. I felt a familiar internal yanking at my gut: the instinctive awareness that someone meant to harm me.

My heart contracted, and my first inclination was to run. But I was desperate, and in that desperation I turned to Jesus and trusted him with my fledgling faith. I grabbed my Bible and looked for some kind of divine message that might apply to this perilous situation. Red-printed text seemed to pop from the page as I looked down: *Why are you fearful, O you of little faith?*[1]

A surge of courage flowed through me, and I spoke aloud: "I have faith in you, God." Then I shut my Bible and dressed in my "hood uniform"—jeans, icy white T-shirt, black Nike sneakers. Meanwhile, I heard three more hard bangs on the door downstairs. Whoever stood behind it knew I was there. So I went downstairs, feeling prepared to face whoever stood on the other side.

I opened the door a crack, then turned the lock button so whoever it was couldn't get inside once I closed the door behind me. I steeled myself for battle mode and knew there'd be no turning back once I opened the door.

My mouth went dry when I saw who waited outside. Mental,

the trouble-making New York drug dealer, stood on the front steps with fire in his eyes. With a well-deserved reputation as a shooter and a fighter, he was big, strong, and quick. He had robbed major drug suppliers in New York. He was a total mental case—hence the street name—and people in New York and Winston-Salem respected him for his toughness. He didn't have the business acumen to be a drug boss, but no one in his right mind wanted to have problems with Mental.

I had fought Mental twice before, so I knew I couldn't trust him to fight fair. We'd had two petty fights a month earlier, and each time we had made things right. That's how things worked in the hood.

But now Mental was at my door, and he had a good reason to be upset.

His little brother had been murdered in New York. Days earlier I had received a call from Royal who told me about his death. Royal had added that I should put Mental on a plane so he wouldn't get worked up and kill someone in Winston-Salem. I took Royal's suggestion and drove Mental to the airport in North Carolina, but I didn't tell him about his brother's murder. Now Mental was back, and I suspected he was livid that I hadn't given him the tragic news before putting him on that plane.

Looking at his features, contorted with rage and sorrow, I figured that he'd come to kill me. He was a loose cannon, ready to fire at any time, and likely armed with a pistol. This would be a robbery and a hit, and Mental probably thought I'd be an easy target because I'd become a Christian.

I glanced out at the street and saw a car with a New York license plate parked about a hundred feet away. A couple of shadowy figures sat inside, probably counting the minutes until Mental returned with a fistful of money and blood on his hands. It was a poor plan, but a common one—shoot, grab, run to New York, and live like a king until the law caught up with you.

But neighborhoods in the South are like small towns; everyone knows everyone. Everyone would know Mental had shot me.

Mental looked at me and said, "Let's talk on the side of the house."

"Okay." I flipped the lock and pulled the door closed behind me, locking him out of the house.

As I walked across the front lawn, I saw Jah waiting for us. The guy could barely conceal how badly he wanted my business, but both Jah and Mental were ruthless idiots. If these two had concocted this scheme, I knew that neither of them planned for me to live another day.

Yet my thoughts kept returning to the Bible verse I'd read a few moments earlier: *Why are you fearful, O you of little faith?*

I had no idea what to expect next, but I knew I had to trust Jesus. Holding on to my little verse, I turned to face Mental and Jah. Mental pulled out what looked like a black .380 pistol and pointed it at my head. As I stood there, a familiar maxim from the street flashed through my mind: "If you pull it out, you'd better use it." He'd shown his weapon, so Mental knew that with all the guns I had, he'd have to kill me. The honor code on the streets dictated that if he backed down now, I would then hunt him down.

He began to talk, working himself up into a lather about how I once disrespected him at a party and how I should have "looked out." The entire story was contrived, but in order for a man to kill, he has to believe he has a good reason, even if he has to fabricate a story to move into the emotional kill zone.

Jesus, you have to get me through this one. With surprising calm, I met Mental's narrowed gaze. "You don't have to come at me like this; if you want something from me, just ask. But not like this."

Only God deserves credit for my ability to even form words in that moment.

The situation shifted from bad to worse as a single tear streamed down Mental's cheek. "My brother is dead, and that is that."

I knew the next moment would be my last. At point-blank range, with the gun aimed at my head, Mental pulled the trigger. I heard the click, but nothing else. Mental pulled the trigger again and again, but each time the gun refused to fire.

Mental gaped at the gun, then threw Jah a nervous glance. "Let's go!" They hurried toward their getaway car, and then the vehicle sped off.

I stood at the side of the house, overwhelmed by the power and faithfulness of God. "Hallelujah!" I shouted loud enough to wake the late sleepers. "Hallelujah!"

Then I dropped into a crouch and prayed. "Anything, God. Anything you want me to do, I will do it. Since you went all out like this for me, I'm going all out for you. I am totally yours. If you comb the whole world over and you need somebody to go somewhere or do something and you make it clear that you're the one asking, I will go and do anything you ask."

That simple prayer changed my life forever.

CHAPTER TWELVE

IN THOSE FIRST MONTHS following my conversion, I walked around praising Jesus. I thanked God for saving me and for delivering me from that horrible situation with the witch. I thanked him for jamming the gun and saving me from Mental—who I learned used that same weapon just two days later to shoot someone else. Even more, I thanked him for delivering me from life as I'd known it.

One night I went inside, woke Renee, and began to tell her everything I was thinking and feeling. "Look," I told her, "I have to serve God all the way. I can't play around. I gotta stop having sex because I'm going to serve Jesus."

She looked at me with no real expression. "Okay."

"Look," I went on, "you gotta come to Christ. Then I can marry you and we can do this right."

That woke her up. "But you've got warrants out for your arrest, you're on the run, you have to lay low—"

"God is working all this out," I assured her. "I don't know how he's gonna do it, but he's gonna do it."

We left the apartment we'd been sharing, and Renee moved back in with her mother. I moved in the house with them, but I was trying to stay on the straight path and not have sex with her. A week and a half later, though, I slipped up.

My spiritual growth seemed to come by trial and error. After I messed up with Renee three times, I went to the pastor and confessed that I was having trouble in the area of sexual temptation. Reverend Newton looked me in the eye and said, "Son, you're a habitual fornicator. You can't be living with a girl and beat that problem. You can't be a good witness either."

I knew the pastor was right, so I went back to tell Renee I was going to move out so I wouldn't be tempted to sleep with her. I gave her some money before realizing I wouldn't have any money coming in for a while.

I put my things in a bag and told her good-bye. "I know I'll be in sin if I live here, and I don't want to disappoint the Lord. So I'll see you around."

I had no idea where I was going to go. I had money, but I didn't have any ID because I was living as an escaped parolee and using Daylight as my name. I couldn't rent an apartment without an ID, so what was I going to do?

I walked down to the corner where the drug spot was, and a woman I knew walked up. She was an addict.

"Daylight, what are you doing out here on the corner?"

I shrugged. "I need a room."

"Well, I have a room." She squinted at me. "Want to stay with me and my boy?"

I squinted back at her and decided that I wouldn't be tempted to fornicate in her house. Besides, I knew how to live with an addict. There's a certain art to it. I knew I couldn't leave valuables out,

I couldn't buy expensive clothes that could be stolen and sold, and I knew to keep my money in my sneakers.

So I moved in with the addict, and soon she and her son were coming to church with me. Not long after that, they became believers, and she started to get cleaned up and off drugs.

And I learned an important lesson—when we get serious about walking with Jesus, he takes care of the obstacles in the road.

*　　*　　*

Once Jah began to sleep with Renee, I realized I was a single man. That was okay; if Renee wanted to be with someone else, she was not God's woman for me.

I went to church and heard a dude stand and give his testimony. He had recently given his life to the Lord, and he told the church that he had a warrant out for his arrest. "I'm going to turn myself in," he said. "There's a verse in Romans 13 that talks about obeying the law of the land, so that's what I'm going to do. After I do my time, I'm gonna come back here and find me a wife in this church."

As the church erupted with shouts and applause, I heard the Lord speak to my heart: *You're next.*

Not today, I answered.

But God had begun to work on me. One of my cousins had borrowed my BMW, so I asked him to watch it so I could go to NYC and turn myself in. "Aw, man," he said, "you need to come hang out with me a while."

I went with him, and he and some of his friends took me to a club. The minute I walked in, I could tell the Holy Spirit within me was grieved. *What are you doing here? You don't belong in this place.*

One day I ran into Soda, who was smoking weed.

After we talked for a few moments, Soda held the joint out to me. "It's not like you haven't been doing it," he said. "C'mon. What will one pull hurt?"

That sounded logical, so I took a hit. Soda looked at me and grinned. "I knew you'd come back around."

I was disgusted with myself. *I totally fell for that one.* Then I walked away, sick at the thought that I could begin a descent back into the darkness that quickly.

With no way to support myself after leaving the drug business, I went to church and asked around to see if anyone was hiring. I found a roofing job and signed on under my brother's name, since I was still a wanted man. I worked under the broiling sun for about three weeks; then my boss, Sam, pulled me aside. Sam was also a minister, so he had insight into the struggle I was facing.

"Look," he said, "roofing is not for you. Look around. You see Charlie over there? And Tom? Those guys were born to do roofing. But not you. You need to return to New York and go back to school. You're the only one serious about God up here, so you need a job where you're thinking and leading, not working with your hands."

Because I was a terrible roofer, I felt like praising God right there on the rooftop.

"Sir," I answered, "I'm going to do it."

That weekend I went to church, stood up, and faced my new brothers and sisters: "Church, I have an announcement—I'm a man on the run."

I blinked when the entire church broke out in laughter. I thought I'd get the same enthusiastic and supportive response they had given that other guy, but everyone was laughing at me.

One dear lady stood up and smiled. "Son, everybody who comes here from New York is on the run. We all knew that."

I smiled in relief. "Well, I'm going back to turn myself in. Outside of a miracle, I'll most likely be doing seven years in jail, but at least I'll be honoring Jesus."

That church surrounded me and wrapped me in arms of love. Some cried, some hugged me, and some police officers stood and looked me in the eye. "Daylight," one of them said, "we have followed your story and watched you. We're going to send letters to the judge on your behalf."

It wasn't just an empty promise—right then, they went back into the church office with a secretary, dictated some letters, signed them, and photocopied their badges. They put those papers in an envelope, sealed it, and gave it to me, telling me not to open it but to give it to my lawyer.

That night I called my mother and gave her the news: "I'm coming home. I'm taking a bus to New York, and I'm going to turn myself in."

That's what I did. My bus pulled into Queens on a weekend. When I arrived home, Mom welcomed me, hugged me, and listened to my story. I was ready to go down to the parole office right then, but Mom caught my hand. "Why don't you wait," she said, her eyes glistening, "until Monday."

*   *   *

I had taken a shuttle van from the bus station to my mother's house. After I had climbed into the van and settled my bag on my lap, someone unexpectedly tapped me on the shoulder. I turned and saw a guy grinning at me. "Hey, mon," he said in the thickest Jamaican accent I had ever heard. "Would ya like to study the Bible?"

I grinned at him. "I would *love* to!"

He told me that his church met in a public school, and then he gave me the time and address. I went home to Mom, and when Sunday morning arrived, for the first time in my life, I went to church in a public school.

I found my Jamaican friend with several other believers in Jesus, all young and energetic. They explained that they were part of a church that required prospects to take a number of lessons, and then they could be baptized.

"I've already been baptized," I said.

One of the leaders grinned at me. "We'll see about that."

We studied the Word a while; then they listened while I explained why I had come back to New York. When they heard my story, they showed me nothing but love. The entire group rallied to support me.

I would draw on their backing later in the day when I unexpectedly ran into Otis, the dealer from Winston-Salem who was in the city to buy weight.

As I marveled at the odds of running into Otis in a city of millions, he jotted something on a card. "Here's my number," he said, handing me the paper. "If you want to get back into the business, just let me know. I'll be leaving tomorrow."

For just a moment, I weighed the options—jail or street god? But then I realized that running into Otis on that precise date was no mere coincidence. It clearly was the enemy's last ploy to pull me off the path of righteous living.

I ripped up the card and silently prayed, *God, you have to walk with me through this.*

On Monday morning, twenty believers from that church went with me to the parole office. They waited outside, praying, while I stepped inside and told an officer I was a fugitive who wanted to turn myself in.

The man looked up and eyeballed me over his reading glasses. "And who are you?"

"Dimas Salaberrios."

He rifled through some papers, tapped on a computer, and then came around to handcuff me. Before long I found myself going to a jail called the Queens House, a holding center near the courthouse and parole office.

Going to jail this time was unlike any other time I'd faced incarceration. I had decided to live for Jesus no matter what happened, so even though the external events were familiar, the feeling inside me was completely different. I went through the usual routine—handcuffs, central booking, toilet-paper roll for a pillow—but this time I was in Christ, so I kept praying, reading, and asking God to help me endure the experience.

I went before a judge who glanced at my records and gave me a court date fifty-six days away. *Fifty-six days?* Man! I was okay with the situation, but fifty-six days was a long time. I was trusting God to work a miracle, but a couple of months of waiting didn't seem like a very promising start.

The routine in Queens House was simple. Each inmate spent the night in a cell. The COs opened the cell doors at six for early risers, and then opened them again later for inmates who liked to sleep a little longer. Once out of our cells, we watched movies and television in an open space for eight or nine hours. If we wanted to, we could work out in the yard or in an indoor gym area. At the end of the day, we went back to our cells for the night.

I figured that if I was going to be in Queens House for fifty-six days, I might as well be productive. They'd given me a little Bible when I arrived, and that was all I needed to start a Bible study.

The next morning when they opened the cells for early risers, I walked down the block banging on the other cells and calling, "Bible study! Starting in thirty minutes, come to the day room for the Bible study!"

Six guys came—three Latino, two black, one white.

There we were—one Bible and seven incarcerated criminals, one of them a guy who didn't know the first thing about preaching or teaching the Word. Since I had no idea what to do, I opened the Bible and created a sermon from the first page I saw. I had opened to the book of Jude, and my gaze fell on the passage where Satan argued with the archangel Michael about the body of Moses. I don't think I could have chosen a more obscure text, and I know my sermon was a homiletic nightmare. "Do you see?" I kept asking. "The devil was arguing about the body of Moses. *Moses' bones*, man! Moses' bones! This means you need Jesus. Jesus cares about you, about everything! Do you see the connection?"

I'm not sure I made much sense at all, but when I asked whether they wanted Jesus, every hand went up. I led them in a one-sentence prayer, and they gave their lives to Christ. Those six men came to Bible study every day, and they brought others. The majority of guys in our Bible study group ended up going home, but others took their places because they wanted to study the Word.

As I became more comfortable, I relaxed and spoke from my heart. Criminals who had been brought up in the church would sometimes try to demean me and discourage others from being a part of the Bible study. They would curse and growl and fight one moment, and in the next they would talk about how they knew so much more about the Bible than I did.

"You know, I may not know much about how to teach the Bible, but I'm living this thing," I'd answer. "You may know more Scriptures than me, but you're not a true follower. I'm a true follower, and that's the difference. You might try to fight me or whatever, but I'm not going to fight you back. I'm following Jesus all the way."

I think the other guys appreciated my honesty, and they wanted to be taught.

Unfortunately, I was transferred out of Queens House to Rikers Island after a few weeks. Inmates usually aren't transferred unless they cause some kind of trouble, and I think the COs liked what I was doing. But apparently someone hated that I was preaching to those guys.

So I rolled into Rikers Island again, knowing things would be different this time. The last time I'd been housed in an adolescent facility, but this time I would be put in the adult population—a much more serious proposition. I'd be with grown men with adult minds, lifetime criminals who were constantly in and out of jail. These were masters of the game, not kids, and they played for keeps. Some of them were men who greeted new arrivals with "I'll cut your throat if you so much as look at me sideways."

Some of them, I knew, would remember me as Slim, but I wasn't Slim anymore.

When I walked in and saw the first familiar face, I told the inmate that I'd been changed. "I'm not Slim anymore. I'm Daylight, and I'm serving Jesus. I'm a new man in the Lord."

*   *   *

The setup in the adult facility was similar to the adolescent facility I'd been housed in earlier. They put me in a fifty-bed dorm in the Otis Bantum Correctional Center (OBCC), a building named after a former warden. As I walked in, the CO pointed out an empty bed with a stack of linens. I nodded and sat on it.

Scarcely a minute later, a big guy with a cane walked over and raked me with an appraising glance. "Let me sit," he said, sinking to the mattress, "and tell you the rules of the house. There are three phones—the Latin Kings' phone, the Ñetas' phone, and the black phone. This guy runs the black phone, Chico—"

I lifted my hand. "I'm not interested in the phones, so I'm not getting caught up in that."

He heaved an exasperated sigh. "Look, I'm just giving you the rules."

"It's okay. I'm not watching TV, and I don't care about the phones."

He sighed again, then rested both hands on the top of his cane. "Well, now you know."

"Okay." I gave him a polite smile. "Thank you."

When he had gone, I stood and started to make my bed. I didn't want to get caught up in any kind of feud or rivalry, but I wasn't sure I could avoid it in this house.

Within a few hours, I understood the lay of the land. The house was more dangerous than it had first appeared. Four Muslims were incarcerated in this group, and they had the first beds by the front. They didn't like me because I announced right away that I was a Christian.

I met one guy from the Bronx and shared the gospel with him. Like me, he was a newcomer to the house. When I urged him to give his life to Christ, he did, but the Muslim guys were trying to convert him as well.

"Why are you following Christians?" they taunted him. "If you come to Islam, we will fight for you; we will defend you. The Christians won't fight."

The guy looked back at me, as if weighing his options.

"Fine, if you want to go with them," I said, shrugging. "But there's no power with them. All power and authority lie in Jesus."

My mother came to visit, and she brought the few things I'd asked for: a Bible and a book to help me prepare for the GED test. I told her I didn't want a lot of money for the commissary. I only wanted a little money and those two books.

Every bed had a locker next to it, so I took a shoestring and a piece of paper and made a little sign that said CHURCH and hung it on my locker. The locker was practically empty, since I kept only my Bible and my GED book in there.

The guy in the next bed was a thief. We called him Shaolin because he was from Staten Island, home to the hip-hop group Wu-Tang Clan. The Wu-Tang Clan refer to Staten Island as *Shaolin*, the name of an ancient Chinese temple. (It's about the same as someone calling you "Tex" if you hail from Texas.) Shaolin began to irritate me by kicking down my church sign every time I turned my back. The more he did it, the more irritated I became, and I found myself struggling against anger. I was saved now, but I still knew how to fight and could be pushed to the point where I wanted to start throwing punches.

"Why are you messin' with my stuff?" I asked him once. "Leave my sign alone."

Some guys told me about another Christian in the house. He was from the Dominican Republic and spoke no English, but he read his Bible and prayed for an hour and a half every day. I went over to him, sat down, and said, "I'm a Christian too." When he saw my Bible, he understood and grinned up at me. "Amen," he said.

Every day I'd visit, and we would pray and do Bible study together. The whole house would laugh at us because neither one of us understood a word of what the other was saying. He was from a Pentecostal background, so he'd yell and shout in Spanish while I talked in English. He'd open his Bible and point to something in Spanish. I'd try to find the same verse in my English Bible. After reading it, I'd smile and nod. "Yeah, that's good."

We worshiped and studied together every day, and for some guys in the house, we were better entertainment than whatever was playing on television. When the guy next to my Spanish friend went home, I took that empty bed because I was tired of Shaolin kicking down my church sign.

Then Eric, another inmate who had accepted Jesus, got into trouble because he used the Spanish phone without permission. The Spanish phone was controlled by a short guy named Edgar. He was skinny and only about five feet tall; but he was in jail for murder, and he was ruthless. He was also the leader of the entire house, a fact that Eric seemed to have missed.

"Yo!" Edgar shouted when Eric used the phone. He started to walk toward Eric, but I stepped in. "He didn't know," I tried to explain. "He didn't know that was the Spanish phone."

Eric was as tall as I was but stronger and more sharply cut. He could probably have handled himself, but I didn't want him to fight if he didn't have to.

"Mind your business, Slim," Edgar said. Then he yelled something in Spanish, and every Hispanic man in the house started to advance on Eric.

"Jesus!" I called out to the Lord in a desperate prayer, and then

I took a step toward Edgar. "He didn't know you were head of the house, man. He's a Christian. He's with me."

My words hung on the air as Edgar and Eric stared at each other. I knew the men behind Edgar were pulling out shanks, razor blades, whatever they had. Their territory had been invaded, and they were ready for a fight.

I held my breath and waited, silently praying. Then Edgar lifted his chin and looked at me. "Only because of you, this time, this is not going to happen."

I lifted my hands. "No problem, man. No problem."

Later that day one of the other guys drew me aside for a quiet conversation. "Yo, three of those guys were planning to stab you. The only reason they didn't was because you called out the name of Jesus. They were going to tear you up, they didn't care, until you said Jesus, then they put their knives away."

I rejoiced that God had gotten the glory.

The next day, one of the Spanish dudes had his fancy watch stolen. Edgar and his guys started turning the house upside down searching for the watch, but when they got to the front of the house, the Muslims leaped up and said, "In the name of Allah, you ain't doin' this," and Eric went with them. I watched the kid go over to the Muslims, who patted him on the back and said, "Man, stick with us. We're action. We'll fight for you."

Impressed that the Muslims faced down the Latin Kings and the Ñetas, Eric fell for that action. His decision devastated me.

Other Muslims came to the door to back up the four—now five—in our house, and then the head of the Ñetas and the chaplain imam of the Muslims said, "We're not having a war over some stupid dude losing his watch."

Everything died down, which was good. And the dude never got his watch back.

One guy—the man who had explained the rules of the house—was in for murder. I knew his case was coming up, so I began to pray for him. He went to court, then came back and told us that his case had been dropped because the evidence against him was circumstantial. His release took three days, so during that time he gave all his stuff away.

Then I started praying for the guy in the bed next to me. I prayed for him, and he was released. Over the course of a week, two more guys occupied that bed. I prayed for each of them, and they went home. The guys in the house started fighting over that spot, calling it the "lucky bed." I told them, "It's not the bed; it's the prayers of the righteous. It's Jesus. Everyone who sleeps in that bed and allows me to pray for them goes home."

Some people may not think it was right for me to pray for the release of prisoners. But in all my prayers, I wanted God's will to be done, and I knew that my fellow prisoners could be profoundly influenced if they saw that God answers the fervent prayers of a righteous man.

Eric asked me to pray for him, so I did, and he went home. Before he left, he wanted to bless me, so he gave me everything he had in his locker: potato chips, drinks, all kinds of snacks. "When you get out," he said, "call me and I'll come to your church."

"Let's do it," I answered, grinning.

Later that night, some of the guys made plans to rob me of my newfound riches. A few of the Muslim prisoners and Shaolin got together and came toward me with threat gleaming in their eyes. "Slim," they said, ready for a fight, "we want your food."

I stood in front of my locker and met their gazes head-on. "Yo, I'm a Christian, but I'm not giving you my food."

"We want your food."

"Really?" I bent and took two bags of potato chips from my locker. "You see these? They're worth twenty-five cents. You want to fight me or kill me for twenty-five cents? For real? You've been reduced that low that you're ready to rob me for a measly bag of chips worth only *twenty-five cents?* Then come and get it."

I stood there, waiting, and one by one, those dudes lowered their heads and walked away in shame. Fighting over a quarter's worth of food made no sense, and everyone realized it.

The would-be thieves left me, and I ate a bag of chips. Then I called over the guys who were in my Bible study, and I shared whatever I had left. Food was always a problem in jail, so maybe it was better not to keep much of it.

Finally, my fifty-six days were up, and they called me to court.

*   *   *

My lawyer briefed me before we went before the judge. "I'm going to try to get this case dismissed," he said, "so you can go home and get a job. I know there's an automatic seven-year sentence for escaping, but with this change in your life, I think we have a shot. Or—" he shook his head—"they could send you away. We'll see."

I went into the courtroom and stood before the judge. I had stood before a judge before, but I had never had such hope in my heart, or such resignation. If the Lord wanted me to go to jail, I was okay with that; I'd be a preacher in prison. But I sure didn't want to spend the next several years of my life locked up.

The judge, an older woman, looked up from the papers on her desk. "I read through your file, young man, and I have only one question. Why did you turn yourself in? You were on the run five years, you had a job under an alias, and you seemed to have created a new life for yourself. So why did you come back here?"

I swallowed and then met her piercing gaze. "Ma'am, I've given my life to Jesus Christ, so I've made up my mind to obey the law of the land. Whether I do it in jail or out of jail, I'm going to follow Jesus."

The judge waved her hand at me. "Take him out of my courtroom right now."

What? Maybe she'd heard my answer a dozen times before, and maybe she didn't believe me. But I couldn't believe what she'd said.

My heart sank and I started to pray. *Lord, I've been faithful to you. You know I didn't look at pornography or use any drugs in jail. I was just faithful to you, so please, Lord, help me.*

I sat in a room with my lawyer for what felt like an eternity. Then a bailiff called my name. We stood and went back into the courtroom, where I stood before the judge again. She looked at me and then at the papers on her desk. She looked at me a second time, then looked at her papers again. For a third time she raised her head and peered at me, then shook her head as she looked back down at her desk.

Finally she took off her reading glasses and studied me a fourth time. "I'm sorry for taking so long, but the man standing in front of me is completely different from the person I'm seeing in these reports. I believe that if I send you away to jail, it will turn you back into the person I'm reading about. So I'm going to set you free. Go back to your parole officer, keep your appointments, and continue to do what you're doing with your life."

Bang went her gavel, and just like that, I was free—or soon would be. I still had to go back to jail and be processed, but my heart was as light as air as my lawyer and I walked out of the courtroom.

Being released from Rikers can be a tricky situation. While you want to scream and celebrate that you're on your way home, you have to temper your joy and be discreet. Good news can be like salt on a wound for the less fortunate, and I'd heard about guys getting cut or stabbed as they were celebrating an upcoming release.

One of my friends pulled me aside when I came back into the house. "Slim, what happened?"

I could barely contain my joy. "God answered my prayer and I'm going home. Can I pray for you?"

He cried while I prayed for him.

When others asked if I was going home, I shrugged. "Man, I wish."

"Aw, you know you're going home. We all know it."

"You know," I answered, struggling, "I'm just going to pray."

While they prodded me, I sat on my bed praying, and about three hours later, the CO came in and told me to pack up; I was on my way outta there.

A couple of the guys started to tear up at my happy news. They told me to hang in there, to keep praying and trusting Jesus.

The tough guy who ran the Spanish phone came over and glared down at me. "Slim," he growled, "if I ever see your face in here again, I'm going to stab you seventy times, and I'm going to kill you real good."

I looked up and met his gaze, realizing that this threat was a way of showing love, of saying I didn't belong in there. At least, not anymore.

"Okay," I answered, nodding.

One of the guys I'd had problems with stopped me on my way out. "Give your heart fully to Jesus," I told him. "Let him be your all."

"Pray for me," he said, momentarily dropping his tough guy routine. "I don't want to do life in jail."

I promised to pray for him, and then the CO said, "All right, Slim, this isn't church; you've gotta go."

"Love you all." I lifted my hand in a last salute. "Love you all, but I gotta go."

When I took my first steps into freedom, I discovered several people from the church waiting for me.

*　　*　　*

After my release from Rikers, I was happy to find that I was again welcomed and accepted by the group from the church. I went to their Bible studies and loved being with people who were so enthusiastic about the Word of God. After attending a number of their sessions, they told me I was ready to be baptized.

"But I've already been baptized," I reminded them.

"Trust us, we know more of the Bible than you do," they said. "You need to be baptized in order to experience baptismal regeneration."

Since almost anybody in church knew more about the Bible than I did, I submitted to their leadership and got baptized again. When I came up out of the water, though, I didn't feel anything—the experience was nothing like the time I'd been baptized in the little North Carolina church.

But the people around me were thrilled. "Now that you're baptized," I was told, "you can date any girl from the group you want."

What?

"Yeah." My mentor laughed at my look of delight and surprise. "Any girl from our group, whether she's from Brooklyn, Queens, Manhattan, the Bronx—you name it. Just keep the church informed about who you're dating."

I felt like a kid in a candy store. I dated all the prettiest girls, asking out as many as I wanted. Every Sunday at church, I'd see a pretty girl and say, "Hey, why don't we go out?"

I didn't even mind that we had to go out on group dates. I found myself surrounded by people who seemed to love God and love talking about him.

I was also given a discipleship partner to whom I was supposed to confess all my sins and from whom I was supposed to get advice about all my decisions.

After a few weeks, however, I began to notice things. The group was extremely moralistic and started to tell me that I couldn't make decisions on my own. What?

"But I've been making my own decisions since I was a kid."

"And did you always make *godly* decisions?"

"Well . . . no."

"That's why you need to follow our Bible counselors. In a multitude of counselors you'll find safety."

They wanted me to seek their input on every decision I made and then submit to whatever I was told to do. I wasn't having that; besides, I had begun to see how people's lives could be shipwrecked by some of the counselors' decisions.

I began to notice other red flags. I had learned what a tithe was in North Carolina, but this church had an annual mandatory special offering based on our tithe, which we had to calculate using a complex equation. I'd just gotten a job that paid $200 a week, and the "special offering" I had to give the church came to $680. Everybody had to come up with that inflated "tithe," so they had garage sales and all kinds of fundraisers. And in meetings, they'd stand up and explain how they'd come up with the cash: "God inspired me to sell all my jewelry," or "God told me to sell my grandmother's antique china."

I thought that concept was nuts. Why would God demand more from people than he'd given them?

The church leaders told me to get a job, but I had trouble finding one that suited me. I decided the $200-a-week job wasn't for me the day another worker cut off his hand in a machine. I was working, listening to the machine hum, and suddenly I heard a wet sound, followed by *thunk-a-thunk-a-thunk* and a bloodcurdling scream. Red lights flashed, the power shut down, and a man was running around with half a hand.

I walked over to the foreman and quit on the spot. Risk losing my limbs for $200 a week? I wasn't down with that.

One day the church threw a party for my small Bible study group. In walked a sister named Lisa, who was wearing a red dress. After seeing the way she looked in that dress, I told myself she was The One. From that point on, I never wanted to date anyone else from the church group. When other girls asked me out, I'd smile and say, "Next month," but I only wanted to date Lisa.

I started modeling because I'd worked out in jail and thought it might be a nice way to earn a living. I had some people take a few pictures for my portfolio, and I started getting jobs. Lisa had a good job too. Things were coming together when I came up with the idea of doing a fashion show. Since my church sometimes rented a Seventh-day Adventist church building for special events, I called someone at that church and explained that we wanted to do a three-hour show on a Saturday night. He gave us a price of one hundred dollars. Then I found some models, had tickets printed, and arranged to have them sold in Brooklyn, Manhattan, and Queens. I found three young designers who agreed to come and supply clothing, and then I taught all the models how to walk.

The place was jam-packed, and the event was a rousing success. Throughout the group, people were whispering my name and showering me with praise and approval.

The next Sunday, I gave my testimony. When I stood and told them how the fashion show had earned my special offering for the church, the place went crazy. I felt great until one of the leaders came to me and said, "You have the money for the special offering?"

I blinked, confused. I'd just made $680 for the church, so what was he talking about?

He narrowed his gaze to an ice pick's point. "You're not ready to lead. You're not better than me, you don't speak better than me, you'll never be better than me."

What was the dude's problem? I stared at him in shock and amazement until he walked away.

Lisa and I had been dating four months when we had sex for the first time. Afterward, we were both devastated because we knew that the Bible said sexual intimacy should be reserved for marriage. In fact, I had told my mother I wanted to marry Lisa. I also reconnected with my father and told him I'd found a girl who really liked me, so what did he think?

His answer was brief: "I don't think you're thinking straight right now."

One of my modeling friends came to a church service with me, and I was eager to see what he thought. Afterward, he drew me aside and shook his head. "You like these girls?" he asked. "You could have one of the best girls in the country, but these girls—I don't know if their heads are right."

I didn't want to hear that. "You don't understand," I told him. "You don't have God."

I went by Lisa's house and told her we couldn't have sex anymore. "I won't even go inside your house. We're going to have a pure relationship before God."

Then Courtney, another friend I had met at a modeling event, got on fire for Jesus. He was fasting and praying and seeking the Lord. We had to spend a night in the train depot after a modeling gig, and the next morning I told him that I was going to see Lisa.

I went to Lisa's house and stood outside calling her name. After a minute, she lifted the window. "What do you want? You really should call before coming over here."

I frowned. "Are you comin' down, or what?"

"I'll be down in a minute."

As she closed the window, I realized something wasn't right. I went in the house and bounded up the stairs to her bedroom. Another guy was in her bed, sleeping.

"You." I prodded the guy with my foot. "Get up and get out of here."

The guy didn't even look ashamed. He mumbled something about me not understanding, then he got up and shuffled out of the room.

I took Lisa's arm in a firm grip. "How could you do this to me? It's over. Call the church and tell them what's up."

She nodded and I left.

A few hours later, a leader from the church met me. Lisa had called them, but she'd told them I hit her and threw her against the wall. I listened with my jaw practically on the ground. The messenger said I had been put out of the church, excommunicated for hitting a sister and fornicating.

"Okay." I nodded slowly, scarcely believing a word I'd heard. "Okay."

I went home completely shattered. I went to my room to pray, and on my knees I cried and told God how sorry I was. I'd messed up twice, but I hadn't hit her. I could get a handle on things . . .

My mother caught me when I came out of my room. "Dimas, are you okay?"

"No, Mom. They threw me out of the church."

She pressed her lips together but didn't say anything.

Then a counselor from the church called and told me to meet him at five the next morning. Though the early hour was unusual, I'd have met him anytime to win forgiveness from people I'd come to love and trust.

That next morning, I found myself face-to-face with the man who'd told me I'd never be better than him. I confessed my sins and told him I was sorry. He listened, then his eyes narrowed. "You're not sorry enough. Have you repented?"

"Yes," I answered. "We have stopped being sexually active."

"Really? You're not broken enough, so I don't believe you."

He told me to go to the Bronx the next morning to talk to another guy from the church. I agreed.

I went home and sat down on the couch. Mom came in and sat next to me, then she touched my arm. "Dimas," she said, her voice gentle, "open your eyes."

"What do you mean?"

"How many old people are in this church of yours?"

I had to think. "Well . . . one guy is, like, fifty."

She nodded. "And nobody is a true disciple unless they go to this church? So everybody I grew up with, all of them older than fifty, all those people and all those churches around the world are wrong, and only your church is right? Are they really the only people God will allow into heaven?"

In that moment, my eyes opened. I had known many Christians, including my sister Dawn, yet by my church's standards, they weren't true believers. According to the leaders, all other churches preached lies.

"Thank you, Mom." I patted her knee. "You're absolutely right."

When the people from the church called again, I told them I was going to attend another church. "Thanks for the impact you had on my life, and God bless you," I finished. They *had* impacted my life— they had loved me, supported me, and taught me to take sin seriously.

But by far the best thing that church ever did for me was kicking me out.

CHAPTER THIRTEEN

AFTER I LEFT THAT CHURCH, Courtney and I visited the Greater Allen AME Cathedral in Queens, a large church with several thousand members at the time. I loved it, but a friend told me about a church in the Bronx that was serious about discipleship. I gave the pastor a call and then went out to visit him. I told him the story of my last church experience, and he said he'd heard that the church was a cult.

I started to attend that church in the Bronx. The experience was incredible. The people seemed committed to seeking the Lord, and the pastor often called for church-wide fasts—a three-day fast here, a seven-day fast there. During these fasts, church members weren't to eat anything but were only to drink water. After going to the church for three months, I had lost forty pounds. The pastor said he would make me a leader in the church, and his support greatly encouraged me.

I was still modeling professionally, and one of my jobs involved a video with Jay-Z. At the gig I met a beautiful girl who'd been singing country music—her name was Mary. Courtney introduced us and said he'd talked to her about Jesus, so we started to date. I brought her to my new church in the Bronx, where Mary garnered mixed reactions from my friends. My pastor loved her and was soon calling her his daughter, but the pastor's wife didn't like Mary one bit.

Then the pastor said he was going to make me a deacon.

"That's great!" I answered. "What does a deacon do?"

"You come in early, clean the church, and have the pastor's back."

"Okay." I was as excited as a puppy with a new toy. "Let's do it!"

As part of my deacon duties, the pastor would often put me on special fasts—if the church was doing a three-day fast, he'd ask me to fast for seven days. He would say, "The Lord told me to tell you to stay on the fast another four days," and, not wanting to disobey the Lord, I'd do whatever the pastor said. Unfortunately, all that fasting seriously cut into my dating life, as I couldn't take Mary out to eat.

The pastor had an attractive female assistant/secretary, and one Sunday morning he pulled me aside. "My assistant's husband is going to come here to the church," he said, "but don't let him in."

Not wanting to question authority, I stood in the back of the church as the service began. Sure enough, in the middle of the worshiping, the assistant's husband pulled into the parking lot and started walking toward the church. I stepped outside to head him off, and when he approached, I said, "I'm sorry, but you can't come in."

I expected him to be angry, but instead he started to cry. "Man, I respect you," he said, "and I know this is what he's telling you to do. But he's messin' with my wife. He can't do this to me."

"I'm sorry," I answered, "but please don't try to come in. Don't make me hurt you. Just go on home."

The man went home, but I wondered why the guy would make those kinds of accusations against his pastor. Something didn't seem right.

A little later, I told the pastor I needed a set of keys. "If I have to come every week to clean before the service," I said, "let me have a set of keys so I won't have to wait for someone else to show up and let me in."

He looked at me thoughtfully, then nodded. "I won't give you the keys," he said, "but I'll give them to Mary."

Didn't he trust me? I couldn't figure out his reasoning, but I wanted to submit to the pastor, so I let it go. But every Sunday morning I'd have to get there early and wait for Mary, and the situation took the steam out of me. Not being considered trustworthy was demoralizing.

The pastor asked me to teach the young group—three kids. I took the class and grew it to fifteen by telling stories about Jesus. Apparently, the pastor wasn't pleased. "Just read out of this book right here," he said, giving me a dull book. "And when the book stops, you stop and walk out."

Within a couple of weeks, the youth group had dropped down to three again. The failure hurt me deeply, but I was trying to obey my authority as I would obey the Lord.

One day, the pastor and I saw his wife leaving the church. She was striding away with determination, though her eyes were wet with tears. "Where are you going?" he asked.

She shook her head. "Don't ask me that."

"You believin' all this garbage?" he said.

"I'm out of here," she said simply, then she got into the car and drove away. I never saw her again.

When I asked a deacon about the pastor's wife, he snorted. "Woman's crazy," he said. "Accusin' a man of God."

I wasn't sure what was up, but I figured everything was okay.

One day I was working in a quiet corner of the church, tucked away so I couldn't be seen. I heard the pastor come in, and a moment later I heard the door open again. I stood and moved into the open space just in time to see the pastor's assistant walk forward, embrace the pastor, and kiss his lips.

I dropped my jaw. "What was that?" I said aloud.

The assistant blushed, then moved away, signaling me to ask the pastor before she left; but the pastor only smiled at me. "Greet one another with a holy kiss," he said. "It's in the Bible. You can look it up."

I may have been naive, but I wasn't stupid. At that point, I put two and two together and figured they were having an affair. But then I searched the Scriptures and discovered that the New Testament tells us to greet one another with a holy kiss no less than four times.

Okay, I told myself. *It doesn't look right, but maybe this is what the husband saw. Maybe it's all been a big misunderstanding.*

After a few months I asked Mary to marry me, and she said yes. "But just so you know," I told her, "I'm not down with the holy kiss thing. That ain't right."

The news of our engagement seemed to make everyone happy. The church was happy. I was happy. Mary was happy.

*　　*　　*

One night after a modeling gig, I was coming home on the subway. Because the subway car was empty, I set my Bible on a seat and began to do chin-ups on one of the bars at the top of the car. When I dropped down, a man was seated across from me, staring at my John MacArthur Study Bible.

"I remember meeting you at Allen," I told him.

"I'm Reverend Johnson," he said, shifting his gaze to me. "And I'm starting a program called 'Rites of Passage.' We're trying to help young men get to know the Lord better." A slow smile crossed his face. "Why don't you come down on Monday and help us get this program started?"

"I'd love to!"

I went down to his church and met Reverend Johnson with about twelve other young men. I shared some of my story with those kids, and afterward Reverend Johnson asked me to be a mentor in the program. I was thrilled.

From out of the blue, my father, an avowed atheist, called to share a bit of wisdom. "Dimas," he said, "as a man, you need three things: a watch, a strong piece of ID like a driver's license, and a passport. You'll need a photo to get the passport."

Because the Lord said we should obey our fathers and mothers, I went out and bought a ten-dollar watch and got a driver's license— for years I'd been driving without one. Then I got the photo and sent off for a passport.

I knew I needed a full-time job, so I began telling family and friends that I was looking.

Trevor, a friend of mine from childhood, called and said, "Dimas, call my aunt right now; she works for the city of New York. Maybe she can help you find a job." So I called her, and one of the first things she told me was that I'd need a birth certificate, a driver's license, and one other piece of strong ID.

"Like a passport?"

"Like a passport."

I went to the address she gave me and got a job with the New York Department of Health.

One day I was driving and listening to the radio when I heard a reporter say that for the first time in ten years, East New York—one of the most crime-infested locations in the city—had experienced a week without homicides. That fact gave me an idea, and I couldn't wait to tell Mary, who lived in East New York.

"Listen," I told her, "we need to do a big event on your block."

Knowing that we'd have to have a permit, we applied for one. Then I went to the church, found an elder, and asked if he could build us a stage. When he said yes, I gave him $150 to do it.

When our permit came through, we stepped out in faith and hired a DJ to play for the event. The date arrived, and our outreach event featured music and preaching. I had invited Reverend Johnson and Reverend Emmanuel from Allen AME Church, and I was thrilled when they showed up with Rev. Paul Leacock, another pastor from the church. By the time the outreach ended, over fifty people had come to Christ. I praised God and gave him the glory.

Afterward, I handed the DJ sixty dollars, the amount on his estimate. "Wait a minute," he said, "the amount wasn't sixty dollars; it was six *hundred* dollars."

Not knowing what else to do, Mary and I began to knock on doors. We knocked on the door of every apartment and house in that block. "Did you see this event?" we'd ask. "Well, we need you to invest in it. We need to collect six hundred dollars."

Little by little, with ones and fives and tens, the block paid for the outreach. By the time we finished canvassing the neighborhood, we had gathered $530, and the DJ accepted it as our final payment—a good thing, because we had run out of doors to knock on.

*   *   *

I went to church the next day fully expecting that everyone would rejoice over the fifty people who had accepted Christ through my outreach. But the pastor was furious when he heard the news. "That was not God," he said, his voice firm and flat. "That was not the Lord."

"With all respect, you weren't there," I answered. "I was, and I believe it was the Lord."

I worried about the pastor—his wife had left him, and I knew he was under a lot of pressure. But he began to do increasingly weird things.

A beautiful new girl appeared in church. She began to hang out with me and Mary, and we liked her a lot. But one Saturday she called Mary in tears. After listening a few minutes, Mary handed me the phone. "That pastor is a fake," the girl shouted through angry tears. "He invited me to his house for a Bible study, then started to take off his clothes. He is a fake."

I tried to calm her down, and I didn't want to believe her. Maybe she'd misunderstood his intentions, or maybe she had made up the entire story. "Come to church with us tomorrow," I told her. "Maybe things will look different in the morning."

The next day the girl met Mary and me outside the church. She was dressed in one of her best outfits, and she led the way into the church and sat in the front row. I kept looking at her and then looking at the pastor, searching both faces for some trace of guilt. The pastor looked like he always did, but throughout the entire service the girl stared at the pastor with eyes as cold as ice.

I felt sorry for her because, at the time, I was sure she had allowed evil to rule her heart.

Shortly after that, the situation between me and Mary began to sour. She, too, seemed to fall under the spell of the pastor, who began calling her at home. When they began spending evenings together, I grew concerned. I got down on my knees and prayed for three hours, seeking the will of God, and then I heard a voice speak to my heart: *Allen AME.*

I called Mary. "I'm going to Allen AME," I told her.

"That ain't God," she said, sounding exactly like the pastor.

After hanging up with Mary, I called Tank, my old hustling partner from back in the day, because I had heard that he had given his life to Christ as well. I told him the entire story, then asked, "Am I hearing God right?"

"Are you kidding me?" Tank was incredulous. "Wake up, man! When you become a Christian, don't throw away the street knowledge and smarts you have. Could you innocently spend the night with someone like Mary?"

"No."

"Exactly. You really think they were having a prayer service all night?"

I groaned. "Are you serious?"

"There are pastors like my dad who are real," Tank explained, "and pastors who are not right. Face it, Dimas, this guy seems all wrong."

"Okay." I took a deep breath. "You know what? I'm going to call Mary and tell her it's all over."

I called Mary next and told her I wasn't comfortable with her going over to the pastor's house.

"It's over, then," she said.

"Really? You're breaking up with me?"

"Yes," she said, and I hung up, happy and praising the Lord.

*　　*　　*

I went back to the Allen AME Church and helped with another Rites of Passage meeting. After the close of the meeting, Reverend Johnson pulled me aside. "I've been hired to do a job in Maryland," he said. "I don't know who can run Rites of Passage, but I feel like the Lord is saying you should run it."

I was surprised but eager and pleased by the opportunity. "Okay! I'll give it a shot."

I don't think Reverend Johnson's other leaders were happy that he'd tapped a newcomer for the job, but I felt that the Lord had put me in the right place at the right time. After all, I'd felt the Lord telling me about Allen AME during my long prayer session a few weeks earlier.

At Allen AME, I stepped into a genuine megachurch (currently, the church has over eighteen thousand members). I was new, yet I'd been given permission to run Rites of Passage. The experience was intense, to say the least. I'd go to a Rites of Passage meeting and preach, and those kids just loved my enthusiasm. We hit it off, and when I suggested that we go on a three-day fast, no one blinked an eye. We began to see great results as those young men learned how to trust God, and they began to bring their friends. Before I knew it, the meetings had grown to include over sixty young men.

I began to implement things I'd learned from the Shock program—we started running together, and we wore military fatigues. We'd set off on a run and cry out to the Lord, just going after Jesus.

One Sunday we marched into one of the services, clearly against normal protocol. By the raised eyebrows and stares that met us as we walked down the aisle, I could sense that I was attracting the wrong kind of attention. My heart sank, and I knew there was a problem. I was only doing what I knew worked, and most young men naturally respond to physical exercises and team effort. This sort of program had helped me, so why couldn't it help these kids, too?

When the last of the young men stood in front of a pew, on my signal they stopped marching and sat in unison. The auditorium was deathly quiet, and I knew I'd soon be facing a tribunal. We had seriously freaked some people out.

After the service Reverend Leacock came to me and said I'd have to meet with the church leadership a little more often to make sure everything was cool with the program.

"Okay, no problem," I said. "Let's meet and do this, whatever. Let's do it."

Our rocky beginning straightened itself out.

I counted it a blessing and an honor to watch a man like Dr. Floyd Flake, Allen AME's senior pastor, up close. What set him apart from most pastors was his incredible willingness to trust other leaders with significant roles and responsibilities. He wasn't one of those men who has to keep his thumb on everything and everyone. Instead, he gave people opportunities to fulfill their callings and exercise their gifts.

More than two hundred different ministries operated under the Allen umbrella, led by men and women who took great strides to avoid disappointing the man who had placed such trust in them.

I began to meet and regularly connect with the church leadership. More men from the church began to participate in the Rites of Passage program, and the group became even more vibrant. Best of all, kids were coming to Christ every week.

After I preached a sermon against hip-hop music, one kid got fired up for the Lord and brought all his CDs to the church. He stacked them next to one of the pastors' cars. Then he began to stomp on those discs and crush them. "Brother Dimas is amazing," the kid said, "and I'm serving God like never before."

The Rites of Passage program was enjoying steady success. During my first year there, nearly seventy young men went through the entire program, and I hit on a recruitment strategy for the next year. I asked the pastors if we could do a brief step presentation in church, and they said yes. So I marched the young men in and out with military drills. They showed off everything they'd learned, and the church went wild with approval. It was quite a difference from the first time we marched into church, but this time the church had known what to expect.

After our presentation, I stood and said, "If you have a young man and want him to be a part of this program, we'll be signing up new participants next week." We quickly filled to capacity, enrolling eighty young men. Some of our first-year graduates came back to serve as mentors while others moved on to college.

Standing before the new group, I couldn't help but get fired up. In one of our first meetings, I started to preach. "I've just finished reading Joshua Harris's book *I Kissed Dating Goodbye*," I told them, "and I think it might have been written for me. I believe I have the gift of Paul—with me and women, it's over. From now on it's going to be me and Jesus." The kids were going crazy with me as I said I was done with women. An awesome young man named Gyasi stood and said, "I'm going all out for Christ. You can count on me as a soldier for Jesus till the end."

A few days later, I had just come into the Wednesday night service when I heard a girl screaming behind me—she was worshiping, but she was shrieking like a crazy woman. I turned to see what that was all about, and beside the shrieking girl I saw another young woman—a woman so beautiful she stole my breath away. But I turned around and reminded myself that I had the gift of Paul, so I wasn't about to fall for a trick of the enemy. My mind was in the game, but reality set in about two seconds later. If I was feeling breathless after seeing a beautiful woman, clearly I did not have the gift of Paul.

The following Sunday morning, I was sitting in the church balcony during a service. I remembered the beautiful young woman from Wednesday night, so when it came time to go down and put my offering in the basket, I thought I'd look for her as I walked down the aisle. As I came back from giving my offering, she was walking up the aisle. We locked eyes for a second that felt like a full minute.

I had asked God if he would let me see her again, and like a father who gives good gifts to his children, he provided the opportunity.

*　　*　　*

I went home after church, and out of the blue my mother asked if I'd met any women at my new church. "Don't ask me that, Mom," I said, gently chiding her. "I'm a man of God, and I'm not going to church to meet women." I lowered my gaze, then lifted my eyes to meet hers. "But there is one who stands out."

She smiled that knowing mother smile. "Really? Tell me about her."

I shrugged. "I saw a pretty girl in the crowd, and that's about it. Nothing has happened, and I don't even know her name."

Mom left me alone after that.

On meeting night, the kids would come to church and hang out on the sidewalk outside the building. I would go outside and ask them to come in, and sometimes it took two or three trips before I got all the stragglers inside the building. Not long after the conversation with my mom, I was running out the doorway to round up some more kids when *the girl* came through the doorway. We nearly ran into each other. I stopped in my tracks. I think my brain stopped too, because after sticking out my hand and saying hi, I stammered, "You, you . . . you really know how to worship God well."

I was thinking about how reverent she seemed next to her shrieking friend, but she didn't know that. She lifted a brow and said, "Really?" but she was smiling when she thanked me.

Her name, I learned, was Tiffany. She had a soft Southern accent, and she had come from DC.

"What brings you to New York?" I asked.

She lowered her head in a modest expression. "Acting, and a little bit of modeling."

"Wow. I do modeling and a little bit of acting. Let's trade phone numbers, and maybe I can help you avoid some of the pitfalls you might encounter on the modeling circuit. I could totally help with that."

"Okay." She reached into her purse, and I couldn't believe it when she wrote her phone number on a piece of paper.

I could hardly wait to call her. We had a good first conversation, and the second time I called, we talked for three or four hours straight—and I'm not much of a telephone person. On that second call, I gave her the test I'd given a lot of women—at the end of the call, I said, "Why don't you close us out in prayer?"

Tiffany began to pray, and I was blown away by the honest and sincere way she talked to God. Clearly she had a solid relationship with Jesus; she was the real deal.

When I hung up, I wore a broad smile. I felt great. She was great.

I knew we could go places together because she not only knew about the Lord but also had a vibrant relationship with him.

I started praying, "God, is she the one?"

One night I dreamed about a girl with spiral curls in a gray outfit and knew the Lord was showing me a glimpse of my wife. The following Sunday, from a distance I saw the back of a woman's head with the same spiral curls and gray outfit as the woman in my dream. When I moved closer, the woman turned around, and I saw that it was Tiffany. She smiled at me and kept worshiping. Right then, I knew I'd received a confirmation from the Lord that she'd be my wife someday.

Tiffany received an assurance from the Lord in a different way. Before we met in the church doorway, she'd been on a forty-day fast. She was going to stay home that Monday night because she was tired, but she heard the Lord tell her, *Your blessing is at the church.* She thought she was going to church to meet somebody like Denzel Washington who'd jump-start her acting career, but as she walked toward the church door, she heard the Lord's voice again: *Your blessing is at the church.*

Then she came inside and met me. From the time she was a little girl, whenever she daydreamed or thought about her husband, she would always meet him at church, shake his hand, and know that he would be her husband. When she shook my hand that Monday night, something inside her clicked, and she knew I would one day be her husband.

She also had felt something on that Sunday when we passed each other on our way to and from the offering basket. She later told me that, when she looked at me, time seemed to stand still, but she wasn't sure what that meant.

Both of us were blessed enough to have received assurances from the Lord, but neither of us shared those assurances with the other until much later in our relationship. We both exercised great wisdom in that regard. I wanted to date her, get to know her, and learn how to honor her. She was unlike any woman I had ever met and was definitely a woman worth cherishing.

Tiffany and I were going out on regular dates, but by this time I knew better than to hurry the relationship. I kept things light and neutral.

After several weeks I told her I was very interested in a long-term relationship that would lead to marriage. "I don't know if you have a boyfriend—"

"I don't," she interjected.

I smiled. "Then I'd love for us to see each other in a serious way."

"That'd be great," she answered. "Let's do it."

Truthfully, I was enamored of the girl. She was beautiful, smart, and successful, so when she spoke, I listened.

My sister Dawn came to visit from California around that time, and she told me about missionaries. She mentioned Hudson Taylor, a missionary who prayed so powerfully that God worked miracles in China.

Missionaries! I thought it would be incredible to have a God-ordained mission, so I cried out to Jesus and told him I'd be a missionary if he wanted me to be one. I'd do anything and go anywhere. Anytime.

*   *   *

One Sunday, Matthew Rees, a writer with *Reader's Digest*, visited Allen AME church because he was writing an article about the church's pastor. Reverend Flake announced that if anyone was interested in talking to him, we could meet him at the end of the service. Reverend Flake then preached a powerful message about families and taking responsibility. During his sermon he said, "If you think you have a child somewhere, you need to take a blood test and find out if that is your child. And if it is, take responsibility."

At the end of the service, I went up to the man and told him that the pastor's sermon had convicted me.

His eyes sparked with interest. "How's that?"

"Well—" I hesitated, but pushed on through my doubts—"I've always had a gnawing feeling that a little girl down South is mine. So I'm going down there to pay for a blood test and find out."

Matthew gave me his card and said to contact him once I knew the results.

So I went down to North Carolina and looked up the mother. Then I told her I wanted to take a blood test to see if her daughter could be mine. "And if she is," I said, "I want to raise her. Can I bring her back to New York with me?"

The mother, who had four kids, said yes. If the girl proved to be mine, I could raise her in New York.

Within a week, I had the results . . . and a daughter. After heading down to North Carolina to pick her up, I drove back to New York with six-year-old Shirley Ann, the daughter I never knew I had.

As you can imagine, a six-year-old would have dreams and thoughts of finally being with her father. So when I came to pick her up, it was like a dream come true. "I'm going to be with my dad!" And so our adventure together began.

When I got home, I called Tiffany and told her I had some interesting news.

"What's that?"

"Um . . . I have a daughter. And she's here living with me now."

"Oh. Wow." Tiffany remained silent for a moment, and then I heard her take a deep breath. "Okay. I look forward to meeting her."

I also called Matthew Rees, the man from *Reader's Digest*, to tell him about Shirley Ann. He included a brief mention of my news in his article on Reverend Flake.[1]

Tiffany was great about supporting me as I stepped up to fatherhood, and my mother jumped in to help too. She had retired from being a school principal, so she watched Shirley Ann during the day. We improvised, and my daughter often went with me as I traveled around town. I rented an apartment for us and also bought a little car so I could take her to school.

When a well-known pastor came to town, I wanted to hear him preach at Madison Square Garden. I mentioned it to Shirley Ann, and she wanted to go too.

So we took the train over to that part of town, then got off and started to walk to the Garden. Shirley Ann was just learning to read, and outside the building she saw a sign that said they were looking for people to serve during the meeting. She'd also heard me preach a sermon in which I'd said, "I'm a minister without a title, so I'll just create one. Call me servant Dimas, because I am here to serve."

Shirley Ann put the sign and my words together and said, "Why don't we go serve, Daddy? You said you're a servant."

Caught by my own sermon, I grinned at her. "Okay, we'll serve."

So we got in the line of people who were willing to help at the meeting, and as we stood there I became aware of a white woman in the line in front of me. She said something in an unusual accent, so I tapped her on the shoulder and asked where she was from.

"New Zealand," she said, smiling at Shirley Ann.

"Really?" I was thrilled. "I would *love* to minister in New Zealand sometime."

All of a sudden that woman began to scream. I looked around, only a few seconds away from panic, because a white woman screaming at a black man is bad news. I knew I could be tackled at any moment. I told her to calm down and that she couldn't yell like that in New York City.

Somehow she managed to catch her breath. "God is so good," she said in a rush of words. "Before departing New Zealand, a man told me he had a message from God for me. He said that when I got to New York City, a tall black man would tap me on the shoulder and say, 'I would love to come and minister in New Zealand sometime.' Then God said it was up to me to get the man to New Zealand."

To prove her point, she pulled out a note and an envelope and showed me what had already been written on the note: *I met the tall black man, and he's coming to New Zealand.*

While Shirley Ann and I watched, she placed the note in a pre-addressed envelope, sealed it, and dropped it into a mailbox. Then she looked at me, her eyes glowing. "God is good, and you're coming to New Zealand!"

We exchanged phone numbers, and then we went on our way to serve at the meeting at the Garden.

But on our way into the building, Shirley Ann squeezed my hand and looked up at me. "Look at that, Dad. Aren't you glad you listened to me?"

CHAPTER FOURTEEN

ONCE SHIRLEY ANN AND I got home from Madison Square Garden, I called Tiffany with the news about New Zealand. She was enthusiastic and willing to help with whatever needed to be done.

The first thing I had to do was make sure I could take time off from work at the Department of Health. I went to my boss and said I needed a leave of absence because I wanted to go to New Zealand for two months. My boss wasn't enthusiastic about me going, but he gave me the time off and promised that my job would be waiting when I returned.

Tiffany and I took four months to plan the trip, and during that time I read lots of books and articles about New Zealand. The materials I read, though, had been written many years earlier, and they described New Zealand as home to the Māori tribe, some of the world's fiercest cannibals. I honestly believed my trip might put me in mortal danger.

Pastor Floyd's wife, Dr. Elaine Flake, got excited about my trip and promised that the church would pray for my dangerous expedition. Tiffany used her writing gift to create all the fundraising leaflets. I couldn't raise a nickel, but Tiffany was a good writer and editor. Her sister, Kim, ran a Christian publishing company and was visiting Long Island on a business trip. So Tiffany took me out to Long Island to meet her family. When Kim asked what we were doing for the holidays, Tiffany said, "Dimas is going on a mission trip to New Zealand!"

After meeting with Kim a couple of times to explain our mission, Tiffany said Kim had sent me something, so we needed to stop at Western Union. We were expecting a gift of some kind, but when Tiffany came out of Western Union, she said Kim had sent $1,100! "Praise God," Tiffany said, wide-eyed.

Finally we had everything ready for my trip. I had money to live on, the woman I had met in line had paid for my transportation, and I had Bibles and books to distribute. I thought I was heading to a place no man had gone before, but I was confident that God would be with me no matter what happened.

With that mind-set, I told dozens of people that they might never see me again and that I was going to witness to the cannibals. "Please pray they don't eat me," I finished.

My mother took care of Shirley Ann while I was gone, and Tiffany stayed behind and prayed.

When I arrived in New Zealand, I found myself in the middle of a very modern city—quite a surprise. But civilization can be just as dark and lost as the jungle. I spoke mostly in churches but became aware of a great spiritual darkness in the area.

The first sermon I gave was in a white church, and at the end of the message I received the shock of my life. While I was speaking, several women kept looking down at the floor as though they were disinterested in what I was sharing. Finally I gave the invitation to come to Jesus, and I was surprised when many of them stood and came to the altar. "I have to confess," one woman told me, "I have been a witch for nine years. Now I know I need to give my life to Jesus."

I was shaking with nervousness, but then the host pastor told the woman to bring her witchcraft books to the church and surrender them. After I'd finished speaking to her, I met three more women with the same testimony.

The pastor who helped coordinate my activities told me he was calling all his friends, and I would preach until I couldn't speak anymore. I'd never preached in a church before, and in New Zealand I found myself preaching in some other unusual places.

The pastor introduced me to one woman who had started a ministry house devoted to evangelism. She asked me to speak there and took me to a large building that had formerly been used as a science lab. "When you get inside," she told me as we parked the car, "just preach the gospel. But until we're ready to start, let me give you a tour of the building."

We walked around that huge building for half an hour. "Let me tell you how I got the place," the woman said. "I saw that it had come on the market, and I told God I wanted the building for our ministry. I called the owner, who told me it cost the equivalent of three million American dollars. So I toured the building with him.

"A week later, I called the owner and said, 'Can I see it again?' and he said, 'No problem.' So we walked through the place again, room by room, and I kept praying.

"I called the owner yet again and said, 'Can I see the building one last time?' and he said, 'Can you pay? Where's the money?' I told him I didn't have any money, but God had told me this was my building. He said, 'Come again?' so I repeated myself. Then the owner said, 'You won't believe this, but God told me I was supposed to give this building to you no matter what you offered. So make me an offer.'

"I offered him a couple hundred dollars, and he said, 'Done.'"

Now that she had a building that could be devoted to the ministry, she asked the Lord what she should do next. "The Lord sent me a girl who said she'd been a witch but had decided to follow Jesus. Her boyfriend, however, was a warlock, and when she found Jesus he and some other Satan worshipers wanted to kill her. I was protecting her in this building, but they found out where she was. They grabbed guns and jumped in a car to come over here and kill me and the girl. By that time I was protecting fourteen people in this facility, so all of us were in danger. But on the way here, the warlock and his friends had a horrible accident—three of them came close to dying."

I could barely believe her story, but I was so enthralled that I nodded, silently urging her to keep talking. She explained that a couple of other Satan worshipers were so intent on killing her and the girl that same night that they came to the building, looking for a way to break in. When they saw a ladder on the side of the building, they climbed up to the roof. While they were on the roof, they stepped on a glass skylight, crashed through the ceiling, and landed on the floor. My host said she and the girl found the injured people, and they quickly grabbed all their guns.

When the intruders came to, they asked the two women, "Why didn't you kill us?" That gave the women an opportunity to tell them about Jesus Christ and to let them know that God wanted them to know who he was. That night they all decided to follow Jesus.

Then the woman led me into a room where several men and women waited for me to speak. But before I could start preaching, I had to know the end of the story. "Where are all those people now?" I asked.

The woman gestured to my audience. Five of them had come out of the hospital. The others had survived falling through the ceiling and landing at the feet of those they had come to kill.

I was so rocked.

A few days later the coordinating pastor challenged me: "I want you to believe that God will do something great at your next meeting." I didn't know what he had in mind because I was a fledgling in faith when it came to miracles. I called Tiffany and told her how the pastor had challenged me. She said, "Believe God for the miracles, then. God will show up. Fast, pray, and get yourself together and watch God move."

Her words lit a fire in my soul.

I began to earnestly pray and felt a strong leading of the Lord to ask a couple of questions the next time I ministered.

I went to the next meeting place and started to preach. In the middle of the sermon, I obeyed a Spirit nudge and stopped. "How many of you—" I scanned the crowd—"are thinking about killing yourself?"

Half of the people in the group lifted their hands.

"Oh, my. Come forward and form a line so I can pray for you. How many of you want to accept Jesus?" I could scarcely believe it when half the hands went up again. "Okay, let me pray with those in the suicide line first."

I prayed with them one by one—more than sixty in all—and reminded them that Jesus has power over the spirit of suicide. During this time of prayer, the Spirit of God filled the place, and one by one, like Peter before God's holiness in Luke 5:8, God's truth and presence caused them to lay down and worship God with awe. Many eagerly prayed for salvation as well. I prayed for two people who had been sick for a while and encouraged them to rest in God's great love.

When returning the next day to that church, I followed up by asking some of them what they felt, and they said they had peace and joy and a desire to live. The youth group in that New Zealand church grew that night, and I spoke to the pastor months later and was excited to hear that those commitments lasted.

I was amazed at the incredible power of God.

I preached next in a church; revival broke out there and lasted for three months, continuing long after I left. By the time I left New

Zealand, I had preached sixty-six days in a row, and on several days I preached two or three times.

When I returned to New York, I stopped at a Rites of Passage meeting. Though it was another pastor's night to speak, he graciously let me preach. During the prayer time, people again responded powerfully to the Holy Spirit. As soon as that meeting was over, though, I felt as if I had stepped out of an invisible suit. The mission was finally complete.

I had seen the Spirit's supernatural work firsthand. He had anointed me for the mission and then showed up with power and grace.

*   *   *

Before I left New Zealand, forty pastors had surrounded me and prayed for me. After that time of prayer, one of them had said, "Dimas, I believe God is calling you to full-time ministry, but this is not going to be one of those stories where you can write out what's going to happen from beginning to end. It's going to be a journey where God reveals step-by-step what he wants to do with your life."

When I returned to New York and told Tiffany what that pastor had said, she said, "You need to quit that dead-end job at the Health Department and go hard after Jesus." Encouraged by her response, I went to my supervisor and said, "Boss, I'm done here. I'm resigning."

My boss shook his head. "You know you won't be able to work here again. Those who resign aren't able to come back."

"That's okay; I'm going into ministry."

I was filled with confidence and zeal. I quit that job and walked straight ahead. I had nothing set up: no donors and no support system, only a few friends and an impassioned belief that God was calling me to an unconventional ministry. I was ready to work with what I had.

I called five of my friends and had them meet me at the church to start a tape ministry. I started to study theological books, and when I felt ready, I invited my five friends and Tiffany into a room set up with a recording system. I preached several sermons, and I preached my heart out. I kept talking about the Septuagint, the ancient Greek translation of the Jewish Scriptures, though at the time I had no idea what the Septuagint was. I quoted from commentaries and notes; I tried my best to sound deep and scholarly.

Then Tiffany helped me write a newsletter. We got the addresses of one hundred people for the mailer, and we made them an offer: "If you like this material, send a gift of ten dollars and we'll send you a free tape."

Not one person responded. *No one* wanted that free tape.

Tiffany sat me down and said, "Let me be honest with you. That tape was pitiful. Are you *sure* you're called to preach?"

"Don't worry," I told her. "I'm going to get better."

How do you get better? You practice.

I would get on the subway at seven every morning, when it was packed with people going to work in the city. While they read their papers and listened to music, I'd stand up, hang on to a strap, and say, "Ladies and gentlemen, I'm going to give you a message from the Lord."

That first week demonstrated just how much I needed to improve. People would pretend they were deaf, put on their headphones, or look away and act as if I didn't exist.

By the second week, however, people started closing their books, turning off their music, and putting down their newspapers. I knew that if I could reach a jaded New York audience, I could learn to captivate anyone.

I kept preaching on the subway, and people came to Christ during altar calls on the train. And I learned that, like many speakers, I feed off the energy of my listeners. If they're enthusiastic and receptive, my energy level increases.

The tape ministry proved to be a nonstarter, but then I remembered a story I'd heard in New Zealand about a man who smuggled

Bibles to the persecuted church in China. The man telling the story gave us examples of miracles—how a box of muffins never emptied and how angels blinded border guards as people walked through the border checkpoints.

After coming back from New Zealand, my heart was hungry for another mission. I prayed every day about what to do next. There I was, in full-time ministry, but I didn't have a mission.

Then Tiffany told me about an organization she'd found online whose missionaries smuggled Bibles from Hong Kong into China. Tiffany found an unbelievably inexpensive round-trip ticket to Hong Kong for only three hundred dollars. I would be an international courier. When she explained how it could work, I was ready. "Let's do it."

So I packed my bags, told the church what I was doing, and flew to Hong Kong. When I landed, no one picked me up. I called a missionary affiliated with the program and got him out of bed, which is probably why he sounded so aggravated when he arrived to pick me up. He took me to the place where I would be staying, showed me a room, and pretty much said, "You're here; go to sleep."

Those were the most unfriendly missionaries I'd ever met, but I thought I could provide a little encouragement. "Why don't we have a meeting for Bible study?" I suggested. "I'd love to speak to y'all."

I held the meeting and nobody came, but I met another missionary named Diane on that trip. She talked a lot about missions in Kenya and said I should go there and take my girlfriend. "Fine," I said. "We'll do it."

I also met a little blonde girl, Linda, who was on fire for Jesus. About twenty years old, Linda was tired and frustrated because her last shipment of Bibles had been confiscated before reaching a safe house. As upsetting as that was, we both knew that the penalties for smuggling Bibles could include flogging or hard jail time.

Most of the smugglers carried Bibles in a rolling suitcase, but because I was so tall, I preferred to strap the books around my body in the same way I'd smuggled drugs in my pre-Christian days. I was over-joyed to use a skill from that time for Jesus. I made fifteen successful smuggling trips over the border, transporting about fifty Bibles per trip.

One day Linda came in and swung her suitcase onto the table. "Busted again," she said, almost at the point of tears.

"Are you okay?" I asked.

She shook her head. "I'm not. I think I need to pray right now." She looked up. "Will you pray with me?"

I prayed with her, but mostly I listened to her cry out to God in the name of Jesus. I'd never seen a white girl so ardent about Jesus; most whom I had encountered were more restrained, but she was crazily passionate. "You've got to shut the guards' eyes," she told God. "The next time I go to the border, there'd better not be a cop there. No border patrols. In the name of Jesus, no one will be at the border."

I thought the girl had lost it, but I couldn't doubt her sincerity.

The next day the organizer said, "Dimas, you're going with Linda." Oh, no. I knew I would get busted when they recognized her.

Linda and I approached the border in a group of travelers, just like we were supposed to. I kept looking around for the border cops, afraid that if I searched too hard, I might mess up Linda's miracle. But I saw no one. Nobody at all. We were coming up to the checkpoint, and I couldn't see a guard anywhere.

When we reached the checkpoint, I looked through the window of a little building and saw one guard eating his lunch. He looked up, saw us, and waved a chopstick as if to say *keep going*.

We did. We made it to the safe house where we were supposed to meet our contact, and we dropped the Bibles. Our contact came in, swept up the books, and left. Then we heard someone yell, "A raid!"

We had to go into another room and slip out a side exit. From a safe vantage point, we saw a group of officers burst into the safe house, but it had been emptied. We'd made it.

When we got back to headquarters, Linda was weeping and

praising the Lord. "My God is powerful. I don't care if nobody else here believes. I know you believe, Dimas, but those other missionaries had better realize that my God is powerful."

She got my heart pumping—I was down with whatever she wanted to do because she had big faith in a big God.

The next day, just before my last trip to the border, I wanted to cross the border with Linda again, but the director said I was going with another guy.

The other guy was as stubborn as a stuck door. I was about to strap the Bibles onto my body when he said, "I want you to put them in the suitcase and wheel them in."

I looked at him in disbelief. "Dude. I'm a six-foot-six black man in China. They're gonna stop me."

He straightened his spine. "You need to learn to submit. This is my team."

"You really need to make this point?"

"You need to learn to submit."

"Okay, man. No problem." I put the Bibles in the suitcase, then put on a fanny pack as a dummy bag (another trick I'd learned from my dealing days). We got on a boat because we were going into China through a back way.

Our leader reached the checkpoint and walked past the guard, so I followed him. I hadn't gone three steps when I heard, "Hey, you!" I ignored the summons as if I couldn't hear, then a short Chinese man ran up and grabbed me. "You. Put your bag through the scanner."

I took off my fanny pack and offered it for the machine.

"No. The big bag."

I had heard about all kinds of miracles—people putting bags through scanners and nothing showing up—so I let them put my bag on the scanner and trusted God to work some kind of creative miracle. I prayed, *Jesus, hide those books*, and then the Chinese guy looked at the scanner and went berserk. He yelled out something in Chinese, then twenty or so guards surrounded me.

The guard at the scanner opened the suitcase and took out a Bible, then brought it over and swatted it toward my face. "Whose book is this?"

"It's mine."

"Do you read Cantonese?"

"No, but it's still mine."

The guards got more aggressive, acting like they were about to hit me or cuff me. One of them had a nightstick with a wire attached, and he began to wrap the wire around his club like he wanted to strangle something.

That's when one of them said, "How tall are you?"

I froze for a moment, and then my slick New York mouth took over. I said, "I'm the same height as Michael Jordan."

The guard looked at me with wide eyes, then they all looked at each other, then looked back at me. They began to grin. Suddenly they all started shouting, "Michael Jordan! Michael Jordan!"

I smiled, shook their hands, and walked past the checkpoint, leaving the Bibles at the guard station. A white Jetta with tinted windows pulled up. Someone threw a door open, and I jumped in as the car whisked me away.

"I can't go back through that checkpoint," I told the driver.

"I know," he said. "There's another one about six hours away; you can leave there."

I was amazed. I felt as if I had just been in some James Bond movie! The Lord had phenomenally provided the miracle I had prayed for, and just as it says in Luke 12:11-12, he had given me the right words to say at just the right time. It was awesome!

The next day I told the Bible-smuggling missionaries good-bye and thanked them for their help. "Keep seeking Jesus," I told them as I left. "Keep going after him. And God bless you all."

*   *   *

I came back from my smuggling trip all fired up over what had happened. I still wasn't sure what the Lord was going to do next, but I was ready for anything.

One day Reverend Leacock asked me to ride with him up to Alliance Theological Seminary, where he was working on his master's degree. We had a good talk on the forty-five-minute drive, and I got to walk around the grounds for a while. I was overwhelmed by the campus and by the idea of seminary—once again, I was like a kid in a candy store, delighted by the idea of being able to study God full-time. Reverend Leacock suggested that I start praying and trusting God for a way to go to seminary.

I had received my GED and taken some college classes, but I hadn't graduated, so I didn't see how I would ever be able to get into a postgraduate program.

"Don't give up," Reverend Leacock advised. "If God wants you to do something, he can do it. You can finish your degree and come back."

I admitted that it would be amazing to go to Alliance. It was connected to the Christian and Missionary Alliance denomination, and I knew that it was theologically sound.

A little later I learned that another New York seminary offered weekend classes for college credit—one on the New Testament and one on preaching. I signed up and paid my tuition, but every day I left those classes feeling nauseated. The instructors struck me as so anti-Christ in their teaching, it was scary. One professor stood and said, "Let me tell you how you need to study the Bible. Put God over here, and put the Bible over there. Put space in between them, because the two are not connected."

Oh yeah? What about "All Scripture is God-breathed"?[1]

Another professor said, "How do we know we have the only way to heaven? Jesus and Allah can coexist, you know."

Until that point I had never heard anything about liberal institutions that basically don't believe in the God of Scripture. I found myself yearning for a school like Alliance.

I told Tiffany, "They can keep the money and keep their school. I can't do this."

Tiffany said, "You paid the money. You finish the school."

I answered, "Okay, but I'm going to be me."

So I went back to those classes and challenged those professors every step of the way. Whenever they said, "I don't know . . ." I said, "Well, I do, because the Bible says so." I went for the jugular time and time again. "Jesus is real," I told them, "and I don't believe what you're saying is right."

I didn't know everything, but I took them on with what little I knew and sometimes ended up being right.

Meanwhile, I kept searching for my next mission. I asked the church how I could serve them with my newfound calling, and they suggested that I attend the missionary meetings—the ones with the women in the white hats. I did. But I noticed that I was the only guy present and that foreign missions were not on their agenda.

Finally Reverend Leacock said, "I know a missionary who serves with The Navigators; let's put Dimas with him." The other pastors agreed, and they hooked me up with Andy Puleo from The Navigators. He began to teach me about evangelism and discipleship, the hallmarks of the Navigators organization. He also got me started on Scripture memorization, planting the Word in my heart.

While we were studying together, Andy said he used to be on the board of Alliance Theological Seminary. "Once in a while," he said, "they can grandfather in someone who has over sixty college credits plus dynamic ministry experience."

"Andy—" hope fluttered in my chest—"I have sixty-six credits. When I took some classes at the College of New Rochelle, they had classes with compound credits."

"Wow." Andy grinned at me. "That's incredible—but you'll have to gather up some great letters of recommendation."

"I think I can do that," I said. "Let me work on it."

I was still itching to undertake another mission, so I told Tiffany about Diane, the woman who had invited me to Kenya while I was in China. "The lady invited both of us," I explained, "and she said it'd be fine if we stayed in two separate areas. I told her I wasn't the kind of Christian who would sleep under the same roof as his girlfriend."

"Great," Tiffany said. "What's the mission?"

I contacted Diane and asked the same question.

"The mission?" She sounded a little confused. "We'll go visit this family I know and minister to them. We'll help them grow closer to Christ."

I remained silent for a long moment. Diane's mission sounded much smaller than what I'd had in mind. So although we'd still work alongside Diane on part of our trip, I began to pray that the Lord would give me a greater mission, a solid purpose for traveling to Africa.

A little later Tiffany and I drove up to Long Island to hear an author whose book had challenged us in our walk with God.

Before he started to teach, the author said, "Whoever traveled the farthest to hear me will get a free book. So who came a long way?"

A man said he'd come from Florida, so he got a smattering of applause.

"Anyone else?"

Someone had come from DC.

"Anyone else?"

Another man stood and said he'd come from Africa. The crowd murmured in surprise and admiration. Then the speaker said, "No, I'm talking about travel in the US."

I blinked. What? That dude flew all the way from Africa, and he couldn't even get a free book?

I told myself to calm down, and at the end of the session I went over to talk to the guy from Africa. When I asked where he was from, he said Kenya. He was a bishop who oversaw the work of several pastors.

"Man, I'm going to Kenya," I told him.

"Brother," he said, his eyes shining, "I would love to host you."

"That would be incredible. But tell me—what would be our mission?"

The bishop didn't hesitate. "We have an orphanage, so we need money for food, and we'd love someone to encourage our pastors. And we need bicycles—my pastors need bicycles so they can ride into areas they can't reach by car."

Hallelujah, we had a mission. I was thrilled.

"By the way," I asked, "where are you staying while you're here?"

He was staying with a friend, but I said I'd love to get with him to learn more about his work. While we talked, the friend he was staying with said that I could host him the next night if I wanted to.

I was living with my mother again. A few months earlier Shirley Ann had said that she loved me a lot but she wanted to live with her siblings. So I had taken her back to North Carolina and moved back into my mother's house.

The bishop stayed with us the night after we met, and in our time together we laid out a plan. I would set up a meeting at our church to ask people to buy bicycles and raise money for the orphanage.

"That," the bishop said, grinning, "would be great."

After the bishop left, I went to the church and explained my mission. They gave me a room for a meeting on the same night that they were having a big event for a football game.

That night I popped into the football meeting to make a pitch and collected about three hundred dollars. Then I went to the room for my fundraiser. I had invited everyone I knew, but only thirty people showed up.

But I had come up with a unique approach. Like an auctioneer, I had printed up signs—one said *$25*, one said *$50*, and one said *$75*.

When the people came in, I told them we were doing something for the motherland and asked who would buy a bicycle for $75. I kept my patter light and fast, and before the night was over we had raised $3,800 for bicycles. Who knew that people would get so excited about raising little auction signs?

We raised enough money to pay for the bikes and for airfare for Tiffany and me, but that was all. We were excited and praising God, but we had no extra money. And I knew we could not come from America and land in Africa dead broke.

Up until the day we were scheduled to depart, I couldn't find or raise any extra money. Tiffany's parents had driven up from DC to see their baby girl off on her first overseas mission trip. When the time came for us to leave for the airport, Tiffany and I got into a cab without even enough money to pay the cab fare. All I had was faith.

Someone had promised to send us funds via a money transfer, so we went to Western Union; but there was no money waiting for us. On the way to the airport, I asked the driver to stop by the church. When we arrived, I had Tiffany wait in the cab. I walked into the chapel and dropped to my knees. "Jesus, I'm going to Africa, but I don't even have enough money to pay this cab driver. I need you to show up now."

I got up off my knees and walked out of the chapel. I nearly ran into Reverend Flake, the senior pastor, who asked, "What's going on, Dimas?"

I explained as we walked to his office but hesitated at the threshold. I had never been in his office before.

"Come on in," he said. "And keep talking."

"Pastor Flake, here's the deal," I said. "We're going to Kenya. I have money for bikes and all kinds of ministry material, but I'm broke. How can I go to Africa with no money? I can show you a VHS tape about what we'll be doing—"

"I trust you," he said, interrupting. "Wait a minute."

He turned on the speakerphone and called Reverend Reed,

whose office was downstairs. "I need you to write a check to Dimas Salaberrios—"

"Pastor—" I hated to interrupt, but I had to—"I can't take a check. I'm going to the airport now, so I need cash."

He sighed. "Then I don't know how I can help you since the office normally doesn't keep cash on hand."

Then Pastor Reed spoke from the other end of the phone. "You won't believe this, but I have cash available. Send Dimas down."

Before I left, Reverend Flake laid hands on me and prayed for me. Then he smiled. "Have a great trip."

Downstairs, Reverend Reed gave me a thousand dollars.

Just before we flew out, I called my mother. "Dimas, I had a dream," Mom said. "When you're in the game park, be careful. Those animals will smell your American scent, so don't get out and walk around."

I told her not to worry. Then I hung up and headed toward Tiffany and the plane.

CHAPTER FIFTEEN

A PRAISE SONG, "Lion of Judah," was blaring through the airport's sound system when we landed around midnight. As our plane taxied to the gate, the runway lights revealed gazelles leaping in the nearby grass. Our first glimpse of Africa was like a fantasy come to life.

Tiffany and I disembarked and walked through the airport, so excited to be there that we felt as high as the stars. We spotted a guy holding up a sign with my name on it, and he helped us with our luggage. We got into the car as he chased away the panhandlers who thronged around us even at that late hour.

We traveled down a dark, narrow road and listened as our driver explained how dangerous the area was. "The robbers out here don't just take your money," he said. "They take your clothes, your under-wear, everything."

He had just finished speaking when we approached a hill. The car began to climb and then sputtered, stopped, and rolled backward. Tiffany looked at me, and in the glow of the dashboard I could see that her eyes were wide with fear. No light brightened the darkness— we were utterly alone.

We started to pray.

While we prayed, the driver explained that it was an old car, and we'd have to jump it to get it started. But maybe somebody would come along to help us. Maybe.

I looked out the window, but I couldn't see anything in the darkness. Who knew what kind of robbers or murderers or wild animals lurked outside? Maybe they could see us and were waiting for the right moment to pounce while we sat helpless at the bottom of a hill.

I stiffened as the car began to roll. The engine remained silent, but I heard the pop and crackle of tires on gravel as the car moved, slowly at first, and then with increasing speed. Thing is, we were rolling *up* the hill. My eyes kept searching intently to see who had come to our aid, but no one was there. Part of my mind noted that we were breaking the law of gravity, but another part waited until we'd picked up enough momentum to start the engine. "Hit it," I told the driver. "Hit it now!"

Supported by our prayers and God's faithfulness, the engine turned over and we were off. What a way to start a trip!

Diane, the woman I'd met on my China trip, was waiting for us at our destination. She walked us to what looked like a cinder-block garage with a flimsy door on it. "I stayed here once," she said, "and one of the workers got in and forced himself on me. He was wrong, but I forgave him, and now it's in the past."

I looked at Tiffany and then back at the woman. Needless to say, I was pretty disturbed.

The woman stopped at the garage and gestured toward the door. "Tiffany, you'll stay here. Dimas will be staying with a family a couple of blocks away."

"Wait—wait a minute." I forced a smile and pointed at the garage room. "Are you talking about this room right here? This room with the flimsy door right outside a game park filled with wild animals? This is where you were assaulted, yet you think I'm putting my beautiful, looks-like-a-model girlfriend in here?"

She shrugged. "If it was good enough for me, it ought to be good enough for her."

"Not in a million years." I shook my head. "I'll stay here, and Tiffany can have whatever room you had for me."

Diane's face flushed. "That girl is not better than me. She can stay there too."

Tiffany stepped into the fray. "You want me to stay in the place where you were raped? What do you think is going on here?"

"Whoa." I lifted my hands in an effort to redirect everyone's energy. "This is not the way it's supposed to go. Let's figure out another plan, shall we? Because there's no way I'm putting Tiffany in this place."

We worked it out. The couple with whom I was supposed to stay stepped up and said they had two guest rooms—one on each side of the house, with their room in the middle. So Tiffany and I could both stay with them because we'd be well separated and well chaperoned.

Whew. I was glad when we settled that matter, but first thing the next morning, another issue arose. Ready and willing to minister, I asked Diane what we were going to do. "We're going to a game park," she said.

I stared at her. My idea of a mission trip was taking the gospel to lost people, not visiting a game park. But Diane would not be convinced otherwise, so we all got into a car with our driver, along with his wife and their three-year-old son.

Everywhere I go—whether to Rhode Island or Rwanda—I always inquire about what predator animals reside in the area. I don't know why; maybe my fascination with wildlife is a result of growing up in the city. When we reached the game park, I asked the attendant that question and he rattled off the names of several big game animals, including lions. I wasn't sure I wanted to see one of those.

We left the attendant, and our host drove us through the game park. He lived across the street from the park and had driven through it countless times. "Don't believe the park attendant," he said, shrugging. "I've never seen a lion here."

Two minutes into the park, we spotted a beach area filled with beautiful pink flamingos. Our driver pulled over, and before I knew it, his wife, their little son, and Tiffany were out of the car and about to walk closer to take photos in front of the birds. I stared at them, amazed at their recklessness, and then my mother's warning flashed through my brain.

I put my window down. "Tiffany! Get back in this car!"

Now—if you knew Tiffany, you'd know that yelling at her like that was not going to fly. She turned and looked at me as if I'd lost my mind, but I was in no mood to argue. "Tiffany," I said, my voice calmer, "get in the car now. You should all get back in the car."

Sighing as if I'd spoiled all their fun, Tiffany and the family members piled back into the vehicle. The driver cast me a sidelong glance and then pulled his keys from his pocket. "I have a word for a man like you."

"What's that?" I asked.

He said something in Swahili, and I had to ask what it meant. "Coward."

"Really?" I twisted to see him better. "Well, don't worry. You can call me that, but I'll believe God and we'll be alive tomorrow."

The driver muttered something under his breath, turned the key, and the engine roared to life. He made a sharp left turn, and in that instant a gigantic male lion walked out of the bush and stood in front of us.

Everyone in the car gasped, then fell silent as realization set in. If they had walked down to the beach area, someone wouldn't have made it back alive. The lion would have been standing between them and the car.

The driver's wife began to tremble and cry. The driver shook his head and murmured, "Oh my."

After the guide had maneuvered the car away, the little boy's mother looked at me and spoke in a hushed whisper: "You saved our lives. There is no way that lion would have sat down and let us pass by."

I didn't answer, but the fact that the lion had popped right out of the bush seemed to imply that he'd been watching and waiting the entire time.

At the time of our visit, Kenya was suffering one of the worst droughts in its history, resulting in a famine that was considered the most critical humanitarian crisis on the planet. Many of the villages we visited depended on crops of maize and vegetables for the people's daily sustenance, but the ground had become unfruitful, dried out, and hard from lack of rain. Grocery items had to be imported and were expensive for the average Kenyan.

Our timing could not have been more perfectly planned. Tiffany and I left Diane and paid the driver to take us to Kitale, where our mission took on a new urgency with Bishop James Wafula Wele and Kenya Christ Gospel Ministries. We delivered food and money to those who ran the orphanage, providing enough relief to feed the children for two months. We also used the bike fund to purchase bicycles for the pastors we'd come to serve. We stayed in the bush and slept in mud huts with no electricity or running water and only an outhouse out back.

I ministered to pastors, some of whom had walked for days to reach our training sessions. Their hunger and thirst for the Word of God inspired me. To be able to bless them with an easier mode of transportation filled my soul with joy. Of course, we distributed the bicycles New York style, calling out the recipient's name with great fanfare: "And now, a bicycle goes to Jonathan Kuala!" The smiling pastor would leap up and run outside to claim his bike with a glee that outmatched most American kids on Christmas morning.

I don't think those pastors could have been more thrilled if we'd given them a Lexus. The bishop explained that they could operate bike taxis in the rural, unpaved areas, so a bicycle was not only a tool for ministry but a tool for business as well.

I preached at two or three churches, and we ministered to people wherever we found them.

The day we prepared to leave, the couple who had hosted us confessed something—they'd been witnessing a miracle during our visit. "We didn't want to say anything," the man said, "because we didn't want to spoil the blessing God was providing."

"Truthfully, we ran out of gas and the money we needed to host you," the wife added. "Our gas can had been empty for three weeks before you arrived, and we get our fire from it. When we decided to host you, we prayed, 'Lord, it's our desire to be hospitable to the man of God. Please provide.' Then in faith, every morning we tried the gas can, and we always had enough to start the fire."

"Not only that," said the husband, "but we had a nearly empty box of Cream of Wheat. That little box fed you, Tiffany, and our family for the entire twenty days you were here."

Upon hearing this, Tiffany and I looked at each other, overwhelmed by the way God had provided for us both back in the States and here in Kenya.

The Christian life was proving to be quite a ride.

*　　*　　*

After months of courtship, I went to see Tiffany's father, Chuck Hinton, to ask if I could marry his daughter. Chuck was a retired Major League Baseball player who'd played with the Washington Senators, the Cleveland Indians, and the California Angels. He was an upstanding man with a great reputation, and I was a little nervous about my errand.

When I asked if I could marry Tiffany, he tilted his head and looked at me. "I know you love her," he said, "but how are you going to take care of her and pay the bills? Love is strong, but financial pressures can put a tremendous strain on a couple and destroy a marriage."

"I'll take care of that, sir," I promised. "Give me a little time, and I promise I'll get a good job."

"All right," he said.

On Christmas Eve, I told both of our families I was going to ask Tiffany to marry me. Then I took her out to eat at one of the top restaurants in DC. In the restaurant, I got out of my chair and knelt on one knee to pop the big question. She said yes, thank the Lord, and I was so happy I announced it to the entire restaurant. We were officially engaged.

Around the same time, I was involved in a huge outreach in New York City. Allan Houston, a player for the New York Knicks, was involved, along with Hezekiah Walker, a gospel singer, and the Newsboys, a Christian rock band. They asked for volunteers who could help with follow-up after the meeting, so I agreed to bring a group to help enter information from the decision cards into a computer so that the organizers could send out letters. Our shift was from three to four, and Youth for Christ (YFC) had the shift after ours.

I called on the young men from the Rites of Passage, and about thirty of them showed up and went to work on data entry. When YFC showed up with six people, Jack Crabtree, executive director of Long Island Youth for Christ, looked around and said, "Where did you get all these sharp kids?"

"They're part of a ministry I help lead called Rites of Passage," I explained.

Jack grinned at me. "Let's have lunch and talk. We need to hire some Youth for Christ workers in the city."

"Great," I answered. "I'm getting married soon, and once I get married, I can't be running overseas doing foreign missions. So serving at YFC would be a great opportunity."

We exchanged numbers, and Jack and I started conversing regularly.

The more we talked, the more I became aware of the fact that, in all the time I spent selling drugs, no one had ever come to witness to me on the block. Now I would drive down the street and see young men who looked just like me hanging out with their friends and hustling to sell drugs. I'd been so hungry back then, but I'd been hungering for the wrong things. I'd wanted to be a street god, but something deep inside me had known all along that I wanted to meet the God of the streets: the God who loved the world so much that he gave his only Son . . .

I now had a burning desire to return to the streets—to let young men on the same dead-end path I'd once walked know that Christ offered the significance and acceptance they craved. I shared my vision with some of the other mentors in Rites of Passage and asked them to join me on a guerrilla evangelism mission to the drug dealers in our area.

I pointed out that most ministries go out to minister early on Saturday mornings, when the streets are at their emptiest and safest. The best time to hit the block, however, was on Friday nights after 10 p.m., when drug sales were booming. "So who wants to go with me?" I asked.

I knew Tiffany was down with the cause. A few others responded, including Kam Howard, an aspiring minister, and Audrey, an awesome evangelist from Allen AME.

At 11 p.m. on a clear Friday night, our team hit the streets for Jesus at 109th Avenue and Guy R. Brewer Boulevard, across from

Abdul's old drug haven. After parking, we spent a few minutes praying and then began pulling out cups, refreshments, and cardboard cartons of hot tea to serve to those gathered on the block. As we set up, I was Daylight again—as alert as ever to the vibe on the street. I certainly didn't want to put my team in jeopardy. What I sensed from the people milling about was curiosity, not hostility. The atmosphere was almost celebratory—just about everyone was dressed up and in a party mood. The sidewalks had filled with people coming out to mingle and talk, and they were caught off guard when one of our team members approached and started talking about Jesus.

Our breath steamed in the chilly air as we offered hot tea. I saw Tiffany talking to a couple out for the night, then I told a young drug dealer that I knew something about him because I used to walk the same blocks and take the same risks. "Some days I was on top," I said, "and other days I was on the bottom. Getting beat, getting threatened, getting robbed—I've been there. But then I met someone who changed my life, and I'd like to tell you about him. He's Jesus, and he knows what you're feelin'."

As soon as we started engaging people, I knew we were doing the right thing. How I wished that a Christian had taken an interest in me when I was eleven or fifteen or twenty and told me to walk with him so that he could show me a better way. A pastor invited me to a church only once—and that was to do a work project for which I was paid. He never shared the gospel with me.

I wasn't surprised when the hustlers told us that no one had ever come out to show them any kind of love during their night shift. We began to share the gospel, and some gave their lives to the Lord right then and there. While we were out on the block, I noticed a drug bust go down. It happened so fast that the other team members didn't even notice. I didn't point it out right then, but I couldn't help thinking about Rikers and what would most likely happen next to that kid.

Some of the dealers tried to hit on my fiancée—truth be told, I didn't blame them. Others couldn't stop talking about how real we were keeping it. They had never seen anything like what we were doing. We stayed out with the hustlers past midnight and then invited them to Allen AME.

At church that Sunday morning, I turned around during the service and saw some of the young men and women I'd talked to on the street. I prayed during the service, asking the Spirit of God to work on their hearts. And then, when the pastor extended an invitation for people to come to Jesus, I felt my eyes fill with tears as some of those young people walked down the aisle in their eagerness to learn more about Jesus. I couldn't help but imagine how much foolishness I could have avoided if someone had cared enough to meet me on the streets years ago.

I was rocked. Knowing that God would show up if we reached out to drug dealers on their turf was a lesson that stayed with me.

Unfortunately, we caught a lot of flak for that outreach. Some well-meaning Christians heard about our unorthodox mission and began to discourage the work. They rebuked us for not thinking about safety first and for putting the women in harm's way. They said we should have gotten permission from the church before embarking on a mission to the streets. I took their concerns to heart and reconsidered the best ways to reach these neighborhoods.

Another obvious place teeming with hustlers was the local jail, so I dove into prison ministry. My mentor, Reverend Leacock, already had a gateway into Rikers Island, in the same section where I had spent most of those fifty-six days after turning myself in. I went to Rikers regularly with Allen AME's prison ministry, preaching in the same chapel I used to visit when I was a prisoner. When I told my testimony to the inmates and shared all the ways in which God had changed my life, dozens of them came to Christ and invited others to come hear my story.

As I searched for missions where I could serve, I made getting into seminary a primary goal. I wanted my doctrine to be solid and my heart to be as prepared as possible for everything God wanted to do in my life. I went to see our new congressman, and he gave me a letter of recommendation that mentioned my trip to Kenya and other ministries in which I'd served. I went to other well-known people and put together an amazing group of reference letters.

I gave the package to Andy Puleo from The Navigators. He went into a meeting of the seminary board, and a little while later he called me. "Dimas," he said, "you are the youngest person this school has ever decided to grandfather into the master's-degree program. Congratulations."

I started attending seminary and loved every minute of it. One day our chapel speaker was Josh McDowell. I didn't know who he was, but I was blown away as he talked about his research into culture, especially when he mentioned that every year his ministry spent over one million dollars on youth research alone.

At the end of his talk, he asked for questions, so I lifted my hand. Kids from the Bloods gang had begun to infiltrate the Rites of Passage groups, and the gang members had a tendency to drive the other kids away. I didn't know how to deal with the problem.

When Josh McDowell called on me, I stood. "I'm dealing with a gang problem in Queens, so can you tell me what your research says about the gangs? They're starting to affect my youth ministry."

After a minute, he answered: "You know, out of all the money we spend each year, we haven't spent anything so far on understanding gang culture. I'm going to give you the number of Fred Lynch, who works with me, and you can call him. We'll see what we can do."

At the end of the chapel session, an older woman pulled me aside. "I'm the chaplain of The Children's Village," she said, "and we're looking for an associate chaplain—I think you should apply for the job. It'd be a great thing for you, and you'd get to preach every Sunday."

I smiled and took her card. "Thank you," I said. "This job probably isn't for me, but I have a friend I'll tell about it. Maybe he should apply."

When I caught up with Tiffany and told her what the woman had said, Tiffany said, "No, that job *is* for you! That's God speaking to you."

"Fine," I told her. "I'll go check it out."

I learned that New York's The Children's Village, founded in 1851, serves approximately ten thousand children and families each year. With a staff of over eight hundred, the organization provides housing, education, foster and adoption services, and day care in order to supply the nurture and love that children need.

So I went to The Children's Village and met the woman who'd spoken to me. "Our chapel is being repaired," she said, leading me toward a little house. "So we'll go to twenty-two different cottages, and you'll preach in each of them."

Preach twenty-two times?

I decided to go for it, so I went into the first cottage and preached a sermon. Then I went into the next and preached a different sermon. I did a couple of repeats, but basically I preached twenty different sermons that day.

"My goodness!" the woman said. "You have a gift! And those kids couldn't take their eyes off you. You really have something."

I smiled, remembering the day Reverend Newton had told me I had the gift of charisma. Maybe he had been right.

"I'm ready to hire you on the spot," the woman said.

"Thank you," I told her, "but I'm going to be married soon, so I'll have to be gone for a while."

"That's no problem. But as far as I'm concerned, you're hired."

Not long after that, Jack Crabtree called and asked me to come in to talk with him. He told me that Youth for Christ was considering me for a part-time position. Because they vetted their staff through all kinds of assessments, he also asked me to take a personality test.

When we met, Jack asked what I wanted to do, and I told him my primary mission was evangelism. In my pre-Christ days I had wanted to be the top dog in the neighborhood, and now I wanted kids to know that Jesus was the top dog. I had turned all my ambition and drive toward evangelism, winning kids who were as confused and lost as I'd been. I was pleased when Youth for Christ offered me the part-time position.

After they had hired me, I started doing figures in my head. Tiffany's father wanted me to be able to support his daughter, and with the income from The Children's Village and from YFC, I was well on my way.

Then Fred Lynch, assistant to Josh McDowell, called and asked whether Tiffany and I could come into the city and meet with Josh. When we arrived at the meeting, Josh invited us to sit down.

"Tell me anywhere in the world you'd like to go for your honeymoon," he said.

I looked at Tiffany and grinned. He had no idea what he was asking—Tiffany had been hinting that she'd like to honeymoon in a romantic tree house in Bali. Since she came from a well-to-do family, there were no limits on Tiffany's ideas. I love that about her.

"Let me tell you what I can offer," Josh said. "I have a house in Colorado that I'd like to offer you for your honeymoon. I can fly you out there with my frequent-flyer miles, since I have more than I can use."

Wow. Tiffany and I looked at each other, then I said, "That's really nice. Thank you."

"After a week, I'll fly you guys back to wherever you want in the States and you can continue your honeymoon there, if you'd like."

What could we say? We thanked him again and thanked God for his provision.

As our wedding date approached, I got a call from the Salvation

Army—they were looking for a chaplain who could work the night shift at the Wayside School for Girls. I accepted that position as well.

I met with Tiffany's father again. "Sir," I said, "you told me I had to have a job before I could marry your daughter. Over this last month, I've gotten three jobs." After telling him my combined income, I added, "I think I've done pretty well."

"Yes, you have." Mr. Hinton stood and gave me a big hug. "Let's do the wedding, and welcome to the family."

Tiffany and I got married at the Newton White Mansion in Maryland, a gorgeous neo-Georgian brick house on a huge estate. After the wedding, we flew to Colorado as guests of Josh McDowell and stayed in his mountain home. We had the time of our lives driving around, looking at the mountains, and enjoying the area. Then we flew to Miami where we could soak up the sun and play in the sand at South Beach.

On the morning of September 11, 2001—ten days into our honeymoon—we were in the hotel's fitness room, working out and thinking about our trip to Jamaica later that afternoon. The TV was on with the sound muted, and we saw pictures of the World Trade Center with smoke around it. "This must be a report on that basement bombing at the Trade Center," Tiffany said, referring to the 1993 truck bombing at the North Tower. "But it doesn't look right."

While we watched the TV screen, we saw the second jet hit the second tower in real time. Both of us screamed, and we hurried upstairs as quickly as we could. Like most Americans, we were in a state of horrified shock. We turned on the TV in our room and stayed glued to the set for the entire day. We tried to call New York but couldn't get through; then, as we stared in terror, we heard that another plane had hit the Pentagon—and that was close to Tiffany's family in DC. Tiffany reached her parents and reported to them everything that was going on. She urged them to leave DC and get to safety at her sister's home in Maryland. Sadly, we later learned that one of the mentors from Rites of Passage was killed in the World Trade Center attacks.

That afternoon, we heard that the terrorists who had flown the planes were Muslims trained in flight schools in southern Florida—not far from where we were honeymooning. Like most Americans in those days, we were tense and alert, anxious for our nation and questioning everything we saw.

The terrorist attack pretty much ended our honeymoon plans because the FAA shut down all flights nationwide. We went home as soon as we were able to travel again.

*   *   *

Once we were back from our honeymoon, I told Tiffany we needed to find a place to plant a church. After that, we'd find a permanent place to live. Brooklyn was out of the question for me. Tiffany didn't want to live in Queens or Harlem, and the best sublet we found was in the Bronx. I had no intention of planting a church in the Bronx, but by God's guidance we found ourselves living there. So we began to learn about the area. The more I learned about it—the more I saw its needs and its people—the more my heart warmed to the idea of planting a ministry there.

Shortly after we were married, I learned about Redeemer City to City, a church-planting effort directed by Dr. Tim Keller. He brought Tiffany and me, along with several other couples, to a church-planting assessment weekend. It was like a boot camp for would-be church planters, and the goal was for the supervisors to see who was best suited for the actual work of church planting. Lots of people dream about starting a church, but few have the commitment and skill set to see it through.

Tiffany and I were excited to attend. We were the only African American couple at the session. Another couple was Hispanic; the other eight couples were white. The supervisors were Presbyterians, and I had never spent much time around Presbyterians. I was Reformed in faith but still trying to figure out the Presbyterian world.

Our weekend was a little like the TV show *The Apprentice*. They threw us prospects into a group and watched how we responded to various challenges. "All right," the leader said to us. "There are twenty of you. Let's say you are starting a church together and you need to choose two leaders. Who will it be?"

We heard the challenge and looked at each other. We all were there to be leaders, so how would we narrow it to two? I knew the directors would be watching to see what tactics we used, what politics we employed, and exactly how we went about taking leadership in this group.

We all discussed a few options, and then I spoke up. Since we were meeting in New York, I said, "I'm from New York; I was born and raised here. If this church is to be planted in New York City for New Yorkers, then I could give the best direction." That's how I became one of the two leaders.

The directors then divided us into two groups, and we were asked to complete exercises related to a church plant. We were supposed to put together a budget for our first year: How would we get funding? What tools would we use? How much would it cost to rent a building? To house our families? What kind of people would we need to meet in order to raise the funds we'd need?

They gave that exercise at the end of the first day, and we were supposed to work on it overnight. As we split up, several in my group mentioned that they were going to meet for drinks at the bar. Tiffany and I were stunned—in the culture from which we'd come, Christians did not smoke or drink.

"Tiffany," I told her, "this is our moment. Let's research everything we can so we'll be prepared in the morning."

The next morning, some of those prospective couples walked in with bleary eyes, evidently suffering the effects of a late night out.

The supervisors took one look and promptly took them to the woodshed for their behavior. "Are you taking this seriously?" they asked. "How in the world can you come to a church-planting seminar and then go to a bar?"

When they had finished, I lifted my hand. "My wife and I didn't do that. We're here to work, and we're ready to present."

Everyone else nodded their assent, so we presented our budget to rave reviews.

After that, every man had to preach for ten minutes so the directors could hear and evaluate him. I preached on the qualifications of a pastor according to Titus 1. When I got to the seventh verse—"For a bishop must be blameless, as a steward of God, not self-willed, not quick-tempered, not given to wine"—the directors burst out laughing.

At the end of it all, the overseeing committee told us that we'd passed with flying colors. "We want to get behind you and help you start a church." Tiffany and I were thrilled to have their endorsement and support. Pastor Tim Keller would train me and guide my preaching; plus, they would give us a monthly stipend for living expenses.

I began to wrestle with ideas about *where* to plant a church. The church-planting ministry would help finance our young church for three years; after that, the church would be on its own.

Tim Keller and Terry Gyger, executive director of the Redeemer Church Planting Center, set up a meeting to hear about where I wanted to plant a church and to discuss my joining the Presbyterian Church of America. I was considering joining the PCA, but I had issues with baptizing babies. When I weighed the pros and cons, I decided to plant a church with the DNA of Redeemer Presbyterian Church contextualized into my community. In other words, the church would resemble the Presbyterian Church theologically, but socially it would reflect the makeup and mores of its community.

I was nervous about presenting my ideas to Tim Keller, but I knew I had to be up-front and honest. So I began to pray, and God used two situations to help me crystallize my vision. First, although a relatively small percentage of New York City's residents live in housing projects, a disproportionate percentage of the crime happens there.[1] Second, the Lord reminded me that T. D. Jakes once said that if a pastor really wants to have an impact, he should start a church in the projects. Tiffany and I discussed the idea of starting a church in one of these neighborhoods, and she agreed we could help a lot of people by going there.

Finally, the meeting day arrived. I took a slow Manhattan elevator at 271 Madison Avenue, and when the door opened, Terry's executive assistant soothed my fears. "Tim and Terry are super excited about this meeting," she said.

The two men sat in a small room, but they both got up and gave me a good Christian hug before asking the big question: "Where do you want to plant your church?"

My throat tightened as I looked at Tim. "I want to serve the poor in a project in the Bronx."

Tim smiled. "That's a demographic we're not touching right now." After a moment, he added, "It'll be a different model. You may need more support longer, but God would bless a church serving the poor."

We talked and laughed, and then Tim promised to help. I left the meeting feeling happy that I could return to the streets where I'd spent so much time in my younger days. I would not go empty-handed, however—I'd be bringing Jesus with me and introducing him to thugs, potential thieves, and drug dealers. With Jesus by my side, I could walk the same path I walked as a kid, but this time I'd be walking in the right direction.

Tiffany and I began to drive throughout the Bronx looking for an apartment and a place to plant a church. We were looking in an area of the Bronx called Marble Hill.

A realtor called one night at about ten. "I know it's late," she said, "but if you want to see this apartment, you should come now." So we went out and drove over there, and by the time we'd finished walking through the apartment, it was eleven o'clock. We stepped outside and couldn't believe our eyes. There were little kids—three, four, five years old—all over the street. I felt like a shepherd staring at a flock of lost lambs.

"We *have* to plant a church in this area," I told Tiffany. "How can these kids be running around outside at eleven?"

We took that last apartment. The people at Redeemer said, "Let us know when you want to start church meetings." We told them we'd be ready in three or four months.

We went to the community center to see if we could meet there. In New York, where slivers of real estate sell for millions, it's a viable option for a lot of churches. A private home is too small and commercial real estate too expensive. Schools and community centers, however, are located in the heart of residential neighborhoods, and for most people, they are only a short walk away.

When we first approached the Fort Independence Community Center, the director, Mrs. Venda, told us we couldn't meet there because of a pending court case. The Bronx Household of Faith, an inner-city church, had asked permission to rent a school for its Sunday meetings but had been denied by the New York City Board of Education. This led to a legal battle that began in 1995. The woman who ran the community center didn't want to rent to any church until the Bronx church's case had been settled.

The news was an unexpected blow, but we didn't give up. If God had closed a door, he was sure to open a window.

Redeemer Presbyterian, Tim Keller's church, announced that Dimas Salaberrios was about to start a church in the Bronx. They said that if anyone lived or worked in the Bronx, they should consider joining our church and tithing into it. Then they invited anyone who wanted to help with the Bronx church plant to attend our organizational meeting.

I was shocked. I had never heard a church express a vision so magnanimous and Kingdom minded. To willingly invite congregants to stop giving to their church and direct them to give to another—I'd never imagined anything so generous.

To let churchgoers know about our first organizational meeting, Tiffany and I printed up "Join the Journey" signs and sprinkled them throughout the church building. About thirty people showed up. We had subsequent meetings at our apartment.

One of our first ideas was a way to get to know the community. "Let's go out on the street and take surveys," we said. "We'll hand out the *Jesus* movie on DVD; we'll ask about church names; we'll survey those folks about every topic we can think of."

We did just that. Armed with surveys and pens, we went into the neighborhood and sought people wherever we could find them. We asked whether they preferred the name Oxygen or Infinity. We asked whether they wanted to meet on Saturday or Sunday. We asked what color scheme they liked best. We went out to meet everyone—the poor, the middle-class, and the suffering. After we came back and tabulated the results of our survey, our team dropped from twenty-two members to seven. I guess some folks were just too discouraged by what they learned about the Marble Hill/Kingsbridge area.

But the seven people who remained were filled with faith. In that small group we had a chief surgeon, a nurse, a social worker, a youth worker, a teacher, Tiffany, and me.

Our group might have been small, but we were dedicated. We met every Monday and kept plowing toward the vision. I returned to the community center to check on its availability and learned that a federal judge had ruled that the city couldn't prohibit Bronx Household of Faith and other churches from holding services in public buildings.[2] That meant we could meet in the community center.

I was still in seminary and hadn't yet been fully ordained, so Redeemer Presbyterian and Bethel Gospel Assembly, a church led by Reverend Carlton Brown, came together and did a joint ordination. They knew the call of God on my life; they believed in me and propelled me forward. Finally I was a full-fledged pastor, able to do weddings and funerals.

We were ready for our first service. Church planting experts had advised us not to hold meetings until we had commitments from forty people, but we'd gotten that many verbal commitments from people on the street.

We launched our first church service at the Fort Independence Community Center on October 12, 2003. We had only thirty people in attendance on our first day, and we met on Saturdays because our surveys had indicated that Saturday would be a good time to meet.

Saturday meetings proved to be a recipe for disaster, however. The idea of basing our church on a survey seemed good but proved foolish in reality. Even so, our church grew to about sixty people. We may not have looked impressive to the world, but we moved forward confidently, knowing that the power of God would more than make up for our weaknesses.

CHAPTER SIXTEEN

THE CHALLENGES WE FACED as a new church plant were different from those of most new churches. For instance, I was glad when about twenty gang members from the Crips started coming to church. As happy as I was to reach them, however, they created a huge problem because they hated outsiders. If you want to grow a youth group, you can't have one group chasing away all the others.

Our efforts to help the poor by giving them jobs, although an admirable idea on paper, also didn't work as we'd hoped. Following the City to City model of church growth through community outreach, we spent $100,000 in renovations at the housing project. We manicured the projects, bought a sound system for the community center, and paid young people to come work for us. Redeemer paid some employees and we paid some. The problem was that people were coming for the fish and loaves but not coming for Jesus.

Perhaps our biggest difficulty was getting permission to meet regularly at the community center. We were trying to teach and preach, but Mrs. Venda, the director, tried to shut down every special event we held.

"Can we have a Bible study?"

"No, you can't do that."

It was hard to get a rhythm when we couldn't establish regular meetings at the center. We did one event where about two hundred kids came. We were supposed to have a discipleship meeting with them the next day, but when they showed up, Mrs. Venda had hung a "Center Closed" sign on the door. We'd have success with one event, followed by a colossal failure with the next. We'd have eighty people one week and very few the next.

As a result, we had something that looked like a church, but it really wasn't one. Still, I didn't get discouraged. I'd just say, "This is tough ground, but we'll do our best no matter what." Then I'd pray about it.

About that time a drug dealer called South returned to the hood. God laid it on my heart to boldly witness to him.

"You cannot come back into this community the same way," I told him. "You've got to change. Forget about these streets, man; this is not going to lead to anything good. Give your life to Jesus!"

South smiled at me with his gold teeth. "I'm good, pastor," he said, laughing as he walked away.

The next day when I arrived at Fort Independence, I found everyone huddled together. When I asked what was up, they told me South had been murdered the night before.

Freddy, a teenager who had seen and heard my talk with South, told the others, "Pastor offered him Jesus just yesterday, hours before he got taken out, but South thought it was a joke and turned him down."

Freddy was one of the toughest guys in the community, with a reputation for violence. I had witnessed to him before and had gotten nowhere.

But the day after South's death, I pulled Freddy aside and shared the gospel with him again. This time, Freddy accepted Christ on the spot.

We had about ten young drug dealers in the church. One of them, a kid who looked about sixteen, was always acting out about something. He'd go up on the stage after worship and start banging on the drum, *bang, bang, bang!* He'd mess everything up, and I found myself wondering what was wrong with the kid. He drove me crazy.

At the end of every service, we'd bring in pizzas. Then I'd sit with the kids and minister to them—talk to them, tell them to stop doing the destructive things they were doing, and so on. Around that time, two brothers who were both drug dealers asked me to come see them because their mother had died. So I visited and prayed for them.

The next day the police conducted a big drug raid, and almost half the guys coming to my church got locked up. One of the few who still hung around was the kid who always drove me crazy.

After the raid, while I was feeling morose because half of my youth group was in jail, that kid came over. "Hey, I need to talk to you."

He acted like he wanted to talk privately, so I got up and went with him.

"First of all," he said, his voice dropping an octave, "I want to say I'm sorry."

"For what?"

"For the hard time I gave you."

I shrugged. "Don't worry about it."

"No, I want you to understand. You're doing a great job here, and I've seen a total transformation in your life and in the lives of these kids."

I stared as his words piled on top of one another. Nothing he said made sense. And why was he talking in a deeper voice?

Then the kid reached in his pocket and pulled out a badge. A police badge. He was an undercover cop, and I was being watched by the feds.

My jaw dropped as understanding dawned. I had a church filled with Crips and drug dealers. I was a former drug dealer and drug boss myself. The feds had to be wondering whether I was dealing under the table and the church was nothing but a front.

I lifted a brow and smiled at the mature, focused young man who now appeared to be twenty-seven or twenty-eight. "I get it."

He lifted one shoulder in a shrug. "You are truly a changed man. I gotta go work on another case now, but I couldn't leave this one without letting you know what was going on."

*   *   *

World missions came calling again. This time, my wife and I traveled back to Kenya with an awesome team from our church: Tara and Laura, both of them sold-out white women, and Frank, a young African American man. En route to Kenya, we had a long layover in Amsterdam.

Tiffany and I had been to Amsterdam a couple of times, so we were delighted to leave the airport with our team and head to a few of our favorite places. While eating at a pancake house in Leidseplein Square, I felt the nudging of the Lord to go out and preach. I shrugged off the feeling because I was enjoying a meal with my friends, but then I felt the nudge again: *Go out and preach.*

Again I ignored the feeling. When I felt it a third time, I knew I couldn't shake it off, so I told my team what was going on. The ladies wanted to fit in a little shopping, so they told Frank and me they'd catch up with us at the market in a few minutes.

Frank and I set off for the center of busy Leidseplein Square.

The scene looked like something I had read about in the New Testament—several weird shopkeepers were calling out to passersby and selling all kinds of New Age and occult items. I took one glance at Frank and asked if he was ready.

"I'm ready," he said. "Let's do it."

When I started to preach, people started to walk away from the shopkeepers, and crowds swarmed around me. The more I preached, the bigger the crowd grew. Then one of the shopkeepers cut through the crowd and blew an odd bird whistle three times in my face.

Frank and I looked at each other. *What in the world was that about?* Then I kept preaching.

A guitar singer came along next. Singing "Fa la la laaaaaa," he stood right in front of me and did his thing. I could tell he was annoyed that his crowd had abandoned him to go hear the gospel. Undeterred, I kept preaching.

Then out of the corner of my eye, I saw a crazed man roaring and moving straight toward me. The crowd backed away from him as he came forward, and no one stopped him as he jumped onto my back, dug his nails into my neck, and ripped at my skin. I ducked underneath him, situated him on my shoulders, and held on to him like a sack of potatoes, never skipping a beat as I delivered the Word of God. Tiffany and the other ladies returned to the square to find me penned in by a crazy man and a folksinger.

Cameras and cell phones flashed as onlookers gawked at the sight. I lowered the raving man to the ground and kept preaching. Frank grabbed the guy by his collar, but I gestured to Frank: *Let him go.* I kept preaching and ended by praying for people and inviting them to come to Christ.

After the crowd began to thin, a young man came up and said he'd been struggling with his faith, but after seeing my gentle response to the forces determined to stop the preaching of the gospel, he now knew he could follow Jesus all the way. He rededicated his life to Christ right then.

Tiffany examined my neck where the crazed man had clawed me and treated the bleeding wound with alcohol and Band-Aids. We all climbed into a cab to head back to the airport. As I watched the streets of Amsterdam pass by the cab window, an overwhelming sense of joy came over me. Just as the apostles rejoiced because they had been counted worthy of suffering disgrace for the name of Jesus, I rejoiced that I'd been able to keep preaching in the face of opposition.

We teamed up with some other missionaries from Mission to the World and ministered in the Kibera slums of Nairobi, the largest urban slum in all of Africa. When we completed that mission, we looked forward to reconnecting with our pastor friends in Kitale from Kenya Christ Gospel Ministries, including Bishop James Wafula Wele.

En route to Kitale, our van broke down on the highway. We told Tara and Laura to crouch down in the van since being white in that area was not particularly safe at that time. Bishop Wele's son, Pastor Simon, kept shaking his head. "This is not good. This road is known for thieves and robbers."

Not good at all. In that part of the world, we looked like a bank on wheels.

We began to pray, and a truck pulled over shortly thereafter.

Two men got out, spoke to our driver, and asked us if we had a rope. I gave them the only thing I could find—a bungee cord I'd been using on our luggage.

Those two men hooked that little bungee cord to the fender of the truck and the front bumper of our van. We sat silent, not daring to hope the cord would hold, and were stunned when the van began to move. As we worshiped and prayed, those men towed us for twenty minutes, taking us safely to the next town.

And the cord didn't snap.

We piled out of the van to thank them, but the men and their truck had vanished. To leave without saying good-bye or giving us an opportunity to pay for their service was extremely unusual in Africa.

We believe that the Lord sent angels to help in our time of need.

*　　*　　*

I wish I could say that our church found its footing and began to flourish, but it didn't. Although I knew we'd chosen a tough area to launch a church, I also realized I had to accept some of the responsibility for our difficulties. I hadn't heeded all the counsel we'd been given from veteran church planters, such as waiting to launch until we had a solid core of forty people. When things hit bottom after about a year and a half, I met with our leaders and told them we had invested a lot into the area but had little fruit to show for it. It was time to give serious thought to our next step.

Then Desmond came around. I had gone to seminary with him, and he was eager to help. "We should fast and pray about what location we should be in," he said. "We should do a forty-day fast."

"Are you out of your mind?" I laughed. "These people are Presbyterians—they've never fasted a day in their lives."

He grinned. "I know, but it could happen."

I blew out a breath and shook my head. "I'll do it, but I want you to rally them to do this thing."

Desmond started to work on every leader. "It's going to be great," he promised. "God does great things when his people fast and pray."

That man could sell ice to an Eskimo. He started teaching everyone about how awesome a fast could be, and all of my major leaders bought into it. The majority of us chose to do liquid fasts, but two people ate only fruits and vegetables, while the surgeon chose to fast from coffee.

At the end of the forty-day fast, we met together again. "What do we feel God is saying to us?" I asked, and every one of us felt that we were supposed to move.

So I spoke to the church and told them we would be changing locations. "If you want this church to remain here," I said, "come on Wednesday night and let's talk."

That Wednesday night, only six little girls showed up. I promised them they could come no matter where we moved the church. Then I announced that the next Sunday would be our last in Fort Independence.

A few years later, I received a call from someone in Mrs. Venda's family. Mrs. Venda was dying but wanted to speak to me before she passed away.

When I went to the hospice to pray with her, she caught my hand. "I wanted to tell you I'm sorry," she said.

"Sorry for what?"

"For how I worked against you." Her faded eyes never left my face. "I worked the community against you and your ministry so they wouldn't come back out. I'm so sorry, but I wanted to tell you the reason was because of me. Forgive me, please. I want to make things right before I die."

I forgave her, and then I squeezed her hand and prayed for her.

*   *   *

My team and I looked for places to move our church. We went to the city housing authority to see what community centers were available, and they told us about two places. We tested the first location by holding a gospel hip-hop event there. Once again, the community center director wasn't interested in working with us. Then it snowed all day on the day of the event, which put a damper on it. Afterward, we leaders looked at one another and said, "This ain't the place."

One spot remained—Bronx River. We met the community center

director, a woman named Becky who said we could hold an event but couldn't pray or have an altar call. "Fine," we said, "but can we do counseling?"

"Counsel all you want. We had a teenager murdered here just last week."

So we held a gospel hip-hop service at Bronx River, and over four hundred teenagers showed up. After the service, I took the microphone and said, "If you want to be counseled, follow me as I leave the stage. We want to talk to you about what you just heard."

Sixty-six people followed me off the stage, and we spent a great deal of time counseling those kids. We told them to return on Wednesday for pizza and juice.

Since I'd been doing ministry for years by that point, I would have been happy if ten kids had shown up on Wednesday. But out of those sixty-six, sixty-three came back. We started a Bible study, and every week we had more than sixty kids studying the Word. We did another outreach event, and again nearly four hundred kids came. We did a third event, and yet another four hundred came.

We started a weekly 5:30 a.m. men's prayer meeting. We prayed against homicides and shootings in the area and asked God to shut all that evil down. We'd meet early and pray, but as the weather grew colder and the men bundled up, some of them began to fall asleep during the meeting. Finally one of my leaders said, "Why don't we just walk? You can't fall asleep if you're walking."

That prayer walk is still going strong. Men from other churches have joined us, and additional prayer walks have been established in other parts of the city.

We were seeing amazing results, but we didn't want to start the church until the people were ready for it. When the Bible study had grown to 120 kids and 4 adults, Becky caught me. "I heard y'all used to have a church," she said. "Why don't you open your church here?"

Bingo.

Our church held its first service at Bronx River on November 13, 2006, and everyone invited their mamas, cousins, sisters, and friends. Over two hundred people showed up. The next Sunday we dropped down to half that—but hey, that was a lot better than thirty.

Bronx River is the birthplace of hip-hop. Though Bronx River had had a strong gang presence for decades, it had also been influenced by the Universal Zulu Nation, which was founded by former gang leader Afrika Bambaataa as a music-centered youth organization. Still, though the names of the gangs change with the generations, the popular ones always seem to find a way into Bronx River. People involved with drugs—producers, buyers, sellers, and users—are rampant there as well. When we launched our church in the area, we regularly saw drug addicts, prostitutes, and dealers fighting over drugs and money.

We went into Bronx River armed with strong strategies of prayer and evangelism. We started a conference-call prayer line that operated Monday through Friday. We determined to share Jesus with the lost wherever we found them.

I'd walk up to drug dealers in the area, shake their hands, and introduce myself as their pastor. Many would remark that they didn't go to my church. I'd tell them that God had led me to their area; therefore, I was their pastor by default.

Whenever I was told about someone from Bronx River being arrested, I'd find out their given name (as opposed to their street name) and visit them in jail. Many of those guys showed up at the jail's visiting area completely shocked to see that I was visiting them. I'd ask them how it was going and whether their friends were showing up to help them out. Most replied that not one of their friends had come by.

"The reason I'm here is that God has called me to be your pastor and be here for you," I'd say. Then I'd share my testimony, and many of them would pray the prayer of salvation. Others began to trust me, and our bond remained when they went back into the community upon their release.

After a few months, I'd walk through the community spots where people congregated to deal and drink and curse, and I'd hear people saying, "Yo, shut up and put that blunt out, man. My pastor is coming." Then they'd stop and talk to me about what was going on in their lives.

I always kept an ear to the ground so I would know which neighborhood kids were aspiring drug bosses. Those people became the focus of my attention. Even when they didn't outwardly convert, most of them began to exhibit a consciousness of God that had not been present before. Violence began to decrease in the community. People began to solve their problems with words rather than fists, and we were beginning to see kids walk away from issues that could have spiraled out of control. I would often show up in the middle of the fray and play peacemaker, asking many a heated dude to walk away with me.

A new culture took root. No longer did conflicts have to end in a war; beefs could be settled by words and an invitation from a believer to make peace.

Our prayer focus shifted. We began to pray for a drug famine to overtake our community. During a prayer walk, Reverend Al Taylor, pastor of Infinity Mennonite Church in Harlem, went into a bodega where drug paraphernalia was sold, bought a large bottle of Crisco oil (sometimes you have to use what's in front of you), and poured it on the sidewalk in the shape of a large cross.

"Lord, shut this drug operation down," we prayed.

The following week on our prayer walk, we saw thirty identical black cars parked in the middle of the street, surrounding the perimeter of the projects. Then we saw federal agents with stacks of pictures in their hands. They'd glance at us, then look at the photos. Other guys were running around trying to escape the blockade. Drug paraphernalia rained from the buildings as people dumped evidence out of their windows, and both men and women were being dragged into what turned out to be black unmarked police cars.

Shocked by the scene we were witnessing, we kept praying. We had an idea of what was going on but didn't know for certain.

Later that day, I saw Becky. "Pastor Dimas, did you hear what happened?"

"Well, earlier I saw a bunch of black cars and people getting arrested."

"Every drug dealer was arrested. Do you hear what I'm saying? *Every* drug dealer except for one who got away only because he wasn't home at the time. They confiscated his car, and now he's on the run. It was a major bust."

I blew out a breath. "Yeah, I figured it was the cops."

"That wasn't just the cops," she said. "That was the feds!"

I later learned that seven drug dealers remained at large, but the people of our neighborhood wholeheartedly celebrated the cleanup. The projects were swept clean, and the church started to grow even more. Some of the people whose loved ones had been caught in the raid wanted to change, so they started coming to church.

Once a place is cleaned up, though, evil tries to sneak back in. Gangs—particularly the Bloods and the Crips—are a potent and virulent force in our community. Because I can't spend time with every dangerous person in our community, I've made it my strategy to target some of the gang leaders—the heads, not the feet. Occasionally, I have no choice but to act. Not too long ago, a young man named Chipper called a meeting with dozens of young guys in the neighborhood and formed an affiliate of a major gang, crowning himself the OG, or head. He then announced that he'd better not find any of those guys attending my church's Bible study.

The following week, attendance at our Bible study dropped by a whopping 40 percent. When I asked the guys what was going on, no one wanted to say anything. One of them finally told me that Chipper had threatened them with serious repercussions if they came to the study, so that's why a lot of the guys weren't coming anymore.

"Forget that," he added, smiling at me.

I had to admire his courage.

Chipper set out to make an example of one of the young guys who violated his edict about continuing to attend Bible study. Chipper targeted him and told his gang members to attack whenever they saw him.

I found out about the situation when the young man's mother called to inform me that she'd had to relocate her son because he was coming to our Bible study. I couldn't believe a gang had issued threats over church attendance and was persecuting people for their faith. That was flat-out demonic.

I told Tiffany about it and she said, "You have to do something."

"Trust me." I nodded. "I am."

We sent out an e-mail blast asking people to pray. The next time I saw Chipper, I was going to take him on.

When I pulled up to the community center not long after, I saw two girls from our Bible study standing on the sidewalk. Chipper rolled up to them on his bike and snatched off one of the girl's glasses. Then his girlfriend joined him and they bullied those two girls.

I felt my blood boil. "Yo, Chipper. Come over here, man!" I called.

He came, swaggering over as if he didn't have a care in the world. For an instant I was taken back to my own street days, when I had swaggered and strutted as if I were the god of the street. This kid reminded me of me.

"May I see those glasses?" I asked.

He gave them to me and then tipped his head back as he waited to see what I'd do next.

I held them out to the girl who owned them, but she refused to take them back. Clearly, she was terrified of what Chipper might do once I was gone.

Chipper grinned. "See that? She don't want 'em."

I decided to cut to the chase. "I hear you ran somebody out of the community because they came to my Bible study. You think you're running people out of the church? Naw, that can't be going down like that."

Have you ever noticed that when some people feel cornered, they get loud? That's what Chipper tried. "What?" he barked, his voice making the two girls flinch.

I got loud right along with him. "You heard what I said. Anybody that wants to come to our church or Bible study, we've got their back. We ain't having you tell them they can't come!"

A crowd began to zero in on our standoff, and I could see people coming closer. Chipper had to see them too.

"Whatever," he said. Then he signaled some of his guys and rode off.

I continued into the center. Angry and slightly embarrassed, I wondered if I had leaned too much on my old Daylight tactics. I decided to calm down and spend some time praying, so I went home.

The next day when I saw Chipper, he rode up to me on his pedal bike and said, "Yo, that dude is all right. He can come back. Ain't nothing gonna happen to him. And I want to tell you something—I'm a Christian too, Pastor." Then he rode off.

A Christian? Naw, what he was was *confused*.

I began to build a relationship with Chipper. I shared the gospel with him, took him out to eat, and spent time getting to know his story. I realized that he was a kid who had been raised with a lot of pain. He prayed the prayer of salvation with me, but I never saw him become a disciple.

After every church service, a group of guys would come to the gym to play basketball. One of them had tattoos all over his arms and neck, so we called him Tattoo. Tattoo was funny, full of charm, and in his midtwenties. He reminded me of myself at that age.

One day another guy laughed at Tattoo, and we saw another side of him. His smile vanished as he spun around and invited the guy to fight. A dark persona seemed to overtake him, one that thirsted for violence, and I identified with that, too. I stepped in to intervene, but through that episode I realized that Tattoo was a ranking member of a New York drug gang.

A guy who helped out at our church told us that Tattoo was a very dangerous dude. So I made it my business to get to know the young man. I knew that if not for the grace of God, I might have been just like Tattoo.

A couple of weeks later, Tattoo got caught up in a bad situation and was arrested, so I went to see him in jail. This time I traveled across that Rikers Island bridge as a visitor, occupying a seat on a bus filled with young pregnant girls. I couldn't help wondering if Satan had worked out a plan to send fathers to jail so they couldn't help their kids.

When I finally made it through all the searches and security checks, I felt like an inmate as well. Many of the COs treated visitors badly, which filled my heart with sorrow. As I watched the COs' rudeness to inmates' family members, I couldn't help but think of my gentle mother, who'd been forced to endure the same process when she came to visit me. I marveled again at her love—she had borne so much humiliation on my account.

I sat in an old blue chair next to the other visitors and saw several women checking me out because they were eager for a fairly decent-looking man to replace their jailed boyfriends and babies' daddies.

Finally, the COs called my name, and I went in to see Tattoo. He looked both shocked and happy to see me. A childlike smile lit his face but vanished when other inmates walked by.

To my surprise, he told people I was his pastor—almost as if he were bragging that a father figure cared enough to visit him. I caught him up on his friends' activities and told him about Jesus. He wanted prayer, and I took comfort in the truth that seeds had been sown in his heart.

A few minutes later an inmate came on the visiting floor and lifted his hand in a sign that was a huge insult to all the members of another gang on the floor—and Tattoo was the highest-ranking member of that gang. He was ready to defend his gang's honor, but he hesitated because I was sitting across from him.

In that moment I realized the power a Christian wields by simply showing up. Who knew what might have happened had I not been sitting there?

Before leaving, I told Tattoo that I had put money into his account and bought him a sweat suit. He was as overjoyed as a kid on Christmas morning. He gave me a huge hug, like a son hugging his father. Then he quickly released me and looked away, hiding his emotions. He mentioned how much he appreciated my efforts and said he'd be home soon.

When Tattoo got out of jail, my rep in Bronx River skyrocketed. People who had once greeted me with mere cordiality began to demonstrate affection and love. Tattoo called dudes into order when I was around because everyone respected Tattoo. Young dudes told me he had massive respect throughout the borough.

My friendship with Tattoo opened doors throughout the hood, and God used him to give me credibility among official gangsters. I learned that going the extra mile for someone often results in unexpected benefits. Teenagers and tough guys started showing up at our services, and some became regular church attenders.

Neighborhood alcoholics began to come to the church. Prostitutes turned their lives around so dramatically that no one would guess their history unless they shared it. Guys came home from prison and got plugged into the ministry. Fathers reunited with their families, and marriages—nearly extinct in the hood—were not only taking place but thriving and lasting. Real life transformation took place.

One Sunday morning, we baptized five young men. We set up our baptismal pool in the center aisle and performed the baptisms in the middle of our service. It was heartwarming, as usual.

During the sermon, I taught on the connection between salvation and the instant response to be baptized. I referred to the Ethiopian eunuch who was converted and immediately got baptized; to Pentecost, when people converted and were baptized; and to the Philippian jailer who converted and was baptized right away. I didn't teach it with the intention of performing immediate baptisms, but I was trying to point out a distinction between the early and the present-day church.

Rhetorically, I said, "Somebody could get baptized right now."

Without warning, a young lady stood up and started to remove her belt and jewelry. "Well, all right," she said, stepping out into the aisle. "Let's do it."

I blinked in surprise but recovered quickly. "Okay, let's do it."

In no time, at least a dozen other people stood up and came down the aisle, all of them eager to be baptized on the spot. Before baptizing them, I asked each of them whether they had committed their lives to Jesus Christ, whether they were ready to abandon their life of sin, and whether they were willing to make Jesus Lord and King over their entire lives. As they agreed, they stepped into the baptismal pool in their church clothes—some in jeans, sneakers, and T-shirts; others in their suits and dresses. They came out of those waters dripping wet without a change of clothes in sight, praising God from the depths of their spirits. There was hardly a dry eye in the place. The whole church broke out in incredible worship. The power and presence of God permeated the church, and that morning was an unforgettable experience.

The next day, I called three other pastors and ran the scenario by them to see if they thought I had violated the Scriptures in any way. Not one of them thought I had, but they encouraged me to follow up with those who had been baptized. We did.

*   *   *

After pastoring the church for seven years, I received one of the greatest surprises of my life. We got a call from the police commissioner, Ray Kelly. He wanted to come see me but couldn't, so he sent his special assistant to Bronx River.

"Do you know the effect you've had on this housing project?" the assistant asked. "Crack dealing is at an all-time low, there are virtually no homicides, people are not nearly as violent, and the entire community has been transformed. We want to work with you. Whatever you're doing, count on the police department to have your back."

I shook the man's hand and smiled, but inwardly I was chuckling. I never imagined the day would come when I would hear those words coming from a cop.

CHAPTER SEVENTEEN

IN OUR NEW LOCATION, our church built relationships with the community by doing creative ministry activities, such as a program we called Extreme Blessings. We'd arrange to go into the apartment of a family who lived in the projects and send them away on a short vacation. Then we did some needed renovations, painting and completely redecorating the apartment with new furnishings and home decor. We'd bring the family back as a couple hundred people gathered outside to applaud and watch them take their walk-through. The neighborhood fell in love with us because we showed love to them, from the stickup kids to the working moms. This program also changed the attitudes of many people who distrusted churches, eradicating the perception that the only thing churches cared about was money. Residents were able to witness the church in action up close and personal, regardless of whether they had ever walked into our Sunday church service or not. The community began to realize that it was better off because of the work we were doing.

After being so blessed and certain we were in the right place doing the right things, we were tested in late 2011 when we were notified by the New York City Housing Authority that the agreement we'd been following to use the community center in Bronx River would soon expire. We would need to find a new spot to hold services by the end of February. At about the same time, the city informed churches meeting in public schools that they would not be allowed to meet there after February 12 because the Supreme Court had refused to weigh in on the Bronx Household of Faith court case. That meant that a June 2011 decision by the Court of Appeals, which upheld the city's ban on churches holding worship services in schools, would stand. Now the New York City Law Department was threatening churches' access to all public spaces. I soon talked with other pastors, like Reverend Joe Fletcher of Bronx Bible Church, who had also been notified that their churches would no longer be able to meet in community centers.

After making a few calls to the New York City Housing Authority and realizing that they were serious about closing the community centers to us, I was stunned. With my emotions in a tailspin, I called Tim Keller, who listened and then promised to call me back.

When we spoke again, he told me that a couple of people at his church worked in the city government. He gave me the name and number of one lady, and I called her right away to alert her as to what was going on.

She already knew the facts and told me that she was sorry.

"Well—" I snatched a breath— "you let them know the projects are coming to the steps of the city's Law Department."

Not knowing what to do, I paced for a while. Then I learned that Rubén Díaz, one of our state senators, was having his Christmas party that day. I decided to go there and talk to him.

So I went to his party and introduced myself. I'd met him before, and he remembered me. When I told him what was happening, he said, "Call my office, and we'll see what we can do."

The last thing I wanted to hear was that I had to wait.

"I'm going to the Law Department in early January; will you come with me?"

"I'll be in Albany and unable to come." He smiled. "Call my office."

Then someone pointed to another gentleman and said, "Have you met Fernando Cabrera? He's a city councilman."

I went over and introduced myself. Cabrera said he was a pastor too.

"Have you heard what's going down?" I asked. "All the churches that meet in public spaces are being evicted. Will you come with me to the Law Department early next month?"

Cabrera said he would, and I wanted to hug him on the spot.

In late December, I talked with Joe Fletcher again and told him about the planned protest in early January.

"Come join us," I told him.

"Well, you know," Fletcher said, "I've been talking to my lawyer, and he doesn't want me to do that. But if you want to go for it, go ahead."

Later, Mayor Bloomberg held his annual New Year's interfaith breakfast. Oddly enough, I guess he thought business would go on as usual. But as the mayor prepared to speak to the group of religious leaders, Pastor Bill Devlin of Manhattan Bible Church called out for everyone to hear: "We love you, Mayor Mike—we love you. But please don't kick out our houses of worship from our city schools!"[1]

Bill Devlin was my kind of guy.

As a further sign of my identification with the body of Christ, I decided to go on a hunger strike at the beginning of the year. As long as many of our local churches were suffering at the hands of New York officials, I would suffer as well.

Meanwhile, I continued to plan for the protest at the Law Department. I went to the radio station, bought some time on the airwaves, and invited people to join the protest the following week.

I began to hear from others who promised to come. Not only councilman Fernando Cabrera but also Pastor Devlin; Michael Carrion, pastor of Promised Land Covenant Church; and Rick Del Rio, pastor of Abounding Grace Ministries, would be on hand as well. A number of people from our church and from the projects, Christians and non-Christians, said they'd come with me. The radio ad drew even more people to participate in our protest.

Later I heard that the head of the Law Department had been caught off guard by our appearance. He hadn't read his e-mail the previous day, so he didn't know to expect us. Coincidentally, Occupy Wall Street was going on at the same time as our protest. A group of reporters and photographers showed up because they'd heard a group would be at the Law Department.

In the end, about twenty people went down to the Law Department on a cold Thursday morning. Some of the people from the projects got pretty radical, screaming, "Leave my church alone!" After about an hour, I pointed to the steps in front of the door and suggested, "Let's end in prayer." I noticed Cabrera hesitate as he understood what I was asking—that we engage in civil disobedience by blocking access. He hadn't let his family, church, or city council office know that he might be arrested that morning.

Then I saw a hint of a smile as he nodded. "Okay, if I'm going to be a part of this movement, I need to go all the way. I'll pray with you."

Seven of us knelt for prayer, and when we stood up, the cops arrested us. We turned around to face the crowd, and it was the biggest paparazzi moment of my life—strobes flashed everywhere. The cops cuffed us and locked us in a van.

Bill Devlin grinned at us. "I've been arrested twenty-nine times for Jesus."

"What? How?"

"Picketing in front of abortion clinics. I wouldn't give them my name, so they'd keep me three days under 'John Doe,' then they'd let me go. That's why it's not on my record."

With a skill perfected by practice, the handcuffed Devlin pulled a phone out of his back pocket and dialed the Associated Press. He told them he was in a van with several pastors and a city councilman, and we were all going to jail.

The next thing I knew, we were in the jail and we started to minister—we preached to the cops, we sang, and we worshiped. We were going hard in there, knowing that God was with us.

When we came out of the jail, even more cameras were outside to record the moment. We told them what was going on.

Soon Bill Devlin went on a fast too. His lasted for forty-two days. When I stopped eating, the Lord began to give me new ideas. He told me to post updates on Facebook, so I did, praying and posting about meetings in the schools. Focus on the Family and *The 700 Club* called for details and updates on our situation.

Before long, our protest had a name: The Right to Worship movement had been born. This situation proved to be a physical trial for me but a spiritual high. People said we couldn't win, but I'd call for a prayer meeting at a church and four hundred people would show up. Pastors from all over the city began to fast and pray with me. Fernando Cabrera had great organizational skills, and he helped us pull things together.

God was moving, but some people believed not even God could fight city hall.

*   *   *

As days went by, I clung to my resolution not to eat unless and until the entire body of Christ in New York was out of danger. The only way I could stay on my fast was to enter a morbid state of mind. I knew I could come close to death, and I had to wrap my brain around that.

I watched movies about a couple of Irish guys who went on a

hunger strike and died in jail—I had to watch those to stay fired up and persevere. This was a fast, but it was a fast without a definite ending, and it was difficult to maintain my determination. I knew my mind and body had to be connected to the body of Christ. The body of Christ was suffering, so my human flesh could suffer as well. "When they're okay," I told Tiffany, "I'll stop."

On Friday, the day immediately after our protest at the Law Department, I got a call from one of the people in Mayor Bloomberg's office. It was the woman connected to Redeemer Presbyterian Church, and she told me they needed me to come down to 250 Broadway on Monday, that I had done enough and that the standoff was over. I was glad to hear it, but I didn't stop for breakfast on my way over.

When I got to the office, I found Reverend Joe Fletcher there, along with another pastor and his wife. The four of us sat down with the head of the NYC Housing Authority, or NYCHA. "We want you to know we got this wrong," they said, "and you guys and your churches are okay to meet. This is over." We pastors looked at each other, then we looked back at the housing authority people. "We want to keep you as residents as long as we can. You're great tenants, and this shouldn't be an issue."

I looked at the other guys and grinned. Wow. Only one arrest, and we had won the victory. This was great.

I had no sooner left the office, though, when I heard that the victory was only *half* a victory. The Housing Authority had allowed churches to meet in community centers, but the churches who met in schools were still facing eviction.

Suddenly the word *victory* sounded hollow.

I went home and decided to continue the fight. We would fight city hall no matter what, and we were going to fight for our brothers and sisters who had no choice but to meet in schools.

Then I learned that Mayor Bloomberg had arranged to give his

State of the City address in the Bronx. What? The mayor was coming to my hood? Let him bring it.

After deciding to invite people to protest at the speech, I got a call from the woman who attended church at Redeemer and worked in Bloomberg's office. Now that she'd helped ensure that churches could continue to meet in community centers, she asked me to leave the school situation alone.

"No way," I told her. "That isn't enough. I'm fighting for everyone. And I'm going to continue to fight until all the churches can meet where they are used to meeting."

The woman didn't sound happy with me when she hung up.

On day seven of my hunger strike, I met with Tim and Kathy Keller in Tim's office to discuss what the hunger strike was about and how far I was willing to take it. They expressed genuine concern for my health. I promised them that I'd keep checking in with my doctors and let them know I was okay.

I left their office and went to the radio station. "Show up in the Bronx," I urged listeners. "Mayor Bloomberg is planning to give his address, but we need the body of Christ to show up, pray, lift up Jesus, and not be afraid to stand for the seventeen thousand Christians who will be on the streets because of a law that the mayor could easily change."

*   *   *

On day twelve of my fast, a writer for the online magazine *A Journey through NYC Religions* came to our house and started to work on an article about our protest. I was weak and tired, and I had struggled just to get out of bed. But day twelve was the day of Mayor Bloomberg's address, and I knew I had to be there.

The skies were heavy with gray clouds, and the heavens released a stream of steady rain. I put on a raincoat and held a bullhorn and watched as several hundred people showed up. Tony Perkins was there representing the Family Research Council, along with other Christian leaders. I was shocked by how many stepped up to support the cause with me in the pouring rain.

I had been inspired by the movie *Gandhi* and his forms of non-violent protest. In one scene, Gandhi sent men in groups of seven to walk toward British soldiers who kept knocking them down. When one group would get knocked down, Gandhi would send another group of seven, and then another.

I looked at the men standing around me. "I need a group of five pastors who are willing to walk toward the place where the mayor's giving his address," I told them. "I need you to kneel and pray, and then you'll probably be arrested. Who's down with that?"

The first five lined up, and Bill Devlin led them in prayer before they moved forward.

The first five walked down. They knelt in the freezing rain and were promptly handcuffed and led away. Then I sent another five, and the same thing happened. This continued as several more groups of five people linked arms and went forward. The only ones left were me, Joe Fletcher, and a teenager from the projects who had walked across the street to join us.

So we three went arm-in-arm toward the mayor, and we knelt on the wet pavement. When the police arrested us, I noticed that some of the cops were nearly in tears. They were arresting pastors they knew and respected, and it was too much. All together, forty-three of us were arrested—ministers, seminary professors, ministry leaders, and young people. This time we weren't booked and treated like criminals. When we got to the police station, they simply called our names and sent us on our way.

A week later, our court dates came up. We all went down to the courthouse, and the bailiff called everyone's name but mine. After the judge dismissed all the charges, I turned and looked around the courtroom. Why hadn't they called my name?

When I asked a court official, he grinned and said my name wasn't even in the system, so I was good to go, a free man. When that news echoed in the courtroom, all kinds of praising the Lord broke loose among the crowd. I had been arrested twice for this cause, yet my name wasn't even in the system.

How things had changed.

*　　*　　*

I was praying when God gave me the idea of taking our protest to the Brooklyn Bridge. On a call with others involved in the Right to Worship cause, I said, "Let's call the body of Christ to meet us on the south side of the Brooklyn Bridge, and let's cross over."

Bill de Blasio, who was a public advocate at the time, got us a permit and came to the event along with others involved in the cause.

At that point, I was so weak that getting out of bed was difficult. I could tell that my body had shifted somehow—my immune system had been compromised, and my body had begun to get its resources from different places, as if it were digesting itself. I felt like I was eating air. I spent as much time as I could resting and trying to conserve my energy.

When I did get up and get dressed, I could barely get my pants to stay up. My cousin Kaaba had come to visit, and he kept trying to talk me out of the fast, saying I shouldn't lose my life for the church. "What better thing to lose your life for?" I asked. "What could be better than dying for Jesus?"

Living for Jesus, I knew. But I didn't feel that I could surrender yet, even though my body was eating itself alive.

I felt terribly low-spirited, but I kept making YouTube videos and keeping people updated on our plans. Not only was I in physical pain, but I was experiencing mental anguish as well. My motives were continually misunderstood, and I was criticized for calling my fast a "hunger strike," which some people perceived as unbiblical, instead of a fast.

From all sides I felt pressure to stop my fast. Friends and relatives urged me to stop, but I'd fasted before—in fact, I think God prepared me for this fast back when I had attended a church where the pastor routinely called me to fast longer than anyone else there. At least Bill Devlin had helped blunt the criticism about my fasting when he announced that he was going on a forty-day fast. Now I wasn't the only one making a point through not eating.

Not only was I hurt by personal criticism, but the indifference of other churches hurt too.

Yet I knew God was with me. I knew persecution was going to come, and when it did, I shouldered it. Some people said I was making it all about me and my dying, but I pointed out that I had placed my life on the line in a very real sense. When you reach that point, your perspective on life shifts. You don't talk just to talk; you're in a more somber and sober place. I wanted to esteem Jesus alone.

I could barely get around, but I rode to Albany with one group to participate in a prayer demonstration. I felt our cause was gaining momentum, but my weakness made it difficult for me to become excited about anything.

I wouldn't stay silent, however. I spent three hundred dollars on brooms, then had over a hundred people show up at city hall and sweep the steps as if we were sweeping away the negative acts of our city government. I stood with my daughter and told reporters that we were going to keep fighting and standing for Christ no matter what it took. "We're not going to give up, and God is going to do a great thing. Just watch and see."

When I went to church on Sunday, January 22, two of the doctors in the church examined me and shook their heads. "Your pulse is so low you could die at any time," the first doctor said.

The second doctor, who believed more in the discipline of fasting, agreed with the first. "It's one thing to fast when you're at home resting, but when you're sweeping and marching and leading prayer rallies, you're using up more energy. It's time for you to stop, Dimas. It's time."

I turned to my wife. "You did a great job," Tiffany said, "and God is going to honor this. But it's time, babe."

I agreed reluctantly, yet I knew my fast had sparked something in the body of Christ. Prayer meetings were taking place all across the city. Pastor Rick Del Rio did a thirteen-day fast. Soon, fasts were sparking all over the city. Everywhere I went, people were announcing how fasts and prayer meetings were taking place throughout the city, across denominational lines. I hadn't seen anything like it—nor had anyone else—in years.

*   *   *

We had planned the Brooklyn Bridge march for the last Sunday in January 2012. Despite bitterly cold weather, I put on my collar, a black suit, and my white trench coat.

I locked arms with Bill de Blasio and John Liu, who were both running for mayor; Rick Del Rio; and Fernando Cabrera. With my daughter propped on my shoulders, we led the walk over the 1.1 miles of the Brooklyn Bridge. I had thought we might get a thousand people to walk with us, but the media reported a crowd of 17,000 on the bridge.[2] I was astounded.

On the other side, we had set up a professional stage and sound system so we could hold a prayer rally after the march. City officials and pastors spoke, and then we led times of prayer together. We could sense that the Lord was with us.

The Right to Worship movement had attracted national attention. After the rally, Mayor Bloomberg went silent on the subject of churches meeting on public property. He had wakened a sleeping giant, and I suspected he didn't know how to handle a united and vocal Christian community.

In February, we heard about a court decision that granted us a stay, meaning that the churches were able to go back into the schools while another court examined the case again. Since then, churches have continued meeting in schools, despite a 2014 court decision to uphold the city's ban. I was disappointed when, in March 2015, the Supreme Court again refused to take up this case after an appeal. A spokesman for Mayor de Blasio, however, announced that New York was committed to permitting churches to meet in schools and community centers.[3] We have no guarantee that future administrations will stand by the current policy, but we'll cross the Brooklyn Bridge again if we have to.

*   *   *

Macy, a woman who was well loved in the community, attended our church. She caught me one day and told me that her son, known on the street as Hawk, would be coming home after many years in jail.

"It was the gangs," she said, her brown eyes staring into mine. "He wasn't a bad kid, but he got into the gangs and—well, you know what they do. He has been away for such a long time, and I don't want to lose him again."

She caught my arm as her voice trembled. "I am not young," she said, "and I will not be around much longer. Please pray that I will be able to spend time with my son . . . before it's too late."

I learned that Hawk had been the violent enforcer of the community. He was often hired to do contract hits and would get into gunfights with the cops. He was also the head of a notorious gang.

Hawk's violent approach hadn't changed during his incarceration; in fact, Macy told me he had exercised significant control over prison life. She was concerned that her son would continue his reign of violence once he came home. She pleaded with me to reach out to him, but what could I do? Even I didn't feel up to the task of turning a notorious gang lord to Christ.

Soon after Hawk was released from prison, Macy brought him to church. He came home with muscles like the Incredible Hulk's and a mind set on the streets. Years of lifting weights had made him far more menacing and intimidating than the average muscleman because he was fast and flexible, not built merely for show. Hawk was polite when his mother introduced him to me, but I could tell he was sizing me up.

In the coming weeks, I watched as young and old alike flocked to him. Most people outside our neighborhood would have feared Hawk, but the kids in our hood thought he was tough, powerful, and awesome. I knew how they felt—at fourteen, I would have idolized him.

As an adult and a pastor, I could see how the kids admired him, so I started praying, determined to lead one of the toughest men in New York City to Jesus. After all, I didn't have to save him; Jesus did. All I had to do was bear witness to the power of God.

I prayed until one day I saw Hawk heading to the store alone. I went over and struck up a conversation with him about working out, and he responded by talking about how he needed to help the young guys organize.

I told him the community had grown much more peaceful, and he mentioned the time when strangers couldn't walk through Bronx River without being verbally challenged or intimidated by gang members. Clearly, he longed for the good old days, but I yearned for a community that had never existed.

A few weeks passed, and then Macy died. With her family's help, our church put together a wonderful funeral that included a moving video tribute. Hundreds came to show their appreciation for Hawk and his mother. Guys with *thug* written all over them went up to thank Hawk for handling violent situations or saving their lives. Some remarked that he had inspired them not to take grief from anyone. Hawk's eyes got misty.

At the end of the video tribute, the community applauded Hawk and his family for the funeral, and the family members publicly thanked the church. When it came time to preach, I stood up and pulled no punches. I looked out at the mourners, including many gang members and drug dealers, and told them the truth about the state of the streets. I told them that I'd seen tough drug dealers break down and weep at the thought of going to prison and breaking their mothers' hearts. I walked them through Ecclesiastes chapter 3 and talked about how there was a time to live and a time to die. I pointed out that Macy had been prepared to die but that most of the people in the seats were not. I told them that Jesus was the only one who would go with them anywhere, even to jail.

After the message, Hawk hugged me and said, "I am with you." From that week he started coming to church on Sundays.

God won Hawk's heart, and he accepted Jesus. The community could not believe his transformation. Everyone was shocked that a gang leader would abandon his considerable personal power to accept the self-control Jesus gives.

Seeing his faithfulness, I invited Hawk to our upcoming men's retreat, which would involve several pastors from the community. He agreed, and when we arrived, some of the pastors' eyes widened. One of them pulled me aside and warned me that Hawk was deadly. "You'd better be careful," he said. "That is one dangerous dude."

I thanked him for his concern, and later Hawk recognized that pastor and went over to engage in some small talk.

A few weeks later Hawk was arrested for violating his parole in what appeared to have been a setup. In no time Hawk was shipped ten hours away. Tiffany and I packed the car with our kids and drove up to see him.

"How you doin'?" I asked when I was finally able to talk to him.

Hawk nodded soberly. "I'm good."

"You stayin' strong? Still with Jesus?"

Hawk nodded again. "I'm okay. My faith is still strong, man."

We talked some more, and Hawk mentioned that he wasn't bitter about being back in jail. After all, he had been in jail that last stretch for a serious crime. And when he got out, he promised me, he was going to walk uprightly before the Lord. True to his word, he followed Christ faithfully upon his release and courageously told many of his former gang affiliates about the transforming power of Jesus in his life.

Why did I go back to the hood? Because every kid walking the cracked sidewalks of my neighborhood is a potential Hawk . . . or Kareem . . . or Dimas . . . and someone needs to reach them. Who better than someone who has walked over those same sidewalks?

CHAPTER EIGHTEEN

I'M STILL DAYLIGHT.

The qualities in me that I had when I was fighting for my life on the streets—the dogged persistence, the willingness to fight, the desire to matter—those will always mark who I am.

But the difference is, my ultimate goal will never again be to become a street god. I know now that I'm not the one who should rule. I've given all of myself—the good qualities and the bad, the victories and mistakes—to the real God, and in his grace he's taking it all and using it for his goals, not mine. It's his job to shine the daylight through me.

Ever since God preserved my life on the day when Mental was determined to shoot me at point-blank range, I have prayed, "Whatever, wherever, or however you want to use me, Lord, I'm yours. I'll take any risk for you, if you'll just make it clear that you're the one speaking to me."

God has honored that prayer, and sometimes he's called me out of one ministry area so he can prepare me for another. For instance, I had served as executive director of Youth for Christ NYC for over a decade when I felt God showing me that my time with this great organization was about to come to an end. I knew that God called some men to be youth leaders for life, but I didn't think I was one of them.

At about that time I began asking him, *Am I maximizing the life you gave me? Is there any more I can do?*

And then I met with Richard Stearns. I was blown away by his story of how he had gone from leading a major china and giftware company to becoming president of World Vision. "Dimas," he said, looking straight into my eyes, "I can sense that one day you're going to be president of a large Christian organization."

Part of me couldn't believe what he was saying. I wanted to ask, Do you know where I've come from, the things I've done? Could God really use me in that way? But when someone you respect that much tells you something like that, you listen. I wanted to be open to wherever God might be pointing me.

Not long afterward, I told Tiffany I was going to go for a run to clear my head. I ran three miles out and three miles back, and while running I heard the voice of the Lord in my heart: *I'm giving you the city.*

Wow. That was weird.

I'm giving you the city.

Okay. Praise God.

I had no idea what it meant. But I had vowed to myself that anytime I heard God speak, I would follow him.

When I got home, Tiffany told me that Gary Frost and Mac Pier, both leaders with Concerts of Prayer Greater New York, had called while I was out. Concerts of Prayer Greater New York is a Christ-centered network of pastors and churches that promotes a culture of prayer across ethnic, economic, and denominational lines.

The mission is to awaken all Christians to the awesome power of united prayer.

These two men told me they believed that I would make a good leader for the organization. I'd been on the board of Concerts of Prayer for about eighteen months by then, and they were well aware of the prayer walks our church had been holding for years. They'd also seen me emerge as a leader in the Right to Worship movement, fasting and praying while mobilizing people and organizing events in support of all our city's churches. Now they wanted me to meet with the organization's board of directors in three days.

Yes, I reminded myself. I told God I would always say yes. Even when the task sounded impossible.

During those three days I prayed, strategized, and developed a ninety-day plan for the organization. At the appointed time, I walked the board through my plan, and then the directors asked me to leave the room. They brought me back in twenty minutes later. They told me they had taken a vote and it was unanimous—I would be the new president. "We've seen what you've done to spur revival and prayer across this city," they said, "and we believe you're God's man for this job."

I couldn't believe it. I thought of the kid I had been, who once sold out everything he had to become a street god. Today I can't imagine a higher goal than to live up to the calling of "God's man for the job."

A few months later I stood on a platform in the ballroom of the Marriott Marquis at Times Square. I looked out on a sea of faces—nearly two thousand ministry leaders from Youth for Christ, Campus Crusade, the Billy Graham Evangelistic Association, Focus on the Family, the Salvation Army, World Vision, the Willow Creek Association, and many other organizations. We prayed together, sang together, and worshiped together.

And in a quiet moment, as I looked around the room, I smiled in reverent wonder. The church leaders I'd looked up to for so long were now asking me to lead them in prayer. Only God could have orchestrated this; only by his power and mercy could I ever have come so far. *Dear God . . . what a miracle worker you are. You took a skinny kid on the streets only a few miles from here and moved him from selling crack to leading your leaders in ministry.*

Who would have thought that a guy who once poured darkness into Queens would stand next to Billy Graham at his historic last crusade in Queens and tell eighty thousand people that Jesus alone is the answer? Who would have ever predicted that God would lead me away from delivering death-dealing artillery in urban communities and toward helping rescue the lives and limbs of people who had been injured in Haiti's devastating earthquake? And who would have imagined that I, the one who used to mobilize kids to sell drugs in the projects, would galvanize them to be some of the first responders after Superstorm Sandy? All I wanted to do was obey God and his Word—to love him with all my mind, heart, soul, and strength— even when doing so was far from easy or convenient. Sharing his relentless love has been everything to me—everything, that is, except boring. I am blown away and humbled by the amazing grace of my Lord and Savior.

Daylight has found a new life.

* * *

When Abdul asked me, "Do you wanna deal?" I said yes, picturing ready cash and instant street cred. I was prepared to do anything to make money and a name for myself, even when that meant lying on the ground, my head spinning and my mouth tasting blood and dirt. I was too naive to realize how easily my life could have been snuffed out. In fact, thirty of my friends died violently in drug wars or in prison. The only difference between them and me is Jesus. So when the Lord asked me, "Will you follow me back into the streets?" how could I say no?

Today when I go for a walk in my own neighborhood, I look at the schoolchildren heading home with their backpacks, and I remember my childhood. The kids who run in and out of bodegas are going to follow the way of the world . . . unless someone tells them that they can find a better path.

As Christ-followers, we are sometimes too quick to write people off. But I can tell you this: Even when my mother couldn't talk sense into her fifteen-year-old son, when someone mentioned Jesus I always wanted to hear more. Unfortunately, no one took it further—until three elderly ladies dared to confront a crazed drug dealer known as Daylight. They pointed me to a better way and to a joy that lasts.

Despite everything I'd done wrong, God preserved and transformed my life, and then he gave me the boldness and passion to return to the streets of New York. I've told my story in the hope that you, too, will be drawn to Christ, who is active, alive, and powerful today. I hope you've come to believe that God can overcome any obstacle in your life as well. Just be real with him. He won't run from your challenges, and he doesn't fear your questions. But he does ask you to entrust your heart and life to him.

Too often I meet people who hesitate when they hear God's call because they haven't figured out all the parts of their journey. I get it. As a man on the run, one of my first questions was simply "God, can you use someone like me?"

He could. He did. He's still doing it.

Dare to offer him all of yourself—even those parts that cause you deep pain or regret. Then just watch what he will do through you.

Watch the break of daylight shine.

Author's Note

GOSPEL IS JUST another word for good news, and I hope this book has brought lots of good news to you. If you have seen yourself in my story—if you have ever felt as frustrated and confused as I was before I decided to follow Jesus—I hope you will consider handing your life over to him now. Jesus loves you, and he wants to give your life meaning. He alone has the power to forgive you for everything bad you've ever done, and he alone has the power to help you create a new life, one centered on and grounded in him.

If you decide to follow him, the God I have described in this book will be just as alive and vibrant in your life as he has been in mine. I encourage you to pray right where you are and ask Jesus to be your Lord and Savior. Then use your life to study God's Word, understand his plan, and give yourself over daily to the things that mean the most to him.

Get ready for the adventure of your life!

If you would like more information on how to grow as a Christian, you can write to me at the address below, and I'll make sure you receive some good information on how to start your new life in Christ. God bless you!

Rev. Dimas Salaberrios
STREET GOD CONTACTS
PO Box 59
Bronx, NY 10470

Acknowledgments

Every single time I have shared my life's story, crowds of all races, ages, and economic backgrounds have told me that I need to share it in a book and that, when I was speaking, it was as if they were seeing a movie.

Ever since I was six years old, my mother repeatedly told me that I was a great storyteller and that I'd be an author someday. My dad always told me not just to read books but to write them. I am forever grateful for my parents.

My beautiful wife, Tiffany, would force me out of our comfortable bed and turn the lights on in the middle of the night, saying, "It's time to get to work." She'd read the book to me *out loud* cover to cover numerous times, poring over details and making sure it made sense. She is my greatest gift and cheerleader, my life partner and heart's desire in every way, and truly the *love* that moves me from merely doing to actually having a life full of what matters most. I love you, Tiffany!

To those who motivated me to write this book:

Sekou Laidlow would randomly text and call me for three years straight, asking, "Did you write your book? How's it coming along? When are you going to finish it?"

Rev. Floyd Flake and Dr. Tim Keller modeled being writing pastors. I read Flake's *The Way of the Bootstrapper* at least four times. In it, he talks about writing in the wee hours of the morning, and that always stuck with me. Tim Keller talked to me throughout his process of writing *Reason for God*; that encouraged me tremendously to step up my writing game. The truth is, Tim and Kathy Keller's impact in my life is immeasurably amazing. I'm incredibly grateful. Thank you for everything and for sharing your family's Thanksgiving and Christmas dinners in your home with me, Tiffany, and our little girls.

My friend Brad Winters coached me on the practical side of how to be a writer and challenged me not to shy away from taking readers into the dark side of my life and the drug world. My great friend Scott Winters made sure I stayed on course with the writing of this book. To Esther Fedorkevich and the Fedd Agency: Thank you for your incredible enthusiasm for this project and for making sure it found the best home to be told. And to Angela Hunt and my incredible team at Tyndale Momentum, particularly Jan Long Harris, Sarah Atkinson, Kim Miller, Sharon Leavitt, and Mark Lane: my sincere appreciation for you all knows no bounds.

Thank you to those who have made great investments in my life: Patricia Lanza for forcing me to think big; Dr. Frank and Sandra Maselli for consistently encouraging me to stay faithful to the vision of reaching people on the streets; Bill Hwang for helping me to crystallize the value of pastoring in an underserved community; Lowell Adrian for challenging Tiffany and me to model being a healthy family before our congregation; Julie Griffin-Fambro and family for sticking by our sides to do grassroots ministry in the Bronx; Christina and Brian Stanton for championing our vision and cause; Dr. Helen Kim and Charlie Westfall for your faithful commitment to sharing the love of Christ through holistic ministry; John Moon for advancing the Kingdom of God even among the marginalized; Dr. A. R. Bernard for granting me personal access to his remarkable wisdom and mentorship; Andi

Brindley for giving us a retreat when we needed it most; and Chuck and Irma Hinton, Andy Puleo, Paul Leacock, Jack Crabtree, Joel Smith, Terry Gyger, Carlton Brown, Mimsie Robinson, Gary Frost, Mac Pier, John Clause, Derwin and Kimberly Stewart, Craig Higgins, Chris Luppo, and Phil Boyce for not only seeing the diamond in the rough in me early on, but for being instrumental in honing it.

I've been blessed with phenomenal friends who sharpen me, hold me accountable, and challenge me to higher heights. Thank you, Tara Flynn, Dr. Randall Owen, Al Taylor, Scott and Brad, Julie, Gyasi Summerville, Sekou and Melinda, Maurice Winley, John and Kyoko Lin, Bob Thompson, Ray Mott, Bill Devlin, Joe Fletcher, John Boyd Jr., Hugh Marriott, Jack Redmond, Mitchell Torres, Larry Acosta, James Puleo, David Ham, Kelvin and Edwina Findley-Dickerson, Norma Saunders, Mark Reynolds, Jamie George, Dennis Bishop, Anthony Coles, Eddie Torres and Kris Hosch, Rick and Jeremy Del Rio, Fernando Cabrera, Nick Hall, Delores Burnett, Yakimiyah Binyamin, Emmanuel Haniah, Vernard Kam Howard, Michael Thomas, and Wayne Barnett.

Special thanks to those who first helped us launch our ministry in the Bronx: Tara, Randy, Al, and Julie; Laura Commins; Pamela McKelvin-Jefferson; and Michelle Shin-Stavrou.

Thank you, Infinity Bible Church, for the privilege of pastoring you.

I am forever grateful for the love we get from the Bronx River Community.

Thank you to Concerts of Prayer Greater New York.

Thank you to my Salem Communications family.

Thank you to all the partners and supporters of the TV and radio broadcasts of *The Dynamic Life with Pastor Dimas*—let's keep making *bold* disciples of Jesus Christ!

A big shout-out to those who helped transcribe my scribblings: Ismatu LeBlanc, Sonia Joubert, Jelani Spencer-Joe, and Kristine Meachem.

Thanks for hanging in there with me, Chad, Emerald, and Dawn. You're the best brother and sisters in the world. You and Mommy never gave up on me, and you made sure I never gave up on myself. I love you all from the bottom of my heart. Love you too, Carolina, Angelo, and Kaaba!

To my dearest Shirley Ann, I love you so much. I thank God for gifting me with you and making sure we didn't miss out on knowing and loving each other.

And to my Dallas and Skylar—before you were even born, we prayed for you. From the womb, I *knew* you'd be Daddy's girls! You'd respond when I'd sing to your Mom's tummy, and when you both came out, our hearts were knit together and I could see forever in your eyes. My precious princesses, run with Jesus all the way! You mean the world to me. I will always love you and am forever thankful for your love for me.

Notes

CHAPTER ELEVEN
1. Matthew 8:26, NKJV

CHAPTER THIRTEEN
1. Matthew Rees, "King of Queens," February 2001, *Reader's Digest*, 34–38.

CHAPTER FOURTEEN
1. See 2 Timothy 3:16, NIV.

CHAPTER FIFTEEN
1. In 2013, Mayor Michael Bloomberg announced that, although only 5 percent of New York City's residents live in apartments of the New York City Housing Authority, 20 percent of the crime is committed by them. See "Bloomberg's Public Housing Fingerprinting Idea Stuns, Infuriates Residents," *CBS New York*, August 16, 2013, http://newyork.cbslocal.com/2013/08/16/bloombergs-public-housing-fingerprinting-idea-stuns-infuriates-residents (accessed April 6, 2015).
2. For background on this lengthy legal battle, see Sophia Hollander, "Court Upholds New York City Ban on Church in Schools," *Wall Street Journal*, April 3, 2014, http://www.wsj.com/articles/SB10001424052702303987004579479922983220310.

CHAPTER SEVENTEEN
1. Kate Taylor, "At Mayor's Interfaith Breakfast, Some Respectful Dissents," *New York Times*, December 30, 2011, http://cityroom.blogs.nytimes.com/2011/12/30/at-mayors-interfaith-breakfast-some-respectful-dissents/?_r=0.
2. "Thousands March to Protest Ban on Using Public Schools for Religious Services," *CBS New York*, January 29, 2012, http://newyork.cbslocal.com/2012/01/29/thousands-march-to-protest-ban-on-using-public-schools-for-religious-services.
3. Sharon Otterman, "Supreme Court Leaves Intact New York's Ban on Religious Services in Schools," *New York Times*, March 30, 2015, http://www.nytimes.com/2015/03/31/nyregion/supreme-court-leaves-intact-new-yorks-ban-on-religious-services-in-schools.html.

For video content, the *Street God* discussion guide, and more, visit **www.StreetGodBook.com**.

About the Author

DIMAS SALABERRIOS is pastor of Infinity Bible Church, which he founded in partnership with Tim Keller and Redeemer City to City, in the South Bronx of New York City. Infinity spearheads numerous outreach events. The church's impact in the Bronx River housing projects has been credited with a notable drop in crime and drug dealing in that community. As a worldwide missionary, church planter, and speaker, Pastor Dimas has shared the gospel on every continent except Antarctica. He is also president of Concerts of Prayer Greater New York, and he holds a master of divinity degree from Alliance Theological Seminary. He and his wife, Tiffany, live in the Bronx with their two daughters.

DR. ANGELA HUNT has authored more than 130 works and sold nearly five million copies of her books worldwide. Her books have won awards such as the coveted Christy Award, several Angel Awards from Excellence in Media, and the Gold and Silver Medallions from Foreword Magazine's Book of the Year Award. In 2008, Angela earned her doctorate in biblical studies and is currently completing her ThD. Angela and her husband live in Florida with their two mastiffs.